RSACS

AUG - - 2001

OKLAHOMA!

OKLAHOMA!

Jay J. Wagoner

THUNDERBIRD BOOKS

OKLAHOMA CITY   TUCSON

1994

About the Author . . .

Jay J. Wagoner grew up in the Oklahoma Panhandle during the "Dust Bowl" days. His keen interest in history stems from acquaintance with many of the first settlers in Cimarron County. His formal education at the University of Oklahoma was interrupted for service in the Army Signal Corps in Europe during World War II. A career high school teacher, he has written eleven books and numerous articles related to Southwest history. He was a Fulbright scholar in Brazil in 1960 and has traveled extensively in this country and abroad to do research.

Dedication . . .

This book is dedicated to the author's mother, Mrs. Emogene Wagoner (1898–1991), who knew what it meant to be a pioneer. As a young girl, the eldest of six children of William and Ada Humphrey, she lived in Cushing, Territory of Oklahoma. Her maternal grandfather, Benton Chappelle, was a Civil War veteran and 89er who later settled in Pottawatomie County.

Special acknowledgment . . .

Charles and Erma Sullivan (Emogene's youngest sister) of Oklahoma City provided much help and encouragement in the preparation of this book. Charles (1914–1991) was a civil engineer for the Water Resources Department, U.S. Geological Survey.

Cover Painting . . .

"Oklahoma Land Rush" by Charles McBarron is reprinted under permission of Amoco Oil Company.

CONTENTS

STATEHOOD

APPENDIX

INTRODUCTION

Oklahoma is a young state with an exciting history. People of many races, nationalities, and cultures have contributed to our heritage. The early Oklahomans had experiences and held values from which we can learn. Maybe we can avoid some of their mistakes and imitate ways of success.

A study of Oklahoma's past also teaches us that change is always going on. With historical perspective, we have a better chance to understand present-day problems and to arrive at decisions that will make Oklahoma an even better place to live. Yes, this generation is part of history too. We should remember the Indian who never got lost because he often looked back to see where he had been.

The state's history can be understood better if we visualize places where the action was. *Oklahoma should be pictured as a meeting place—not only for people of many different origins, but also as the place where several of the nation's geographic regions come together.* The western Great Plains, the central Farm Belt lowlands, the eastern forest zone, and the southeastern Coastal Plain stretch into Oklahoma. Thus, this state is a transition zone with a great variety of landforms, plant life, and climates.

A knowledge of geography came naturally to Native Americans who have called the Oklahoma area home for about 600 generations. The early natives hunted for a living. They also gathered wild food and, eventually, learned to farm. They lived in harmony with nature, neither spoiling nor wasting the environment. *Is there a lesson in the Native American culture for this generation?*

Oklahoma was involved in the struggle of European nations for colonial empires. In the 1500s, long before the Pilgrims landed at Plymouth, the King of Spain claimed a vast empire in the New World. His explorers traveled north from Mexico. They blazed trails, named rivers, and raised the Spanish flag in present-day Oklahoma. French-

men came next. They trapped for furs and traded with the native tribes. Finally, in 1803, the French government sold Louisiana to President Thomas Jefferson. All of Oklahoma, except the Panhandle, was in the Louisiana Purchase and became part of the United States.

American explorers and traders soon arrived from the States. Soldiers came to build Fort Gibson and Fort Towson. Settlements grew up near these forts. Then the federal government began moving the Five Civilized Tribes from the Old South. These tribes were promised most of the Oklahoma land area "as long as grass shall grow and rivers run." The tribal members cleared land for farms. They organized as nations with governments, built schools and churches, and started newspapers.

Progress in Indian Territory, however, came to a halt during the Civil War (1861–1865). This war was a turning point in Oklahoma history. The Five Nations were punished for siding with the South. Congress forced them to give up what is now western Oklahoma. Much of the lost land was given to other Indian tribes, though a large area around present-day Oklahoma City was unassigned. Land-hungry "Boomers" persuaded Congress to open the unassigned land to settlement.

On April 22, 1889, an army of people raced wildly for homesteads and townlots in what is now central Oklahoma. The next year, Congress gave them a government by creating the Territory of Oklahoma. During the 1890's, more and more Indian tribes were persuaded to give up tribal ownership of their lands and to take individual allotments. Outside settlers moved in to fill up the surplus lands. Finally, on November 16, 1907, the Oklahoma and Indian territories were combined to form the 46th state.

Since statehood was granted, Oklahoma has changed from one of the nation's last frontiers to a modern industrial state. By the 1960s, new industries—aerospace, electronics, mobile homes, plastic products, and many others—highlighted the state's growth. Thousands of skilled rural people and newcomers moved to Oklahoma's cities to work in factories. Oklahoma's boosters began describing the state's economic changes with such phrases as "tepees to towers" and "from arrows to atoms."

Completion of the McClellan-Kerr Arkansas River Navigation System made shipping an important Oklahoma activity. Barges now move along the Arkansas waterway with heavy loads of raw materials and manufactured goods. Also, a system of manmade lakes throughout the state has made tourism another important industry. Oklahoma, called "America's frontier lake state," has more shoreline than the Atlantic and Gulf coasts combined.

Today, Oklahoma is in the mainstream of American life and is changing with the times. So what sets this state apart? Every proud Oklahoman could give a good answer. One state booster said Oklahoma is unique because of "our Native American culture (the nation's second largest Indian population), our Western heritage, and our opportunities for outdoor recreation, particularly water recreation." A recent governor's list includes "pure air, four seasons, plenty of elbow space, and the people—their independent spirit, belief in family life, and involvement in church-oriented activities." Despite many changes around them, Oklahomans are likely to hold on to these traditional values and to revere the state's heritage.

1

OKLAHOMA IS A LAND OF CONTRASTS

Oklahoma has a great variety of scenery. A traveler can see mountains, hills, broad *plains,* rolling *prairies,* and *plateau* land.

Oklahoma's crazy quilt pattern of landforms can be divided into ten *physiographic regions,* each with its own *relief.* Three of the regions have mountains: the Ouachitas, Arbuckles, and Wichitas. One, the Ozarks, is called a plateau. Two regions have a hilly relief. Four areas are mainly plains or prairies.

Sometimes, when we are riding in a car, we know exactly when we go from one region to the next. Usually, however, the change is gradual. The dividing line is not as clear as a line on the map. Similar vegetation can make one region look like the next one until relief differences become obvious. This point is illustrated by the *Cross Timbers,* a scrub tree belt in central Oklahoma. The Cross Timbers is found mainly in the Sandstone Hills region, but it also reaches into the Western Red Plains.

Each of the physiographic regions in Oklahoma is a part of a larger zone that covers several states. The East meets the West in Oklahoma. The North and the South come together here. That helps to explain why Oklahoma has more kinds of country than most other states.

1. THE LAND SURFACE OF OKLAHOMA HAS BEEN CHANGING FOR BILLIONS OF YEARS.

How old is the earth? The earth is more than four billion years old. It has been changing constantly since it was created. How? Seas flowed in and deposited silt. *Earthquakes* buckled up layers of rock. *Volcanoes* erupted, spreading lava over the land. Wind and water eroded the earth's surface. These changes have been at work on land where Oklahoma is today.

Geologists can tell us what the earth was like at different times. They have divided the past into "ages."

Paleozoic Age (550 to 200 million years ago). Geologists say Oklahoma changed greatly during the *Paleozoic Age.* The state was underwater during the early part of this age. A sea laid down silt that formed stone. As a result, Oklahoma now has deposits of sandstone and limestone.

Ever wonder why the soil in central and western Oklahoma is red? The color came from red sands left by the sea that covered this area.

In later Paleozoic times, Oklahoma was swampy. Streams washed in mud and sand that covered plants. Some of this vegetation slowly changed into coal. In modern times, coal mining became an important industry in eastern Oklahoma.

Earthquakes shook Oklahoma near the end of the Paleozoic Age. These quakes warped and uplifted the earth's inner layers of stone. A good place to see uptilted, once horizontal, stone is in the Arbuckle Mountains near Ardmore.

Dinosaur Age. Huge *dinosaurs* once roamed through swampy marshland. *Archaeologists* have uncovered dinosaur bones near Enid. Other dinosaur remains were dug from pits northwest of Boise City in the Panhandle.

The Dinosaur Age is known to geologists as the *Mesozoic Age* (200 to 70 million years ago).

Changes in the Panhandle. In more recent geologic ages, the Panhandle area was covered by rock debris washed down from the Rocky Mountains.

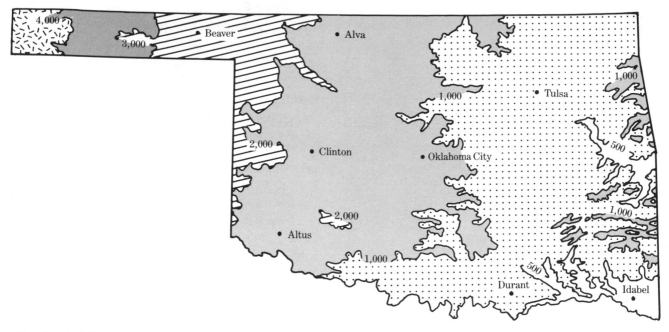

Elevations in Oklahoma

Also, lava flowed in from a volcano in present-day New Mexico. This lava formed the Black Mesa.

2. OKLAHOMA IS A SOUTH CENTRAL STATE THAT IS DRAINED BY THE ARKANSAS AND RED RIVER SYSTEMS.

Oklahoma is the first state south of Kansas, the geographical center of the first forty-eight States. Thus, Oklahoma can be called a south central state.

Culturally the state is tied to several sections of the nation. The northern Oklahoma wheat country has much in common with Kansas and other Midwest states. Many eastern Oklahoma people have roots in the Deep South. Western Oklahoma cotton and cattle areas often are identified with Texas and the Southwest.

Shape and size. Oklahoma is shaped like a saucepan with a long handle. The state boundaries also resemble a butcher's cleaver. The Red River forms a dented cutting edge. The cleaver was favored for the state seal by a few delegates at the constitutional convention in 1906, according to "Alfalfa Bill" Murray, a former governor.

Oklahoma contains 69,919 square miles. It is the eighteenth largest state in area.

Elevations. Oklahoma tilts from the northwest to the southeast. The highest point is on the Black Mesa in Cimarron County. It is 4,978 feet above sea level as measured by the U.S. Geologi-

Highest point in Oklahoma—on the Black Mesa in Cimarron County. (Oklahoma Tourism photo by Fred Marvel)

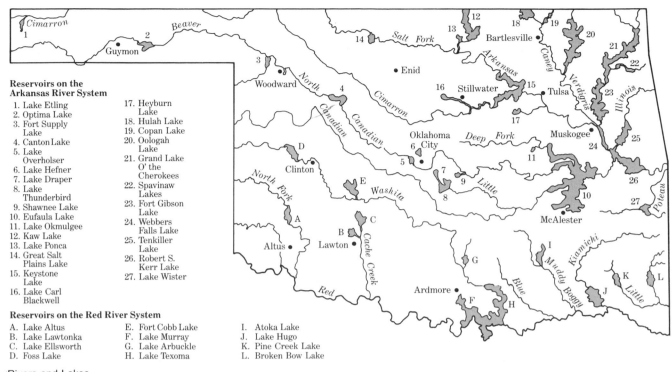

Reservoirs on the Arkansas River System

1. Lake Etling
2. Optima Lake
3. Fort Supply Lake
4. Canton Lake
5. Lake Overholser
6. Lake Hefner
7. Lake Draper
8. Lake Thunderbird
9. Shawnee Lake
10. Eufaula Lake
11. Lake Okmulgee
12. Kaw Lake
13. Lake Ponca
14. Great Salt Plains Lake
15. Keystone Lake
16. Lake Carl Blackwell
17. Heyburn Lake
18. Hulah Lake
19. Copan Lake
20. Oologah Lake
21. Grand Lake O' the Cherokees
22. Spavinaw Lakes
23. Fort Gibson Lake
24. Webbers Falls Lake
25. Tenkiller Lake
26. Robert S. Kerr Lake
27. Lake Wister

Reservoirs on the Red River System

A. Lake Altus
B. Lake Lawtonka
C. Lake Ellsworth
D. Foss Lake
E. Fort Cobb Lake
F. Lake Murray
G. Lake Arbuckle
H. Lake Texoma
I. Atoka Lake
J. Lake Hugo
K. Pine Creek Lake
L. Broken Bow Lake

Rivers and Lakes

cal Survey. Most of the Panhandle is above 2,500 feet in elevation. Some of the land there is so level, water cannot run off.

The lowest point in the state, 287 feet above sea level, is on the Little River in McCurtain County in southeastern Oklahoma.

In between these extremes, central Oklahoma is approximately 1,000 feet in elevation. Imagine a north-south line along Interstate 35 passing through Ponca City, Oklahoma City, and Ardmore. Most of the land west of this line is above 1,000 feet. Most of the land to the east is below 1,000 feet.

River systems. Two river systems drain Oklahoma—the Arkansas and the Red.

The Arkansas River begins as a mountain stream in the Colorado Rockies. It winds across Kansas and northeastern Oklahoma on its way to the Mississippi River. The Arkansas drains the northern two-thirds of Oklahoma.

The Salt Fork, Cimarron, and other *tributaries* that empty into the Arkansas from the west have a high mineral content. On the other

hand, water of excellent quality flows from other feeder rivers: the Verdigris, Neosho (Grand), Illinois, and Poteau.

Most of the runoff water in southern Oklahoma empties into the Red River system. Tributaries include the North Fork, Washita, Blue, Muddy Boggy, Kiamichi, and the Little River.

Kiamichi River in flood near Sawyer in Choctaw County, 1923. (U.S. Geological Survey photo by H.D. Miser)

3

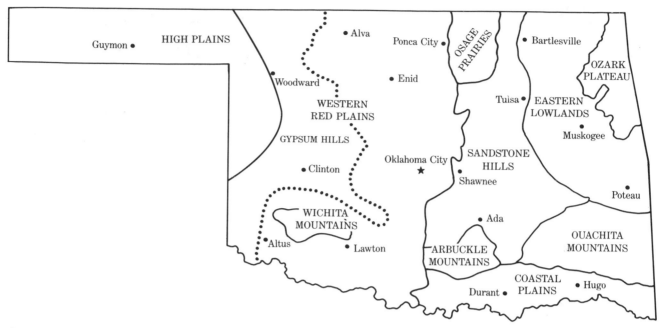

Geographic Regions

A complete list of all the rivers and streams in Oklahoma would have about 500 names. The flow of water in these streams varies greatly.

Streams in eastern Oklahoma are likely to have a steady flow. Plenty of rain keeps them rippling out of the Ozark Plateau and Ouachita Mountains.

Western Oklahoma rivers are usually dry, though water may be flowing beneath the surface. During rainy weather these rivers can become muddy-red, swirling torrents. They may overflow their banks and destroy farm land. Pioneers who tried to cross these flooded streams were sometimes drowned or sank in quicksand.

Little Sahara State Park near Waynoka. The dunes form when winds whip sand from the dry Cimarron riverbed. (Fred Marvel)

3. EASTERN OKLAHOMA CAN BE DIVIDED INTO SIX GEOGRAPHIC REGIONS.

Ozark Plateau. This region is in northeast Oklahoma and parts of Arkansas and Missouri. It is bounded on the west by the Grand River and on the south by the Arkansas River Valley.

The Ozark region is famous for its wild, rugged beauty. Forests of oak, hickory, and other trees grow here. Rivers have cut steep-sided valleys in the flat tableland.

"Our mountains aren't very high, but our valleys are deep," goes an Ozark expression.

Pure, cold springs feed the Illinois, Spavinaw, and other rivers. Lakes along the Spavinaw are one source of water for the city of Tulsa.

Broad flat areas in the Ozarks are suitable for grazing and farming. Specialty crops are planted that hold the loose soil in place. These include strawberries, grapes, vegetables, and fruit trees. An annual Strawberry Festival in Stilwell attracts many visitors.

The Ozarks became Cherokee country in the 1830s. The Cherokees were forced to move west from the southeastern part of the United States. They established their capital at Tahlequah. The tragic story of the Cherokee removal is told in a musical drama called *Trail of Tears*. It is performed on summer nights at the Tsa-La-Gi outdoor theatre south of Tahlequah.

The Cookson Hills make up the rugged southern part of the Ozark region. From the 1870s to the 1930s, these hills were a popular hideout. Outlaws and moonshiners felt safe there. Today, Lake Tenkiller draws many visitors to the Cookson Hills.

Eastern Lowlands. This region is west and south of the Ozarks in northeastern Oklahoma. It has two parts. The "Prairie Plains" stretch west of the Ozarks as far as the cities of Tulsa and Bartlesville. The lower Arkansas Valley, from Tulsa to Fort Smith, is also part of the Eastern Lowlands.

Rivers are important to this region. Manmade lakes on the Verdigris and Grand provide recreation and a thriving tourist business. The lakes also furnish water for the McClellan-Kerr Arkansas River Navigation System. Freight barges come inland on this waterway to the ports of Muskogee and Catoosa.

The best farmland is in the broad flat river valleys. Spinach and other vegetables grow well in the Arkansas Valley. Local canneries buy a lot of the vegetables.

Cattle ranching is an important industry in the Eastern Lowlands. Tall grasses provide excellent grazing on the rougher prairie lands. Will Rogers, the popular part-Cherokee actor and humorist, grew up on a cattle ranch at Oologah near the Verdigris River north of Claremore. Rogers was already doing rope tricks when he attended secondary school at Vinita which he later called "my college town." Rogers was buried at Clare-

Family fun on the Illinois River near Tahlequah. (Fred Marvel)

more where thousands of people visit the Will Rogers Memorial.

The spirit or pioneer farm and ranch life along the Verdigris was captured in the plays of Lynn Riggs, a part-Cherokee. Riggs grew up on a farm near Claremore. His *Green Grow the Lilacs,* a folk opera, was used by Richard Rodgers and Oscar Hammerstein to produce the great musical comedy *Oklahoma!* The Lynn Riggs Memorial at Claremore's community college contains a famed "surrey with the fringe on top" and other memorabilia.

Some of the other cities in the Eastern Lowlands are Pryor, Nowata, Wagoner, Muskogee, Sallisaw, and Poteau.

Ouachita Mountains. The Ouachitas (Wah-she-taws) are a scenic paradise in southeast Oklahoma and in Arkansas. They are a series of parallel mountain ranges. The ranges have interesting names like Winding Stair, Jackfork, and Kiamichi. Rich Mountain is the highest point in the Ouachitas. It is nearly 3,000 feet above sea level.

Many people visit the Ouachitas for outdoor fun. They fish, hunt, camp, or just enjoy the scenery. The Ouachita National Forest is popular with tourists. Beavers Bend State Park is one of the most beautiful places in Oklahoma. The Broken Bow Reservoir is nearby.

All of the Ouachita region is good cattle country. Farming is done mainly in the valleys. Lumbering is the most important industry. The timber comes from pines and other trees on the mountain slopes.

Coastal Plains (Red River Plains). This strip of land along the Red River is about forty miles wide. It stretches from the Arbuckles to the Ouachitas in southeastern Oklahoma. A land of nearly level slopes, it is part of the coastal plain that extends north from the Gulf of Mexico.

Some parts of the Coastal Plains are still wild. Even elephants are hard to find in the dense vegetation. In 1975, two of these escaped from a circus wintering in Hugo. The elephants wandered for days before they were found.

Much of the farmland on the Red River plain is worn out. In the past, heavy rains washed away soils and formed gullies. Now, farmers try to conserve the land. They use *contour plowing* and other methods to improve their farms.

Since World War II, towns in this region have created jobs by bringing in manufacturing plants. Durant, Hugo, Idabel, Madill, and Marietta all attracted new industries. A large mill in Valliant boasts of having the biggest papermaking machine in the world.

Sandstone Hills Region. This region is a fairly rough area of land in east-central Oklahoma. It stretches from the Red River Plains on the south to eastern Osage County on the Kansas border.

The sandstone hills were formed by *erosion* of water, wind, and frost. For millions of years these forces wore away the soft shale and clay that surround the harder sandstone. The hilly slopes were eventually covered with blackjack oak, post oak, and hackberry as well as a tangle of underbrush.

"Cross Timbers"—that's what early travelers and settlers called the scrub timber belt that separated eastern Oklahoma from the western part. Washington Irving, a famous New York writer who visited here in 1832, also used another term, "forests of iron." The Cross Timbers was hard to

penetrate. The jungle of short trees, briars, and vines "tore the flesh of man and horse that had to scramble through them."

In the 1890s, pioneer settlers began clearing the land. They removed blackjacks and other vegetation to plant crops. During rainy seasons, runoff water washed away the thin sandy soil and cut deep gullies in the fields. Erosion was destroying the land.

By the 1930s, farmers were learning that the fragile soils should be left in grass or trees. Experts at Oklahoma State (formerly A. and M.) showed them how to smooth out the sides of large gullies and to plant native grasses. Erosion was checked. Before long, beef cattle grazed on lush grasslands. Farmers also improved land still under cultivation by using crop rotation and other conservation methods.

Petroleum attracted many people to the Sandstone Hills country. Some of the biggest producing oil fields in the world were discovered in this area. Nearby cities grew rapidly. These included Cushing, Drumright, Sapulpa, Shawnee, Seminole, Ada, and others.

Osage Prairies. This region is in western Osage County and parts of adjoining counties. It is an extension of the Kansas Flint Hills.

Great herds of buffalo once munched on the Indian grass, cordgrass, and bluestem. The grass was belly high to a horse. Today, large ranches occupy much of the land. The cowboy and his cattle have hardly changed the tall grassland. Fences are few. Roads are far apart.

The most important activity, other than ranching, in the Osage Prairies was the Burbank oil field discovery in 1920.

4. WESTERN OKLAHOMA CAN BE DIVIDED INTO TWO PLAINS AND TWO MOUNTAIN REGIONS.

The Arbuckle and Wichita mountain regions are in southern Oklahoma. The High Plains cover the Panhandle and the northwest corner of the state. The rest of western Oklahoma is in a region identified by its red soil.

Western Red Plains. This rolling plains region of red soils is between the north and south

Yearling steers grazing on Osage Prairie bluestem grass near Pawhuska. (USDA, Soil Conservation Service)

boundaries of the state. It slopes down from the west to central Oklahoma. Four major rivers flow across it: the Cimarron, North Canadian, South Canadian, and Washita. The Western Red Plains is the largest physiographic region in Oklahoma.

Agriculture is a major industry in the Red Plains. The region gets 20 to 30 inches of rain annually—enough for dry farming. Wheat and grain sorghums are grown in the fertile red soil. Cotton, peanuts, hay, soybeans, and other crops do well in the southern part of the Red Plains. Some of the cropland is irrigated. Many farmers derive income from beef cattle. Ranchers use the rougher land in the west almost entirely for cattle grazing.

The Western Red Plains Region has the biggest population. Oklahoma City is the most populous urban area. Other cities in this region are Enid, Ponca City, Stillwater, and Alva in the north. Guthrie, Edmond, Norman, and Chickasha are in the central section. Altus, Duncan, and Lawton are some of the cities in the southern part of the Red Plains.

The Gypsum Hills are sometimes classified as a separate region. The white gypsum in these hills stands out in contrast to the red earth of western Oklahoma. Some of the "Gyp Hills" have a round gypsum dome. Others are *buttes* with a flat ledge of gypsum on top.

In some places, layers of red shale are mixed in the gypsum. Visitors at Roman Nose State Park have a good view of red and white *bluffs*. This park is near Watonga in Blaine County. In pioneer days, outlaws hid out in the cool valleys of this area after they stole horses from homesteaders or robbed a country store.

Today, the Gypsum Hills are important to several towns in Blaine County. In Southard, a *company town,* the U.S. Gypsum Company makes wallboard from gypsum. The town of Okeene sponsors an annual spring Rattlesnake Roundup in the Gypsum Hills. Hunters compete for prizes given for the "longest snake" and the "biggest snake."

The Glass Mountains, near Fairview in Major County, are unusual. They contain a clear gypsum called *selenite* that sparkles in the sun like glass. The Glass Mountains are easily spotted by the Flying Farmers group who attend the annual Fairview Fly-in.

Other rows of gypsum hills are found between Woodward County in the northwest and Harmon County in the southwest corner of Oklahoma. Wallboard is made at a gypsum plant in

A gypsum butte in the Glass Mountains. (U.S. Geological Survey photo by G. I. Adams)

Oklahoma City skyline. (Oklahoma City Chamber of Commerce)

Duke. This town, located west of Altus, is also known for its underground high school. The school doubles as a community storm cellar.

High Plains. The Panhandle and northwest Oklahoma are part of the *High Plains.* This region is the highest, driest, and flattest part of Oklahoma. A solid carpet of short buffalo grass once covered the High Plains.

Most of the level, treeless High Plains in Oklahoma is divided into huge farms. The soil is good, but crops have often failed for lack of rain. In the 1930s, *drought* turned this region into a "dust bowl." Strong winds blew away the topsoil. Today, many farmers pump ground water to irrigate their fields.

The cattle industry is also important on the High Plains. The rough land in western Cimarron County is ranching country. Guymon, in Texas County, is one of the biggest cattle feeding centers in the United States.

Guymon is also close to the huge Hugoton Natural Gas Field. The nation's largest helium plant is at Keyes in Cimarron County.

The Arbuckle and the Wichita Mountains Regions. The Arbuckle Mountains are in south-central Oklahoma. The Wichita Mountains

Turner Falls in the Arbuckles. (Fred Marvel)

8

are in the southwest near Lawton. Millions of years ago, both of these mountain areas were much bigger. They were worn down by erosion.

Mount Scott is the highest peak in the Wichitas. This peak is 2,464 feet above sea level. It rises about a thousand feet above its base. A scenic drive up Mount Scott provides a birdseye view of Lake Lawtonka. This lake supplies Lawton and Fort Sill with water. A wildlife refuge in the Wichitas protects a buffalo herd and some longhorn cattle.

The Arbuckles are famous for swift, clear streams and waterfalls. Visitors enjoy Lake Arbuckle south of Sulphur. The Chickasaw National Recreational Area is nearby. In season, the redbuds and wildflowers are beautiful here.

The Arbuckles and Wichitas are known for beautiful scenery, but are also a source of stone. Good granite in several colors is quarried. Limestone is crushed for cement. The sand and gravel is needed for many things. A high-purity sand found in the Arbuckles is used for glassmaking.

The bluestem grass country around the Arbuckles is called "Hereford Heaven." Some of the finest cattle and horses in the world are raised here. The most famous animal was a bull named "Old 81." He is buried in a tile-lined vault. The bull belonged to ex-Governor Roy Turner.

ROUNDUP

1. Define the following: plain, prairie, plateau, relief, and physiographic region.
2. When was the Paleozoic Age? List the important changes that occurred during that age.
3. What are the highest and lowest places in Oklahoma and their elevations?
4. Name Oklahoma's two river systems. What area is drained by each?
5. Fill in a chart with columns labeled: Ten Physiographic Zones; Location; Main Characteristics; and Unusual Events, Places, or People.
A. Think about it! "Each of the physiographic regions of Oklahoma is a part of a larger zone that covers several states." Look at a physical map of the United States and explain this statement.
B. "Tourism is a growing industry here because Oklahoma's geography has much to offer visitors and outdoors people." Explain.
C. Try this! See the list of "motivating projects and activities" in the appendix.

2

CLIMATE, FLORA, AND FAUNA

Will Rogers was exaggerating about Oklahoma weather when he said, "If you don't like the weather, wait a minute!"

The weather in Oklahoma, of course, can change very quickly. One reason is the state's location. When cold polar air from the north collides with warm southerly winds, the result can be a storm. Few states, however, are blessed with as many sunny "Indian summer" days. The *weather* can be changeable but the yearlong *climate* is mild.

The state has a variety of plant life (*flora*) as well as weather. Forests in eastern Oklahoma contrast greatly with the western short grass plain. The most unusual flora is the belt of short trees and tangled undergrowth known as the Cross Timbers.

Wildlife (*fauna*) is as varied as the plant life and weather. The coming of settlers took away the habitat of many animals, including the buffalo, elk, and black bear. Oklahoma, however, still has a wide assortment of *vertebrates*: mammals, birds, fish, and reptiles.

1. OKLAHOMA HAS A MILD CLIMATE AND A GREAT VARIETY OF WEATHER.

Oklahoma is "a land of spangled sunshine with variations." The sun shines two-thirds of all daylight hours in Oklahoma City and slightly less in Tulsa.

Climate is the general pattern of weather over a long period of time.

In comparison to the rest of the nation, Oklahoma's climate is mild. What makes it so different is the great variety and sudden changes of weather.

Oklahoma is in a transition zone. Two air masses meet here. Cold, dry *polar continental air* moves in from Canada. Warm *tropical air* comes from the Gulf of Mexico.

The northerly winds predominate during the winter. Periods of extreme cold are infrequent, however. Winters here are shorter and less severe than those in the northern Plains states. Winds from the south prevail most of the year in Oklahoma. They make the hot summer days more comfortable.

The southern and eastern sections of the state are affected the most by the tropical air. These areas have higher *humidity* and get more rain than the western and northern parts of the state.

Weather depends on the temperature, humidity, amount of sunshine or clouds, wind, and *precipitation*.

Every county in Oklahoma has stations to record weather data. On any given day, a variety of weather might be reported by these stations. It would not be unusual to hear that a cold wind is sweeping over the Panhandle while people in the southeast are basking in the sun.

Changes in the weather. In April, 1938, hundreds of students were caught in a weather turnaround at Enid. They came from three states for a spring band festival. The bands were enjoying a beautiful sunny day. All of a sudden, a cold *norther* rolled in. Snow drifts blocked roads. Icy telephone lines fell down. Parents were worried. Happily, Enid people took the thinly-clad young visitors into their homes until the roads were cleared.

Most of the damaging storms come in the spring. Oklahoma's most destructive *tornado* on record hit Woodward on April 9, 1947. More than a hundred people were killed, 95 of them in Woodward. The state's worst hailstorm struck Oklahoma City the night of May 23–24, 1968. The hail caused more than $20 million property damage.

The tornado is a terrible storm. It is made of

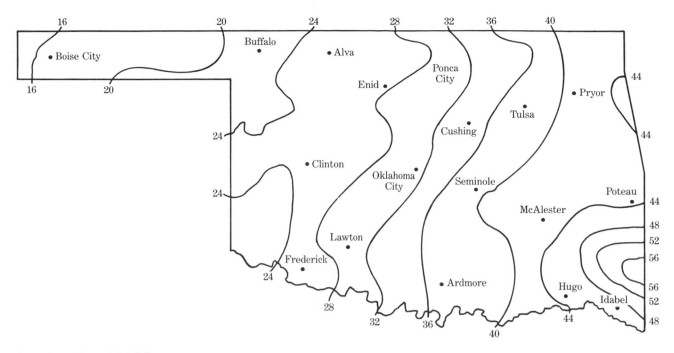

Approximate Annual Rainfall

strong winds whirling in a circle at high speed. The storm itself may travel slowly but strikes with a loud roar. It can destroy buildings, uproot trees, and toss cars into the air like toys. A number of Oklahoma towns have seen the need for storm shelters. The "Duke Plan" for underground schools has been followed in Blanchard, Comanche, Seiling, Wellston, and other places.

Oklahoma's weather is hard to predict. A folk story about a farmer exaggerates this point. On a hot, sunny day he was plowing with a team of horses. One of the horses overheated and fell dead. While the farmer was removing the harness from the dead horse, a *blizzard* moved in. The other horse froze to death.

Rainfall. In Oklahoma, the farther west one goes, the less the amount of rainfall. The Ouachita Mountains in the southeast get over 50 inches a year. The west end of the Panhandle averages less than 16 inches. Those are the extremes. The central part of the state receives about 30 to 40 inches.

A record 84.47 inches of rain fell on Kiamichi Tower in LeFlore County in 1957. The least amount was 6.53 inches in Cimarron County in 1956. Rainfall is light on the High Plains because this region is not in the path of moist, tropical air from the Gulf of Mexico.

Snow. The snowfall pattern in Oklahoma is just the reverse of rainfall. The amount of snow increases from about two inches in the southeast to approximately 20 inches in the western Panhandle.

The record seasonal snowfall in Oklahoma was 87.3 inches at Beaver in the Panhandle. That was in the winter of 1911–1912.

A tornado cloud. (National Severe Storms Laboratory, National Oceanic and Atmospheric Administration, Norman)

11

Temperature. Southern Oklahoma is the warmest part of the state. In the southwest, the temperature rises above 90° about 120 days a year. It drops below 32° only 55 days a year.

The Panhandle is the coldest area. In western Cimarron County the temperature goes above 90° only 85 days a year. On the cold side, this area has 125 to 140 days of sub-32° temperature.

The growing season, or freeze-free period, ranges from 220 days along the Red River to 170 days in the western Panhandle. Farmers wait until the danger of a hard frost is passed before planting spring crops.

Recreation. The climate of Oklahoma is favorable to a long vacation season. People who like the outdoors can enjoy a wide variety of recreation. Sparkling lakes, parks, and resorts provide boating, fishing, camping, hiking, and other activities.

2. OKLAHOMA HAS A RICH VARIETY OF PLANT LIFE.

Oklahoma has more different kinds of native plants than most states. Why? The chief reason is the state's variety of climate, soils, and terrain.

The natural vegetation of Oklahoma can be

Having fun at Lake Texoma State Park. (Fred Marvel)

divided into three groups. These are *grasslands, savanna-woodlands,* and *forests.*

Grasslands. Grasses are found in all parts of Oklahoma. They are the main vegetation in the drier western counties where few trees grow.

Short grasses grow with as little as ten inches of rain a year. Buffalo grass, grama, and wire grass do well on the High Plains in the Panhandle and the counties of Harper and Ellis. The short grasses provide good grazing for livestock.

Most of the once-vast carpet of buffalo grass has been plowed up. In the spring and early summer it is now an ocean of wheat. The Russian thistle, a weed, is also seen in many places where grass once grew. Thistles got started in the farm country years ago. Thistle seeds were in wheat seed brought from Russia. When the thistle dries it becomes a "tumbling tumbleweed."

Mixed grasses. A variety of short and tall grasses grow in northern and west-central Oklahoma. This area gets 25 or more inches of rain each year. Most of the sea of grass that once covered the Western Red Plains region, however, is gone. The plains are planted in wheat, cotton, and other crops.

Tall prairie grasses grow chiefly in eastern Oklahoma where there is lots of rain. Bluestem is the main tall grass. Bluestem Lake in Osage County is named after this grass. Now cattle country, the Osage prairies were once grazed by great herds of buffalo.

The bluestem also grows in many valleys, including the Eastern Lowlands west of the Ozarks. Some farmers cut the tall prairie grasses for hay.

Smith Paul, the first white settler in Pauls Valley, told about tall bluestem along the Washita River in 1847. "A man on horseback was almost hidden," he said. Paul had come west with the Chickasaw tribe. He lived in a log cabin while farming and ranching thousands of acres in "Smith Paul's Valley."

Savanna-woodlands. A *savanna* is a grassland that is partly covered with trees and bushes. The trees are usually shorter than forest trees. In some parts of the West, these short trees are called chaparral.

Much of the *Cross Timbers* belt is savanna-woodland. This belt has many scrub trees. It is the largest natural vegetation area in Oklahoma. The belt covers parts of central, eastern, and southern Oklahoma. Blackjack oak, dwarfed post oak, and hackberry are trees that grow in the Cross Timbers belt. The wood is not much good. It is used for fence posts and firewood. Bushes, vines, and briars made the Cross Timbers a real barrier to early explorers in this area.

Western Oklahoma is too dry for most trees. Desert plants such as the sagebrush, yucca, and cactus are more common. Shim oak, however, is found in the Antelope Hills. Junipers and pinyons—scrubby, pine-like trees—grow in the northwest corner of the Panhandle. Mesquite trees are seen in the southwest part of the state. The mesquite roots are strong. They grow far out in search of water. Little moisture is left for grass.

An old story is told about a greenhorn cowboy in Greer County. He had to dig mesquite roots for firewood. Then he climbed up to repair a windmill to get water for cattle. "I don't understand a country," he said, "where you have to climb for water and dig for wood."

Forests are found only in the eastern part of Oklahoma. These forests are important to us. They provide lumber and places for outdoor fun. The forests also protect wildlife, the soil, and water.

In the Ozarks, oak and hickory are the main forest trees. These hardwoods are used to make furniture and many other things.

The Ouachita Mountains have dense forests. Shortleaf pines grow at higher elevations. This soft pine is Oklahoma's main lumber tree. Oak and other hardwood trees are also cut for lumber in the Ouachitas.

Oklahoma has many trees that are not in forests. More different kinds of trees grow here than in all of Europe. Even in the drier west, the cottonwood, willows, and salt cedars grow along streams. The tall, white-branched cottonwood was a welcome sight to pioneers crossing the grassy plains.

Many trees in wet southeastern Oklahoma are like those found in the lower Mississippi River states. Miles and miles of loblolly pines grow in sandy soil. Others are the white oak, sweet gum, hard maple, pawpaw, and tulip tree. The holly tree stands out in winter with its bright red berries. Magnolias give some of the streets in Durant the fragrance of a charming "Old South" city.

Oklahoma has some famous trees. The "million dollar elm" is in Pawhuska. Many oil leases in Osage County were sold under its branches. The largest chinaberry tree in the United States is at Carnegie in Caddo County.

McCurtain County can brag about several record trees. The oldest living tree in the state, until it died, was a 2,000-year-old cypress at Eagleton, east of Broken Bow. The state's tallest tree, a sweet gum, grows in McCurtain County. The biggest redbud is also there.

The redbud is the state tree. Blossoms of the redbud and dogwood are pretty in the spring. Mistletoe clings to many trees in Oklahoma. Its blossom is the state flower. Pioneers used the mistletoe at funerals when they had no flowers. Today, some mistletoe is cut and sold.

3. OKLAHOMA HAS A WIDE RANGE OF WILDLIFE.

Prehistoric reptiles and animals. Millions of years ago, *dinosaurs* lived in Oklahoma's swamps.

Thousands of years ago, this area was the home of the elephant-like *mammoth*. The giant bison, the small horse, and camels also lived here. All of these animals are now extinct.

The buffalo. Millions of buffalo (American bison) roamed the plains in the 1880s. The coming of the railroad to the West changed that. Buffalo hunters killed the beasts for hides. Carcasses were left to rot. The grasslands were soon covered with bleached buffalo bones.

The few remaining buffalo in Oklahoma are in captivity. One herd can be seen at the Wichita Mountains Wildlife Refuge near Lawton. Other buffalo are on the grounds of the Pawnee Bill Museum, a state-owned park in Pawnee. The Pawnee

Gordon W. "Pawnee Bill" Lillie. (Archives and Manuscripts Division of the Oklahoma Historical Society, hereafter abbreviated OHS)

park was formerly the buffalo ranch of Gordon W. Lillie, better known as "Pawnee Bill."

Lillie came to *Indian Territory* in 1882 as a nineteen-year-old adventurer. He hunted buffalo and worked at the Pawnee Indian Agency. Lillie joined Buffalo Bill's Wild West Show and later formed his own show—the Pawnee Bill Wild West Circus. An old restored 10-by-66 foot billboard poster at the park advertises a Pawnee Bill show in the town of Lamont, Oklahoma. The poster features Bill, his wife May, cowboys, cavalry, and a herd of buffalo.

When flickering silent movies ended the popularity of wild west shows, Pawnee Bill retired to his sprawling ranch near Pawnee in 1913. There he soon developed the world's largest privately-owned buffalo herd.

Other big game animals. The large American elk and the smaller antelope were once plentiful in Oklahoma. Elk are now protected at the Wichita refuge. Some have been turned loose in forest areas. Only a few antelope are left in

Oklahoma. Young antelopes are usually killed by coyotes.

The black bear is another animal not seen here in the wild any more. The whitetailed deer, however, is one big game animal that is still hunted in Oklahoma.

Smaller animals in Oklahoma. The coyote, whose name means "barking dog," is perhaps the most adaptable animal in the state. Coyotes eat a wide variety of small animals, insects, carrion, and plants. They thrive on the plains and prefer the rabbit for food. Coyote pups are born blind in March or April. By fall they are on their own. Coyotes multiply fast and are a problem to farmers because they kill small livestock. No amount of hunting, trapping, or poisoning can wipe them out.

The badger has been known to be a hunting partner of the coyote. The badger hunts mice, gophers, and ground squirrels. It is found in central and western Oklahoma.

The bobcat also hunts smaller animals, snakes, and birds. But it will kill chickens and small livestock too.

Small furbearing animals abound in Oklahoma. Cottontail, jack, and swamp rabbits do well here. The state has three *species* of foxes. The red fox is a mouse catcher. The gray fox likes cottontail rabbits for food. It also climbs. The swift fox is being killed off fast because it is not as sly as most foxes.

Squirrels might be seen in any tree area. The gray squirrel likes hickory forests and city parks. The southern flying squirrel can glide. Loose skin on its long legs flattens out like an airplane wing. Most squirrels are up early, but not the fox squirrel. On cold days it may stay in the nest until noon.

Furbearing muskrats, beaver, and mink like water and trees. Mink are also raised in captivity for their valuable furs. Raccoons, which also live near water, wash their food before eating it.

The opossum looks like an oversized rat. Young 'possums are carried in a pouch. Another animal, the striped skunk, might be found anywhere in the state. Whew!

The armadillo is one of Oklahoma's unusual

Scissor-tailed flycatcher, the state bird. (A painting by Wallace Hughes)

animals. It has an outer covering of shell-like plating. The armadillo likes the rocky country in the western part of the state. Its main diet is ants and beetles.

Birds. Oklahoma has several hundred species of birds. They help farmers by eating insects that destroy crops. Sparrows, finches, robins, and larks are very common.

Some species of owls, larks, blue jays, and cardinals stay here year-round. Many other birds are *migratory*. The scissor-tailed flycatcher, the state bird, goes south for the winter. So do orioles, catbirds, warblers, and the ever-singing mockingbird.

Birds in the unusual category include the turkey buzzard and the comical roadrunner. The roadrunner can't decide if it is a bird or a land racer. It frequently races cars along the roadside. Unlike most birds, the roadrunner eats lizards and snakes. Two other unusual birds are the sand hill crane and the blue heron which visit Oklahoma in the spring and fall.

Bald eagles winter in Oklahoma. The bald eagle is on the *endangered species* list. That means there are fewer of them now and they could become extinct. A small number of golden eagles nest in western Oklahoma. They are protected by state and federal laws.

Crows are a nuisance. Several million spend the winter in the Fort Cobb area. The crows eat tons of feed grains and peanuts. Farmers usually welcome crow hunters.

Game birds. Prairie chickens nest in grassy, open country. They are hunted in northern Oklahoma. The males have air sacs on the throat that enable them to make a loud mating call.

Ring-necked pheasants live in grain farm areas in the north part of the state. The male has a green head and a ring around its neck.

The bobwhite is the most common quail in Oklahoma. At night a covey of bobwhites form a circle. Their heads face out. Another species, the scaled quail, is found mainly in Cimarron, Harmon, and Greer counties.

Mourning doves are found statewide. The dove weighs about four ounces. The woodcock is mainly in the southeast. It weighs about six or seven ounces and has large eyes and a long bill.

Wild turkeys are the biggest game birds. The Rio Grande turkey in western Oklahoma is smaller .than the Eastern turkey. Both are more scarce than they used to be.

Reptiles. Many kinds of turtles, lizards, and snakes are found in Oklahoma.

The most common land turtle is the painted box tortoise. The mud turtle and the soft-shelled turtle live in the water. Snapping turtles, the largest species, weigh about 75 pounds.

Lizards range from the collared lizard (mountain boomer) to the sand swifts in western Oklahoma. The horned toad is a small, flat lizard—not

Roadrunner.

15

Rattlesnake hunt near Mangum. (Fred Marvel)

Sport fish. The white bass (sand bass) is the Oklahoma state fish. White bass travel in large schools in open water. One female can lay up to a million eggs.

The striped bass is a big relative of the white bass. It can weigh up to forty pounds. State fish hatcheries cross the striped bass and white bass. This striped bass *hybrid* grows fast. All the bass like shad fish for food.

Largemouth bass have been stocked in nearly every lake in Oklahoma. This fish helps to control the sunfish and blue gill populations. These smaller fish often multiply too fast.

Smallmouth bass prefer cool, clear streams in eastern Oklahoma. They seldom weigh more than two pounds. Spotted bass also like flowing streams. But they live in still, warmer water too.

The white crappie is a small, flat fish. Crappie fish are in most lakes and rivers of Oklahoma. People like the crappie's sweet meat.

Catfish don't mind muddy water. Huge blue catfish are native to the Red and Arkansas rivers. They are bigger than the channel catfish. The channel cat feed on almost anything. Fishermen have good luck with worms. The flathead catfish feeds on smaller fish in larger streams.

The large walleye has been put in Oklahoma's bigger lakes since the 1950s. The walleye stay in deep water during the day. They don't like the bright sun.

a toad. Lizards are harmless. They help us by eating insects.

Most snakes in Oklahoma are also harmless and useful. They gobble up insects and rodents that damage crops. The worm snake, green snake, blue racer, garter, and black snake are common. The bull snake is one of the largest. This snakes helps farmers by destroying mice, gophers, moles, and insects. The blow snake, also called hog nose, scares people by swelling its head and hissing. The king snake and water snakes are other nonpoisonous snakes.

Beware of poisonous snakes! The water moccasin, called cottonmouth, is found in southern and eastern Oklahoma. The copperhead is dreaded in timber country. This snake is seen around old buildings or on stream banks. It strikes without warning.

Rattlesnakes? There are several kinds in Oklahoma. The timber rattler is mainly in eastern Oklahoma. The prairie rattler is a small, gray snake. The diamond-backed rattler likes the rough country in western Oklahoma.

Several towns sponsor annual rattlesnake hunts. Snake hunters comb the hills near Mangum, Okeene, Waurika, and Waynoka for rattlers. They compete for prizes. The hunt is part of a weekend of fun activities.

A happy fisherman with a big catfish. (Russ Boshart)

16

Rainbow trout are not native to Oklahoma. Trout are stocked in the cool Illinois River below Tenkiller Dam. The Blue River, near Tishomingo, is stocked with keeper-size trout from November through March.

Oklahoma is a fisherman's paradise. About three dozen large lakes and hundreds of small ones give the state more than a million acres of water playground.

ROUNDUP

1. Define: weather, climate, flora, and fauna.
2. Explain why Oklahoma has a great variety of weather.
3. Which parts of Oklahoma are the wettest, the driest, the warmest, and the coldest?
4. List Oklahoma's three main natural vegetation groups. Give examples of each.
5. What reptiles and animals lived in the Oklahoma area before buffalo roamed the plains?
6. Make a chart of Oklahoma wildlife with these column heads: Big Game Animals, Small Game Animals, Birds, Game Birds, Poisonous Snakes, Other Reptiles, and Sport Fish.
A. Try this! Draw a map of Oklahoma or construct a bar graph to show the high and low temperatures on a given day in five Oklahoma cities, located in different parts of the state.

3

AGRICULTURE

Agriculture is one of Oklahoma's basic industries that produce wealth and provide jobs. The other basic industries are mining, manufacturing, and lumbering. The tourist industry does not produce goods but is an "unsung hero" in the state's economy. Thousands of Oklahomans have jobs or businesses that depend on tourists and travelers.

Agriculture has been an important basic industry in Oklahoma since prehistoric Native Americans planted crops along the rivers. Today, beef production is the biggest source of agricultural income in Oklahoma. Wheat and cotton are the leading cash crops. A variety of other crops are grown: grain sorghums, soybeans, corn, peanuts, vegetables, nuts, and fruits. Farmers now often plant a diversity of crops.

Agriculture has undergone many changes, especially since the "dirty thirties." Farms are larger today. More efficient mechanical equipment is used than in the past. Production has been increased by improved seeds, fertilizers, insecticides, and irrigation in some parts of western Oklahoma.

Some things, of course, have not changed. Farmers are still at the mercy of the weather, interest rates, and market prices for their crops and livestock.

Effect of physical geography on agriculture. Agriculture in Oklahoma is as diverse as the physical geography. Many factors determine how the land in a given area is used. The amount of rainfall must be considered. How long is the growing season? How level is the terrain? Hilly country may have thin, rocky soils that should be left in grasses. The sandy soil in some areas requires special tilling to conserve moisture and to prevent erosion. A farmer must know all these things and much more to use his land properly.

Oklahoma land use areas. Oklahoma can be divided into *agricultural land use areas.* Crops vary from region to region, though cattle are raised everywhere. Farmers in the northwest grow wheat and grain sorghums primarily. In the southwest, cotton and wheat are the main crops. The northeast-central area is a mixed farming region: corn, alfalfa, oats, soybeans, vegetables, and other crops. The southeast is a cotton and mixed farming region.

1. AGRICULTURE WAS OKLAHOMA'S FIRST IMPORTANT INDUSTRY.

Native American farmers. Early people in Oklahoma were farming here at least a thousand years ago. They grew corn, beans, squash, and pumpkins.

The economy of the Five Civilized Tribes was based on agriculture. After their forced removal from the Deep South, tribal members cleared land in Indian Territory. They grew crops of corn, vegetables, wheat, oats, barley, and cotton. They planted fruit trees and gathered berries and wild pecans in the woods.

At first, the tribes practiced *subsistence farming*—growing only what they needed. Soon, however, the Creeks and Choctaws were selling surplus corn to white emigrants and the U.S. government. In 1836, the Choctaws shipped 500 bales of cotton down the Red River to market.

Commercial farming grew rapidly in Indian Territory (eastern Oklahoma) after towns were founded and mines developed. The coming of the railroads in the 1870s made it easier for farmers to ship their crops to market for a profit.

Non-Indian farmers. Non-Indian farmers were allowed to settle in Oklahoma in the late 1800s. Pioneers who came to this last frontier were eager and hard working. What they needed most was capital—money to buy farm implements, seed, livestock, fencing, and other things.

Most settlers in western Oklahoma were from states that had greater rainfall. Despite occasional droughts and poor farming methods, however, many farmers were prospering before Oklahoma became a state in 1907. By trial and error, farmers learned how to cultivate the soil. They saw the need to conserve moisture and to prevent erosion.

2. OKLAHOMA'S AGRICULTURE HAS BEEN CHANGING.

The dirty thirties depression was the beginning of many changes. Farming progress came to a screeching halt in the 1930s. Drought, erosion, and low prices for crops and livestock all took their toll. Many farmers lost or deserted their farms and moved away—some to the cities to look for jobs.

Oklahoma, like the rest of the nation, began changing from a rural to an urban society. Eventually, many rural people found jobs in manufacturing and other occupations.

Statistics tell the story of urbanization. By definition, the U.S. Bureau of Census classifies anyone living in a town or city with more than 2,500 people as *urban*. Technically, then, any county which has no town with more than 2,500 people is 100 percent *rural*.

In 1930, about two-thirds of Oklahoma's population (2,396,040) was rural. By 1980, only one-third of the population (3,025,290) was rural.

Bigger farms and fewer farmers. In 1950, Oklahoma had 142,000 farms averaging 253 acres each. Since then, the land has been consolidated. An agricultural census in 1982 showed that the average size farm had almost doubled to 446 acres. The number of farms was down to 72,000.

Many of the people who left farming were tenants. The number of tenants dropped from nearly half of all farmers in the 1940s to about 11 percent in 1982.

Irrigation. Irrigation of crops is one of the most important developments in Oklahoma agriculture since World War II. Irrigation farming got underway with the opening of the Altus-Lugert project in 1947. Water for this project comes from the North Fork of the Red River. Deep wells also provide water in the Altus area.

Ground water is used in most other irrigated

Center pivot irrigation system in alfalfa field on Ralph Triplett farm in Woodward County. (USDA, Soil Conservation photo by James H. Shearhart)

areas in Oklahoma. Farmers in the Panhandle pump water from the Ogallala Aquifer where it has been collecting for millions of years. In the Anadarko area, peanuts as well as some cotton, wheat, and other crops are irrigated with water from the Rush Springs Sandstone Aquifer. In the southeastern part of the state, the Antlers Sand Aquifer is the source of ground water for some irrigation.

To help conserve water in the aquifer, the City of Guymon built a wastewater treatment plant. The treated water is used to irrigate wheat and bluestem grass. By the time the water trickles down to the aquifer, it is clean and purified.

3. CATTLE PROVIDE OKLAHOMA'S LEADING SOURCE OF FARM INCOME.

Beef cattle. Beef production is the leading source of farm income in Oklahoma. Cattle are raised everywhere—on both farms and ranches.

The main ranch areas are in the mountainous country of southern Oklahoma, the western Panhandle, and the Osage Hills north of Tulsa. The traditional breeds are the Hereford, Angus, and Shorthorn. Exotic breeds include the

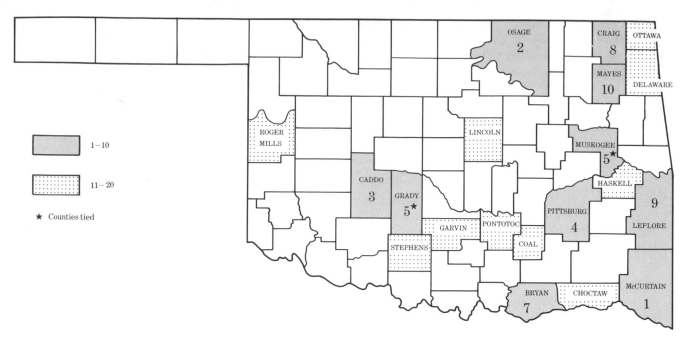

BEEF COWS: Top beef producing counties, 1987 ranking.

Legend:
- 1–10
- 11–20
- ★ Counties tied

Charolai and Limousin. The Brangus and other mixed breeds are common too.

The modern cattle industry in Oklahoma is a mixture of the old and the new. Cowboys still wear wide-brimmed hats, boots, and blue jeans. They ride the range as they did in earlier times. Cattlemen today, however, use more machines— electric pumps to fill water tanks, hay loaders,

Cowboys in the 1880s. (National Archives)

and tractors. The pickup truck is the symbol of the modern cattleman.

Branding has changed. The squeeze chute has replaced the old method of roping and stretching the animal on the ground. Now the branding iron is more likely to be heated with butane instead of a cow chip fire.

Feedlots. Cattle raising is a business today. Many ranchers run their cattle on grassland for awhile and then take them to feedlots. There they are fattened rapidly on special feed. In some areas, wild hay and alfalfa are mowed and stored for winter feeding. Fattened cattle are shipped by truck or train to the stockyards for slaughtering.

Feedlots have been the most important development in the cattle industry since World War II. Cattle feeding grew especially fast in the Oklahoma Panhandle. An abundance of hybrid grain sorghum is available there. The first of many big feedlots in this region was built on the Hitch Ranch near Guymon in 1953. Today, hundreds of thousands of cattle are fed from huge stocks of grain and trench-stored ensilage.

Dairying is even more specialized than beef production. Dairies are now concentrated in urban areas near the markets. Dairy products from

20

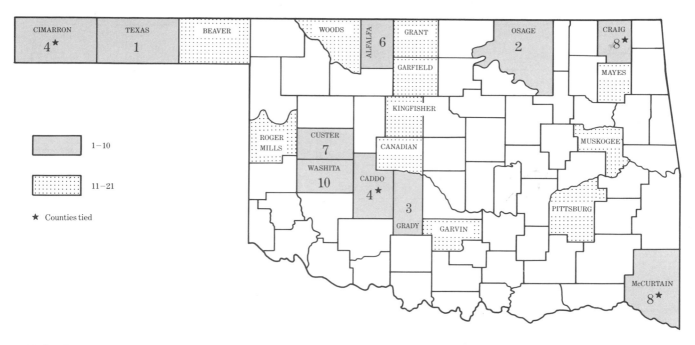

CIMARRON 4★	TEXAS 1	BEAVER		WOODS	ALFALFA 6	GRANT	OSAGE 2	CRAIG 8★

ALL CATTLE AND CALVES: Top producing counties, 1987 ranking.

1-10

11-21

★ Counties tied

Oklahoma's herds are a big source of farm income.

4. FARMERS RAISE THE CROPS THAT ARE BEST SUITED TO THE LAND AND CLIMATE WHERE THEY LIVE.

Wheat is the leading cash crop in Oklahoma. It is grown chiefly in the northern and western parts of the state.

Winter wheat is planted in the fall and is sometimes grazed in the winter. Vast fields of golden wheat are harvested in June. Brightly-colored combine harvesters are a symbol of the wheat belt. These combines cut and thresh the wheat. Then the grain is fed through a spout to the bed of a truck. The wheat is hauled to a bin or taken to an elevator near a railroad. Huge storage elevators in cities like Enid, El Reno, and Okeene are "skyscrapers of the plains."

Before combines were invented, wheat harvesting was a longer process. A binder cut the grain, tied it into bundles, and dumped the bundles on the ground. The bundles were stacked into shocks. Each shock had ten to twenty bun-

dles. Later, the grains of wheat were separated from the straw by a threshing machine.

The heyday of steam-powered threshers was from 1890 to 1915. Memory of these "good old days" is kept alive by the Oklahoma Steam Threshers Association. Organized at Waukomis (near Enid) in the 1950s, this small group now meets every July at Pawnee. After highly mechanized farm equipment has the wheat har-

Wheat harvest in western Oklahoma. (USDA, Soil Conservation photo by F. Dwain Phillips)

21

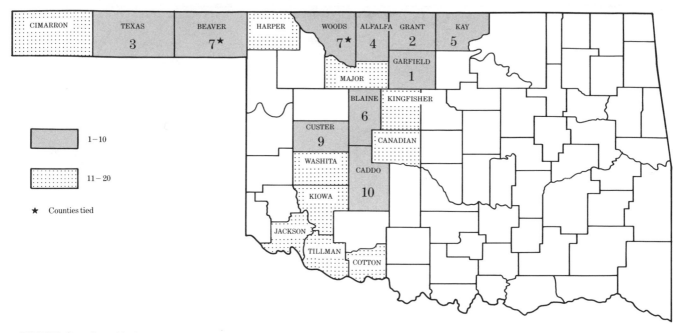

WHEAT: Counties with the most production, 1986 ranking.

vest safely in the bins, the members load up their antique farm machines and head for the annual bee.

Cotton ranks second in value among Oklahoma's crops. It was once grown in many parts of the state. The economy of southern Oklahoma was especially geared to cotton.

In the early days, cotton required a lot of hand labor. In the spring and summer, cotton fields were cultivated along the rows with horse or mule-pulled plows. Workers followed with hoes to thin out the plants. Called "chopping cotton," this process had to be repeated several times.

The plants began flowering in August. A few

An early wheat harvesting crew near Woodward. (Plains Indians and Pioneers Museum, Woodward, Oklahoma)

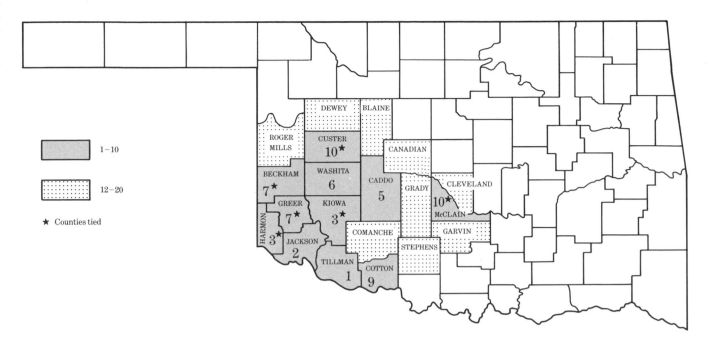

COTTON: Counties with the most production, 1986 ranking.

weeks later the bolls on the lower stalks popped open, showing the white, fluffy cotton fibers. Then cotton picking began. Rural schools had fall vacation during cotton picking season. A family, with the help of migrant workers, might be kept busy picking cotton well into October or November before all the upper bolls had opened. Men, women, and children walked down the rows with long sacks. Picking cotton was slow, hard work.

The fluffy fiber was hauled in a wagon with high sides to a cotton gin. Every town in southern and central Oklahoma had at least one gin in those days. A ginning machine with sharp teeth separated the fiber from the sticky seeds. Other machines pressed the cotton into bales weighing about 500 pounds. A lot of the seed was shipped to an oil mill and crushed into cottonseed oil or cottonseed meal.

Until the 1930s, cotton was the most important cash crop in Oklahoma. This crop, however, exhausted the soil. The harvested cotton land has declined from nearly 800,000 acres in 1950 to about 350,000 acres in the mid-1980s. Most of the acreage is in the southwest part of the state.

Cotton crop yields have been increased by the use of fertilizers, pesticides, improved varieties, and irrigation. After 1950, mechanical cotton pickers gradually replaced seasonal hand pickers.

Corn and other crops. More corn was planted by pioneer Oklahoma farmers than any other crop. But hot July winds and droughts shriveled corn plants. Today corn is grown mainly in wetter valleys and on irrigated farms.

Other important feed or food crops are oats, barley, rye, and soybeans. Grain sorghums are

The whole family was needed to pick this cotton crop near Fort Cobb. (Courtesy of W. D. Finney, Fort Cobb)

23

Machines made cottonpicking an easier job. (Photo by Susan Luebbermann)

Peanut harvest in southern Oklahoma. (F. Dwain Phillips)

grown for both the grain and dry forage feed for cattle. Sorghums are planted mainly in the Panhandle and western Oklahoma wheat counties.

Peanuts are widely-grown in the central and south-central parts of the state. An annual Peanut Festival is held in Caddo County. A huge aluminum peanut on a granite monument in Durant honors the peanut industry in Bryan County.

Broomcorn was once a big specialty crop around Lindsay. Farmers in that area began planting it in the 1920s. Why? Their cotton crops had been ruined by two years of drought and a season of boll weevils. In the early years, broomcorn was cut by harvest hands known as "broomcorn Johnnys." The crops were hauled to sheds for drying. Farm women worked from sunup to sundown keeping the Johnnys fed.

Fruits, vegetables, and nuts. Some crops are identified with a particular place. Strawberries bring to mind Stilwell, the county seat of Adair County in the Ozark flint hills. Blackberries do well at McLoud on the North Canadian River east of Oklahoma City.

Watermelons are grown in widely-separated sandy areas. Rush Springs south of Chickasha is a melon center. Other well-known melon producing areas are Cleo Springs west of Enid and Crescent near Guthrie on the Cimarron River. Lamont, on the Salt Fork in Grant County, and Weleetka on the North Canadian also grow good melon crops.

Tomatoes are produced in quantity along the Red River in southeastern Oklahoma. Spinach does very well in the Arkansas Valley, particularly in Sequoyah County. Truck garden farms line the Arkansas, downstream from Tulsa, and the lower Canadian.

Pecans, both native and hybrid, are harvested in the state. Okmulgee County is a leading pro-

Happy visitors at the Rush Springs Watermelon Festival. (Fred Marvel)

ducer of wild pecans. Peaches are a cash crop in the Ozarks and sandy river valleys. Both the pecan and peach harvest varies greatly from one year to the next.

ROUNDUP

1. In what ways has agriculture in Oklahoma changed since the 1930s?
2. Define: subsistence farming, urban, and rural.
3. Explain how the census reports of 1930 and 1980 show Oklahoma has changed from a rural to an urban state.
4. Where did irrigation get started in Oklahoma? What is the source of most irrigation water used elsewhere in the state?
5. What has been the most important change in the cattle industry?
6. Where is wheat grown in Oklahoma? Describe how wheat harvesting has been speeded up.
7. Which part of Oklahoma is especially suited for cotton farming? How do farmers increase cotton yields?
8. List five specialty crops and the best-known places in Oklahoma where they are grown.
A. Think about it! Explain why irrigation with ground water may not be a permanent solution for western Oklahoma's need for more rainfall.
B. Try this! Do a resources map showing where different crops are grown in Oklahoma. Use actual samples, pictures, or drawings.
C. Do a line graph showing changes in crop or beef prices over a period of time.

4

MINING

Mineral production is an important source of income for the Oklahoma economy. In general, a *mineral* is any substance that can be extracted from the earth for use now or in the future. The minerals may be subdivided into mineral fuels, metals, and nonmetallic ores.

Mineral fuels burn easily. The fuels found in Oklahoma are oil, natural gas, and coal. The mineral fuels may be regarded as solar energy which was stored by plants and animals at the bottom of the sea millions of years ago.

The most important *metals* which have been mined in Oklahoma are zinc and lead.

Nonmetallic minerals found here include stone (sandstone, dolomite, limestone, marble, and granite), sand and gravel, tripoli, clay, gypsum, volcanic ash, salt, and natural asphalt.

1. OIL AND NATURAL GAS ARE IMPORTANT MINERAL FUELS PRODUCED IN OKLAHOMA.

Oklahoma is an oil state. It was once the leading state in oil production. Contrary to popular belief elsewhere, however, very few Oklahomans have become rich from the oil industry. But the industry has provided many jobs in the oil fields, in refineries, on pipelines, and in oil-related industries. Thousands of farmers and ranchers have received royalties from leasing their subsurface mineral rights to oil companies.

Finding oil. Great pools of oil and gas have been discovered in Oklahoma. A pool, in this sense, is not like a lake. Oil and gas fill crevices in porous rock or sand. They are kept from rising by a solid cap of rock.

Wherever oil is found, lightweight natural gas will be above it. Heavier salt water is below the oil. Drillers know they have a "dry hole" if they strike salt water without first finding gas or oil.

Oil companies hire *geologists* to map the rock structure where a hole is drilled. An experienced geologist knows which kinds of rock formations are most likely to contain oil and gas. *Seismograph* and other technical devices are used to study the earth below the surface.

2. THE DISCOVERY OF BONANZA OIL FIELDS MADE OKLAHOMA ONE OF THE LEADING OIL PRODUCING STATES.

First oil discoveries. The Native Americans in eastern Oklahoma burned oil in lamps and used it for medicinal purposes. They dipped the bad-smelling substances from oil springs that seeped to the surface. Little did they realize that the black, gummy oil would someday be one of the most important needs in modern life.

In 1859, the first commercial well began producing at Titusville, Pennsylvania. That same year, oil was accidentally discovered in the Cherokee Nation. Lewis Ross found oil while drilling a water well at Grand Saline, now in Mayes County.

Several *wildcat drillers* struck oil in the 1880s and 1890s. The Choctaw Oil and Refining Company hit oil near Atoka in 1887. Two years later, a white man named Edward Byrd drilled some shallow wells near Chelsea in the northeast. He paid royalty to the Cherokee Nation on the few barrels produced. Oil was also found near Tahlequah, Ardmore, and Muskogee.

In 1897, the Cudahy Oil Company struck oil at Bartlesville's "Nellie Johnstone No. 1." The well was capped, because of the long distance to market, until the Santa Fe Railroad reached this area.

Bonanza oil fields. The exciting period of oil discoveries in Oklahoma got underway in the early 1900s. Oil began spouting from the derricks. Promoters rushed in. By the summer of 1905, there were 255 producing oil wells in eastern Oklahoma. Later that year, Oklahoma's first

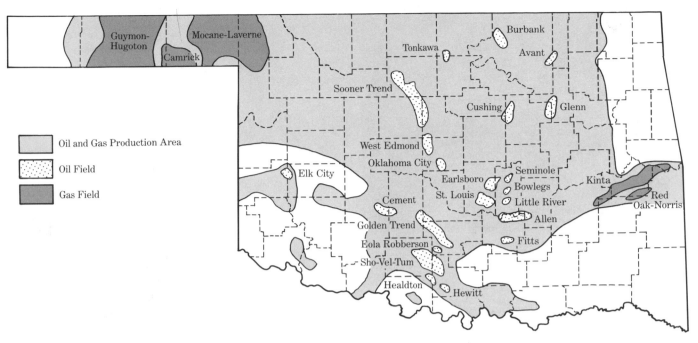

Giant Oil and Gas Fields

great oil pool was discovered on the Ida Glenn farm near Tulsa.

Glenn pool. Within two years, the Glenn pool was tapped by 516 wells. More than 100,000 barrels a day were produced. With so much oil, transportation was a problem. Millions of barrels were caught in earthern tanks or flowed down

Tom B. Slick, the "King of the Wildcatters."

the creeks. Eventually, pipelines were built to refineries at Whiting, Indiana and on the Gulf of Mexico coast.

Cushing field. Each new strike brought in dozens of new speculators—just like a gold rush. The big Cushing discovery of 1912, however, was kept a secret for awhile.

Thomas B. Slick, a young Chicago lease promoter, busily paid a dollar an acre for leases within a ten-mile radius of the first well. To keep anyone else from filing, Slick rented all the livery rigs in Cushing and paid the *notaries* to take a day off. He retired at the age of 26, for awhile.

At its peak, the Cushing pool produced oil for half the gasoline refined in the United States. Unfortunately, most of the natural gas was wasted. Hundreds of wells looked like giant torches. It is estimated that they burned away an amount of gas equal in heating power to five million tons of coal a year.

Other bonanzas. The Cushing bonanza was followed by other big discoveries. Near Ardmore, the Healdton and Sho-Vel-Tum fields were opened. Ponca City boomed with the Burbank pool discovery in 1920 and the Tonkawa field in

27

Oil boom town of Three Sands. The main street divided Kay from Noble County. (Courtesy of Allan Muchmore, Ponca City News)

State Capitol. (Fred Marvel)

the next year. The Seminole was discovered in 1926.

The Oklahoma City field opened in 1928. It proved to be one of the richest in the world. More than 90 percent of the wells drilled in this field produced oil and gas. In 1942, oil was reached in "Petunia No. 1" at 6,618 feet. This well was under the State Capitol. It was drilled three degrees off center from a flower bed south of the building.

Many smaller fields were also opened. The oil derrick became a common sight on the Oklahoma landscape.

Decline of the oil industry. Oil and gas production began declining in Oklahoma in the late 1960s. An increase in world oil prices after 1973, however, made *stripper wells* profitable. Stripper wells produce very little, usually less than ten barrels a day. They are often located in older oil fields that have had better days. Higher oil prices also led to more costly exploration for new oil and gas fields.

Then came the bust in 1982. Drilling nearly ceased when crude oil prices suddenly dropped. More than half the workers in the oil and gas industry were laid off. The petroleum industry was becoming less and less important in the Oklahoma economy.

The future? Oklahoma still has large reserves of oil and natural gas. There is more oil to be found in new fields. More oil can be pumped

from old fields. On the average, less than half the oil in a reservoir is already removed.

As in the past, oil and gas production will increase when prices on these products go up.

3. THE PRODUCTION OF NATURAL GAS IS AN IMPORTANT PART OF OKLAHOMA'S PETROLEUM INDUSTRY.

Natural gas is an ideal fuel. It burns cleanly with intense heat and can be carried great distances by pipelines. Natural gas has many uses besides heating. Carbon black is just one important product manufactured from natural gas. Carbon black is used in tires and as a pigment in inks and paints.

Gas fields. The Hogshooter pool near Bartlesville was the first big *dry gas* field. Discovered in 1907, the pool supplied fuel for smelters and towns in northeastern Oklahoma. Dry gas is gas that is not associated with crude oil.

Oil drillers.

"Wild Mary Sudik" oil well.

Five giant gas fields have been discovered in Oklahoma. The Guymon-Hugoton field in the Panhandle is part of the largest gas field in the United States. An important side industry there is the manufacture of *helium,* a lighter than air gas that does not burn. The U.S. Bureau of Mines built a large helium plant at Keyes in Cimarron County.

Two giant gas fields are in the eastern Panhandle area. Two others—Kinta and Red Oak Norris—are in eastern Oklahoma near the Arkansas River.

Wet gas. Many wells in Oklahoma have produced both natural gas and oil. Gas from these wells is called *wet gas* or *casinghead gas.* It can be piped into a feeder line attached to the casinghead of a well.

In the early days of automobiles, some casinghead gasoline was made from liquids found in wet natural gas. This gasoline was very volatile until blended with naptha or kerosene. On a hot September day in 1915, gas excaped from casinghead gasoline tank cars at Ardmore. A spark somewhere ignited the fumes, causing an explosion. Nearly every downtown building was destroyed or damaged. More than forty people were killed and several hundred injured.

Much natural gas was wasted. When oil and natural gas were found together, most early day oilmen regarded the gas as a nuisance. It was wasted.

After a driller bores a hole through rock and strikes oil, gas pressure forces the oil to the surface. Gas is wasted if a well is allowed to flow wide open or if wells are drilled too close together. When the gas pressure diminishes, the oil is pumped.

Vented gas posed a danger at the Cushing and other oil fields. On damp, cloudy days, the gas settled in low areas. Any kind of spark from a car or cigar would cause an explosion. Signs were placed on roads to warn motorists of "gas pockets ahead." Oil rigs sometimes exploded when gas formed where kerosene lamps, called *black dogs,* were burning.

An unbelievable amount of gas was lost in the Oklahoma City oil field. Enough gas was wasted each day to heat every home in the state for several days. The most famous well, the "Wild Mary Sudik," spewed out millions of cubic feet of gas and thousands of barrels of oil during an eleven-day rampage in 1930. The threat of fire was so great, people didn't dare light a match.

Conservation of oil and gas. In 1945, the Oklahoma legislature empowered the Corporation Commission to set a spacing pattern for each oil field. The commission could also limit the amount of oil pumped from each well.

The commission was given power to order a *unit plan*, choosing one company to develop a field for all the operators who had leases. The commission first applied a unit plan in 1947. The Sohio Company was selected to manage the West Edmond field.

Proper spacing of wells and production limits can save oil and natural gas. There is no way, of course, to bring back resources already wasted.

The future for natural gas. Geologists believe that a vast reserve at deep levels will provide natural gas for generations. A well near Elk City set a world record at 31,441 feet (nearly six miles deep). Deep well drilling began in the Anadarko Basin in the early 1980s.

4. COAL DEPOSITS ARE ONE OF OKLAHOMA'S GREAT RESOURCES.

Modern society depends on fuel. Oklahoma is lucky in this respect. When oil and gas are used up, the state can rely on coal to heat homes and provide fuel for industry. Huge deposits of coal are found here.

Coal is stored sunshine. Coal is the sun's energy that has been preserved in the earth for millions of years. Coal was once plant life that absorbed carbon dioxide from the air. With a microscope, vegetative tissues can be seen on coal.

Oklahoma was once level and swampy. When the short, stubby trees and ferns of that era died, they were covered with mud and sand. Gradually this vegetation changed to peat, then to brown lignite, and finally to soft coal. Meanwhile, the sand hardened into sandstone and the mud turned to clay and shale.

Where are Oklahoma's vast coal reserves? Coal is found in eastern Oklahoma from Craig County to the north to Coal County on the south.

McAlester was named after the first commercial mine developer in that area. J. J. McAlester hauled coal by wagon to Kansas before the M-K-T (Missouri, Kansas, and Texas) railroad was built across Indian Territory in 1872.

Ups and downs of the coal industry. In the 1870s, railroads furnished both transportation and a hungry market for coal. Production rose rapidly.

Underground shaft mining increased coal output. By the time of statehood in 1907, more than a hundred mines were producing about 3 million tons of coal yearly. The biggest coal companies were owned by railroads.

Production reached a peak of nearly 5 million tons in 1920. The tonnage then declined as oil and gas took the place of coal.

Two things revived interest in coal. One was the need for energy during World War II in the 1940s. The other was the high price of oil after 1973.

Mining methods and regulations have changed. *Strip mining* has replaced underground shaft mining. Huge shovels now scoop up yards of coal at a bite. Surface mining is preferred for several reasons. It costs less. More coal is recovered. Working conditions are safer for miners.

After all the coal in a mine is scooped out, mining companies are required by state law to restore the land. Where possible, the original topsoil is graded over the coal pit. The Oklahoma Department of Mines enforces the law.

Coal miners. The coal industry had a strong

Strip mining of coal.

30

social influence on Oklahoma's heritage. When the Choctaws and Chickasaws shied away from underground mine work, thousands of newcomers came to the Indian Territory. Native whites and blacks as well as foreign immigrants took jobs in the coal mines.

Many of the immigrants had worked in eastern mines before moving to Oklahoma. Most of their sons became miners too at an early age. Patrick J. Hurley, son of an Irish immigrant, began working in a Coalgate mine at age eleven. He grew up to become a lawyer for the Choctaw Nation and a famous American diplomat.

An *ethnic* mix was added to Oklahoma by the British (Welsh, Scots, and English), Irish, Poles, Slovaks, Russians, Italians, and others. Peter Hanraty, a Scot immigrant, became a well-known union organizer for the United Mine Workers. He was a delegate to the state constitutional convention and served as the first state mine inspector. Hanraty later owned his own coal mine and lost both legs in a mine accident.

Many miners lived in company towns. They were paid in *scrip* that could be exchanged only at the company store. It was not unusual for miners to work twelve hours or more a day, six days a week for two dollars a day.

Underground mining was unhealthy and dangerous work. In the early days, mining was done with hand tools. Miners sometimes had to work stooped over and on their knees in water several inches deep. Ventilation was poor. Cave-ins and explosions caused many deaths. An explosion at Krebs in 1892 killed 96 miners and crippled over twice that number.

Unsafe mine conditions and low wages caused the miners to form a strong union. Under the leadership of men like Hanraty, the union got an eight-hour day and other benefits for the miners.

5. LEAD AND ZINC WERE FOUND MAINLY IN THE TRI-STATE AREA.

Except for lead and zinc, Oklahoma has never been noted for metal mining. This state led the nation in zinc production between the two world wars. By 1970, however, the zinc and lead mines had played out.

Gold prospectors have searched the Wichitas and other areas. No bonanza gold mines were discovered. A large copper mine in Jackson County yielded some silver as a byproduct. This mine was shut down in 1975.

Iron-bearing minerals in small amounts are found in the Wichitas and Arbuckles. Limonite is used in special cement. Hematite is a paint pigment.

Lead and zinc in northeastern Oklahoma. The Miami-Picher area in Oklahoma's northeast corner is part of the Tri-State mining district. This district, where Oklahoma joins Kansas and Missouri, was once the richest lead and zinc mining region in the world. Lead and zinc were often found together. Zinc was at the deepest level.

Lead was discovered in the Tri-State area in frontier days. Fur trappers picked up lead ore, melted it over open fires, and molded it into shot for their rifles.

The first commercial lead mining in this area began in 1891. Peoria, east of Miami, became a boom town after prospectors made a rich strike. A few years later a farmer south of Miami found a rich lead deposit while digging a well.

In 1914, the richest zinc ores in Oklahoma were discovered accidently near Tar Creek in Ottawa County. The strike was made by a prospect driller for the Picher Lead Company. He was returning to company headquarters in Joplin when his drilling rig got mired down.

While waiting for relief, the driller sank a wildcat hole. Eureka! Cuttings from the hole showed signs of rich ores. News of a bonanza zinc field spread like a prairie fire. The Picher and other companies rushed in to lease land from the Quapaw Indians. A quiet region of isolated farms suddenly changed.

Within a year, the town of Picher had about a thousand people. The Picher Company hired a deputy sheriff to run out bootleggers and the usual boomtown riffraff. For awhile, the Red Apple gambling den thrived on the wages of miners. Living conditions in the mining camp

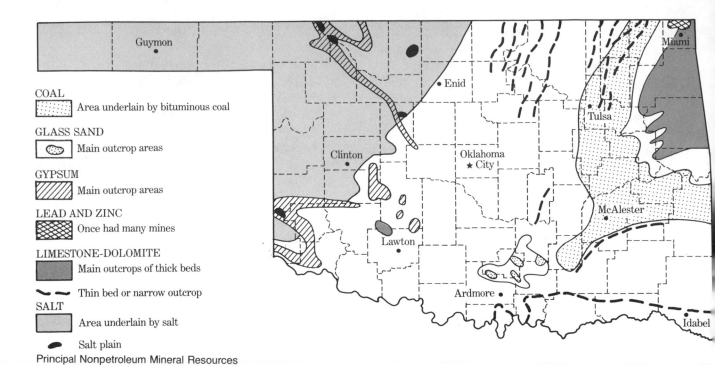

COAL
[image] Area underlain by bituminous coal

GLASS SAND
[image] Main outcrop areas

GYPSUM
[image] Main outcrop areas

LEAD AND ZINC
[image] Once had many mines

LIMESTONE-DOLOMITE
[image] Main outcrops of thick beds

[image] Thin bed or narrow outcrop

SALT
[image] Area underlain by salt

[image] Salt plain

Principal Nonpetroleum Mineral Resources

were primitive. Quickly-built shanties had no public utilities. Water was delivered to a barrel in the front yard. The open barrels, according to a 1917 article in *The Daily Oklahoman,* were "receptive to whatever germ or strolling bacillus comes that way."

In the early 1930s, the world's largest zinc and lead smelter in the world was built in Cardin. Quapaw, Commerce, and other towns in the county also grew and prospered. During the glory days, thousands of miners worked in the underground shafts.

Zinc smelters. The first Tri-State *smelters* were in Kansas and Missouri. In 1907, however, three smelters were built in Bartlesville. This city was ideally located on two railroads. It was only 65 miles from the Miami mines and even closer to a major gas field. Caney Creek provided a good water supply.

The smelters at Bartlesville operated around the clock, seven days a week. The men worked a twelve-hour shift starting at 4 A.M. or 4 P.M. The hours of work were not cut until the 1930s depression when jobs were spread out among more workers.

National Zinc, one of the 1907 companies, op-

erated a smelter in Bartlesville until 1974. In that year, the plant was sold to Engelhard Minerals, a New York corporation. This smelter and others in Blackwell and Henryetta processed ore from out-of-state mines after the Tri-State mines played out.

Polish workers at Bartlesville. Many Polish immigrants were hired at the zinc smelters. The Polish families lived in Smelter Town, the southwest corner of Bartlesville. These people worked hard to make ends meet and to provide a future for their children.

Some of their first homes were built out of huge boxes. These wood crates were used by the railroads to keep zinc ore from shifting as trains bounced along. Dirt was banked up against tarpapered walls to keep out wind and rain. Inside, the walls were covered with old newspapers. The floors were dirt.

The Poles bought their groceries at stores run by people with names like Mnich, Schalski, Blongewicz, or Depalski. Single men went to town on Saturday night, when not working. They watched boxing matches or whirled with dime-a-dance girls on a platform where the Phillips building is located now.

Polish smelter workers at Bartlesville.

End of the mining era. In the 1960s, the lead and zinc mines in Ottawa County were closed after the rich ores gave out. The population began to decline. Buildings were abandoned. Mills fell into ruin. Rails rusted. The mining centers began to look like semi-ghost towns. Piles of refuse (chat) dotted the countryside near the deserted mine tunnels—like one gigantic prairie dog town.

New industries are slowly replacing mining in Ottawa County. Manufacturing plants in Miami and other places produce a variety of products and provide jobs. Agriculture is diversifying. Tourism is developing as more visitors discover the natural beauty of the Tri-State area. Some tourists take tours through the shafts and caverns of the old mines.

6. OKLAHOMA HAS GREAT RESERVES OF NONMETALLIC MINERALS.

The leading nonmetallic minerals produced in Oklahoma in 1980 were Portland cement, crushed stone, and sand and gravel. Others included clay, glass sand, gypsum, dimension stone, tripoli, volcanic ash, and helium.

Oklahoma is rich in nonmetallic minerals. The high cost of shipping bulk minerals to distant markets, however, has held back development of many Oklahoma deposits.

Stone. Oklahoma has a variety of stones for buildings and other uses. Sandstone is the most widely distributed stone in the state. The best grade is found in eastern Oklahoma. Sandstone has been used in buildings at Vinita, Muskogee, Okmulgee, Sallisaw, McAlester, and other cities. The Creek Museum in Okmulgee was built of native sandstone as a capitol in 1876.

Dolomite is a hard stone. It weathers well. The purest dolomite is quarried in the Arbuckles. Other deposits are found in the Wichitas, Ozarks, and in western Oklahoma. Visitors at Boiling Springs State Park near Woodward have seen buildings made of dolomite. This stone is used also in glass manufacturing and for other purposes.

Limestone is plentiful in the northeast and southeast. It is also found in the Arbuckle and Wichita mountains. Limestone can be cut into blocks and used for building. Crushed limestone is important in highway construction. Cement is made by grinding limestone with a smaller amount of clay or shale.

Marble is described as a limestone that will take a polish. Marble City in Sequoyah County got its name from nearby quarries. The original Bell Telephone building in downtown Oklahoma City was built of Sequoyah County marble.

Granite—red, pink, gray, and black—is quarried in Oklahoma. This stone takes a good polish. Its principal use is for monuments and ornamental building purposes. Granite was used in part of the State Capitol. The Chickasaw Council House at Tishomingo, later the Johnston County courthouse, is another granite building. The reformatory at Granite was built from stone quarried nearby.

Sand and gravel. These minerals are essential in the building industry and highway construction. They are found in all parts of the state. The greatest demand is in the urban central and northeastern areas.

High-purity silica sand for glass-making comes from the Arbuckles. It is shipped in closed railroad cars to glass factories, located mainly in eastern Oklahoma.

Tripoli. This stone is a soft form of silica rock. It is ground into a fine powder called "flour." This flour is used as an abrasive and filler in polishing pastes and other products. The automobile industry uses tripoli in preparing car bodies for painting and in polishing chrome trim.

Tripoli is mined at small pits in Ottawa County. It is hauled in dump trucks to Seneca, Missouri for processing.

Clay. A valuable raw material, clay is plastic when wet and stone-hard when fired. Clay suitable for manufacturing is found near the surface in many places in Oklahoma.

Before the Civil War, the Five Civilized Tribes in eastern Oklahoma built schools with bricks made right on the grounds. In territorial days, good clay beds were found along the route of the present-day Turner Turnpike near Chandler, Stroud, and Bristow. Brick was used extensively in some cities, especially Guthrie. The first brick home in the Oklahoma Territory was the Heilman House in that city. Built in 1895, it is now preserved. Another brick landmark in Guthrie is the Co-operative Printing Company's four-story building. It was constructed in 1902 by the *Daily State Capital,* Oklahoma's first daily newspaper. Bricks with "Don't Spit on Sidewalk" stamped on the top were used for paving in front of the Guthrie opera house.

Bricks are still one of the principal clay products made in Oklahoma. Bentonite clay, found in Dewey County, is very absorbent. It is used as a filler in putty, sandpaper, soap, and crayons.

Gypsum. This mineral is a soft, white rock composed of calcium sulfate. Western Oklahoma has enough gypsum reserve to supply the whole nation for thousands of years. It has not been developed fully.

A hundred different gypsum products are manufactured in Oklahoma. At present it is used mainly for sheetrock (dry wall) and plaster. Ground gypsum is used as a soil conditioner and as a filler in paint, paper, and cloth. Gypsum is a good source of sulfur. For that reason, chemical companies may have great use for it in the future.

Volcanic ash. Large deposits of volcanic ash have been located in western and east-central Oklahoma. Ash mined in Beaver County makes a good abrasive for soap, toothpaste, and polishing products. Volcanic ash is packaged at Gate and sold mainly to soap manufacturers.

Salt. Trillions of tons of salt underlie western Oklahoma. Only a small fraction of it has been processed. In fact, Oklahoma still imports salt. A few solar-evaporation plants provide some salt for livestock, to recharge water softeners, and to de-ice roads.

Asphalt. Large natural asphalt deposits are located in the Ouachita and Arbuckle mountains as well as other parts of the state. Not mined extensively in Oklahoma, natural asphalt is found in rocks that once contained crude petroleum. It is similar to petroleum asphalt, a byproduct of oil refineries. Asphalt is used for paving roads and for making shingles and roofing products.

Oklahoma's large deposits of nonmetallic minerals will eventually be developed more fully.

ROUNDUP

1. What is a mineral? Name three types of minerals.
2. For what reasons has the oil industry been important to Oklahoma?
3. Where was Oklahoma's first great oil pool discovered? Where were other bonanza pools found? What kind of wells became profitable in the 1970s? Why?
4. What was the first dry gas pool developed in Oklahoma? What is helium and where is it manufactured in Oklahoma? Why was much natural gas wasted in the early days?
5. Where are most of the state's coal reserves located? Who was J. J. McAlester? How has coal mining changed? Why did the miners form a strong union?
6. List five towns that prospered in the lead-zinc area. What immigrant group found jobs at the Bartlesville smelter? What new industries are replacing mining in the Tri-State area?
7. What important stones are quarried in Oklahoma? For what is high-purity silica used?
8. Clay is used in making which products? List six other nonmetallic minerals mined in Oklahoma.
A. Apply your knowledge! Explain how Oklahoma's mining industry is important to manufacturing in this state. Give ten examples of factories that could use Oklahoma mineral products.
B. Try this! Do a resource map of Oklahoma showing where different minerals are located. Use actual mineral samples if possible.

5

MANUFACTURING AND LUMBERING

Manufacturing is the changing of raw materials into goods that have greater use and value. Oklahoma has hundreds of factories ranging in size from a small bakery or broom factory to an automobile assembly plant.

Factories are located in all parts of the state. They are often near the source of a needed raw material. Flour mills are in the wheat belt. Cotton gins are close to the cotton farms. Canneries are located mainly in the vegetable-producing areas in eastern Oklahoma. Sawmills are in the southeastern timber country. Refineries are in the central oil-producing section.

Most large factories are built where the population is concentrated. They depend on a plentiful supply of labor. Fuel and water have to be available. Good transportation is another reason for locating in or near the bigger cities. Companies also look for places with good schools, churches, and recreation for their employees.

Lumbering is another important industry in Oklahoma. Lumber companies now practice conservation. They replant cut areas to assure a permanent supply of trees. Logs are needed for lumber and paper making.

1. THE HISTORY OF MANUFACTURING IN OKLAHOMA GOES BACK TO THE FIRST PEOPLE WHO OCCUPIED THIS AREA.

Early manufacturing by Native Americans. Prehistoric people in this area made arrowheads and tools from stone. They made baskets, cradles, rugs, and pottery from other materials.

Plains Indians processed the buffalo into meat and other products. The hide was tanned and made into clothing, shoes, tents, and blankets. The bones became hoes, needles, knives, and augers. Tendons were used for thread and bow strings.

Pioneer manufacturing. By the early 1800s, white pioneers and Cherokees were operating salt works near Mazie (north of Muskogee).

As Oklahoma was settled, basic manufacturing was done by blacksmiths, wheelwrights, gunsmiths, leather tanners, brickmakers, flour millers, and sawmill operators.

Manufacturing has been important in the economy of this area for a long time.

2. MANY OKLAHOMA FACTORIES GOT STARTED BEFORE WORLD WAR II.

"Manufacturing is in its infancy, but it is certainly a hopeful youth and offers great inducements," said William C. Renfrow, the territorial governor, in 1903.

Local raw materials were used in early factories. After oil was discovered, petroleum refining became the number one manufacturing in-

The pioneer blacksmith made horseshoes and other items from iron.

35

Refinery with lights of downtown Tulsa in background. (Metropolitan Tulsa Chamber of Commerce photo by Don Sibley)

A 1918 Geronimo. The Antique Car Club of Enid found this car in a Kansas wheatfield and restored it. (Courtesy of George McCamey)

dustry in Oklahoma. Gasoline was the most important product of the *refineries*.

Other leading industries were zinc smelting, lumber milling, food processing, and glass making. Manufacturing relied heavily on Oklahoma's natural resources—oil, zinc ore, forests, farm products, beef cattle, and stone products.

Automobile manufacturing. Cars, trucks, and tractors have been manufactured in Oklahoma almost since statehood. The Pioneer Car Company had a plant in El Reno from 1909 to 1911. This company made a few lightweight four-cylinder Model-B Surrey cars. Two other early Oklahoma vehicle manufacturers grew to prominence.

The Geronimo Motor Company in Enid made more than a thousand cars between 1916 and 1920 when the plant was destroyed by fire. The four-cylinder "Geronimo" was a big seller at $895. It came in black, red, or blue. The engine developed 37 horsepower and a top speed of 40 miles per hour. The car got 20 miles on a gallon of gas.

A French car dealer bought a hundred six-cylinder Geronimos in 1918. He sold them under the name "Wing." The six-cylinder car could do 50 miles per hour with a tailwind on a downgrade. They were sold under the advertising slogan: "Speed You'll Never Dare Use." An unusual ac-

cessory on this car was an air pump. To put air in the huge 32-inch tires, a driver started the engine and pulled an air hose from a concealed compartment under the fender. This device was very useful since tires were not dependable in those days.

The Oklahoma Auto Manufacturing Company produced O-K trucks between 1916 and 1929. The plant was located at Okay (north of Muskogee). The company made one-ton, 1½ ton, and two-ton trucks and some tractors. The one-tonner was a four-cylinder, 29.8 horsepower truck with three-speed transmission. It had solid rubber tires and wooden-spoked wheels. The price tag was $1,295 F.O.B. Muskogee.

The Ford Motor Company had an assembly plant in Oklahoma City. Ford assembled the Model T (1916-1927) and the Model A (1928-1931). Today, the Fred Jones Manufacturing Company makes parts for the older Fords in Oklahoma City.

Two automobile factories now operate in Oklahoma. The big General Motors assembly plant was built in Oklahoma City in the 1970s. Another car manufacturer makes a classic Auburn V-8 at Broken Arrow, a Tulsa suburb. Every part of the Auburn is manufactured in Oklahoma except the 365 horsepower engine and the transmission.

General Motors Assembly line in Oklahoma City. (Courtesy of GMC)

3. WORLD WAR II GAVE MANUFACTURING A BIG BOOST IN OKLAHOMA.

The United States got into World War II after the Japanese bombed Pearl Harbor in 1941. At that time, manufacturing accounted for only 20 percent of Oklahoma's income. Agriculture and mineral production were still the leading industries.

War contracts. Manufacturing got a big boost during the war. Many war contracts were awarded in Oklahoma. Why? The state has many advantages: moderate climate, inland location, and a mechanically-minded labor force.

The most spectacular wartime factory was the Douglas bomber assembly plant at Tulsa. Other new wartime factories included a tire plant near Miami and the Tinker Field bomber repair and assembly depot at Oklahoma City. There were many more.

Top industries at the end of the war. World War II gave manufacturing in Oklahoma a big boost. In 1945, however, the earlier types of Oklahoma factories still employed the most wage earners. The top five industries were petroleum refining, newspapers and publishing, wholesale meat packing, bread and other bakery products, and oil field machinery and tools.

The next five industries at the end of World War II were sawmills; the production of stone, clay, and glass products; flour milling; metal smelting; and ice manufacturing. The manufacture of structural steel and power boilers was not far behind.

4. THE STATE GOVERNMENT BEGAN PROMOTING MANUFACTURING.

Oklahoma Planning and Resources Board. The legislature created this board in 1937. Its job was to sell Oklahoma's industrial possibilities to outside investors.

With the board's encouragement, 62 Oklahoma cities cooperated in a 1947 project to promote the state. The cities prepared a train exhibit to show to out-of-state industrial leaders. Four carloads of materials were taken to cities in the North and East.

O. K. I. E. In the 1960s, Governor Dewey Bartlett launched a campaign to bring new industries to Oklahoma. Thousands of OKIE lapel buttons summarized the program. The words on the button were "Oklahoma, Key to Industrial Expansion." Local chambers of commerce helped by stressing Oklahoma's advantages for industry.

The list of companies that began locating in Oklahoma reads like a blue ribbon list of American manufacturers: General Motors, Xerox, Sylvania, Westinghouse, Uniroyal, and many others.

5. OKLAHOMA HAS A GREAT VARIETY OF MANUFACTURING TODAY.

Transportation equipment. Spartan Aircraft was manufacturing airplanes in Tulsa before World War II. Since the war, Spartan has made house trailers.

Other companies manufacture a variety of transportation equipment for travel by highway, air, water, or railroad. This type of industry is now an important part of manufacturing in Oklahoma.

Machinery. The number of factories that make machinery products, both electrical and nonelectrical, has grown rapidly in Oklahoma.

Spartan Executive and Zeus planes in production at Tulsa, late 1930s. (Spartan School of Aeronautics, Tulsa)

Thousands of Oklahomans are employed in the manufacture of electronic, computer, and oil field equipment as well as many other machinery products.

Spartan mobile homes are manufactured in Tulsa. (Spartan School of Aeronautics)

Fabricated metal products. Metal barrels, cans, hand tools, heating equipment, truck springs, and many other metal products are manufactured in Oklahoma.

Most of the metal products are made from pig iron and iron plate shipped up the Arkansas waterway from eastern steel mills. Local scrap iron, however, is melted down in huge furnaces at Sand Springs to make reinforcement bars.

Petroleum refining and chemical plants. Petroleum refining has been a leading industry at Tulsa, Bartlesville, Ponca City, Oklahoma City, and other places. Oil is piped to the refineries from fields in Oklahoma and Texas. The principal products are gasoline, fuel oil, lubricating oil, road oil, tar, and asphalt.

Chemical plants also use oil to make synthetic fibers, detergents, plastics, and many other items. This type of manufacturing is very scientific.

Products made from stone, clay, and sand. *Cement.* Oklahoma has several large cement plants. One is near Pryor in Mayes County. Another plant is east of Tulsa. A plant at Ada receives its limestone from a quarry miles away by a long conveyor belt.

The cement factories crush the stone, mix it with other materials, heat it, and grind it to a powder. A special type of cement is made for the oil wells.

A cement plant at Dewey was the town's largest employer until it shut down in the 1960s.

Glass factories. The first glass bottle in Oklahoma was made by the Great Western Glass Company in Bartlesville in 1910. Today, large glass plants are located in Sand Springs, Sapulpa, Muskogee, Okmulgee, Henryetta, and Ada. Glass factories have operated at Blackwell, Poteau, and other places.

High purity silica sand is treated to make glass and fiberglass. The sand is cleaned and mixed with soda, lime, fluorite, or other chemicals. This mixture is melted into a heavy liquid and then poured into molds.

Oklahoma's glass factories make containers (bottles and jars), window panes, pyrex, tableware, and other items.

Clay products. Pottery is made from Oklahoma's clay. The pottery is shaped and baked in plants at Sapulpa, Perry, Frederick, and other places. Plates, bowls, and vases are shipped all over the world.

Thousands of people turn off Interstate 44 at Sapulpa to visit the pottery plant founded by John Frank. Dozens of craftsmen work there on Frankhoma Pottery. This creative, western-oriented pottery is internationally famous.

Other factories in Oklahoma use clay to make bricks, tile, sewer and drainage pipe, ceramics, and other products.

Food processing. This type of manufacturing is still important in Oklahoma. Meat packing plants are located in Oklahoma City and throughout the state. Fresh meat is the main item produced. Other products include dried beef, canned meat, lard, hides, soap stock, and dried-bone meal.

Oklahoma's largest flour mill is in Enid. Other mills are located in towns in the north-central part of the state. Wheat, by the millions of bushels, is run through grinders and separated into flour, bran, and shorts. Bakeries are the principal users of flour. The large bakeries use machines to mix and knead dough. In some bakeries, pans of bread are baked as they move slowly through huge ovens on belts.

Rural areas welcome factories. The greatest concentration of factories and jobs is in the areas of Oklahoma City and Tulsa. However, many companies have built new factories in smaller cities. Clothing factories, for example, were located at Woodward and Cherokee in the northwest, at Madill and Temple in the south, and at Holdenville, Checotah, and Coalgate in eastern Oklahoma.

Rural areas often have a surplus of labor because farms have been enlarged and mechanized. Factories are welcome because they provide jobs and keep young people from moving to other states.

6. LUMBERING IS AN IMPORTANT INDUSTRY IN OKLAHOMA.

More than a fifth of Oklahoma is classed as forest land. About half of this area, five million acres, is suitable for commercial *lumbering*. Most of it is in the Ouachita Mountains and the Ozark Plateau.

Early use of the forests. Native Americans have made use of the trees since prehistoric times. When the Five Civilized Tribes were removed to Indian Territory, they cut timber to build log houses. They made furniture from rough-cut wood.

In 1868, Chief Allen Wright, a Choctaw, built the first steam sawmill at Boggy Depot. A lack of transportation, however, limited the market for lumber.

Railroads gave lumbering a boost. Two mainline railroads provided needed transportation for the lumber industry. The M-K-T was completed across the Indian Territory in 1872. The second railroad, the St. Louis and San Francisco, was running trains in 1887. This line ran from Fort Smith, Arkansas along the Kiamichi Valley to Hugo and on to Paris, Texas.

Stringtown (north of Atoka) was the first lumber center along the M-K-T. Logs were cut on the mountain slopes and hauled by ox teams to Stringtown's steam-powered sawmills. Many other mill towns developed on the edges of the Ouachitas where plenty of water was available for steam power and log cleaning ponds.

Lumbering became big business. After lumber companies cut all the timber near the mill towns, they built portable sawmills in the back country. Then they hauled the lumber to railheads in huge wagons and trailers pulled by four to eight oxen.

Other lumber companies built *tramways* to haul logs to town for sawing. Companies at Antlers, Atoka, and Fort Towson got their logs by tramway.

The cost of hauling the logs or lumber from the back country was too much for most small companies. Good trees on the steep slopes were hard to get. Rivers for floating logs didn't run in the right direction. As a result, one large company got control of the commercial forest areas in the Ouachitas.

Dierks Lumber Company. The big company that eventually did most of the lumbering in southeastern Oklahoma started out as the Choctaw Lumber and Coal Company in 1888. It became the Dierks Lumber Company in 1921. By that time, most soft pine logs were sawed at the company town of Bismark (Wright City). Hardwoods were milled at Broken Bow. Both towns were connected to Valliant by a private railroad.

Weyco. In 1969, the Weyerhaeuser Company purchased the Dierks Company. Weyco, as it is called, now owns about half of McCurtain County.

Weyco enlarged the Wright City facilities to handle both pine and hardwoods. At Valliant the company installed the largest paper-making machinery in the world. The plant makes boxes, sacks, and other paper products.

Forest conservation—better late than never. In the early days of the lumber industry, the lumber companies gained control of the Choctaw Nation's timberlands. They bought forest lands that had been allotted to individual tribal members. Also, after 1912, the lumber companies

Lumbering is an important industry in eastern Oklahoma.

were able to buy unallotted Choctaw land. The federal government sold much of this land to the highest bidder.

Unfortunately, most companies followed a "cut out and get out" policy in the Ouachitas. They destroyed forests without replacing the trees. The same wasteful policy was used in the Cherokee Nation's Ozark forests. Prime white oaks, for example, were cut. Only the poorest trees were left.

By contrast, Weyco now uses modern *conservation* techniques to assure a permanent timber supply. They "clear out" a small area of several hundred acres. All the trees are cut. Then the cleared land is contour plowed so it will catch rainfall. Pine seedlings, which grow faster in the sun, are planted. After several years, the growing trees are thinned. This *"high yield"* forestry provides enough logs to keep sawmills in continuous operation.

ROUNDUP

1. Define manufacturing. Give examples of Oklahoma factories that have been located near the source of a raw material.
2. Explain why manufacturing has been important to Oklahoma for a long time.

40

3. Why are Geronimo, O-K, Model T, GM, and Auburn important names in Oklahoma's history of manufacturing?

4. Why were many wartime factory contracts awarded in Oklahoma? Give three examples of these factories.

5. List the five types of factories in Oklahoma that employed the most people in 1945.

6. Who started the O.K.I.E. program? Evaluate its success.

7. Make a chart to show the great variety of products produced in Oklahoma factories. Label the columns as follows: Transportation Equipment; Machinery; Fabricated Metal Products; Petroleum Refining; Chemical Plants; Products from Stone, Clay, and Sand; and Food Processing.

8. Where are factories concentrated in Oklahoma? Give two reasons why many factories are being located in outlying towns.

9. Explain why each of the following was important in Oklahoma's lumber industry: Chief Allen Wright, first railroads, Stringtown, tramways, Bismark, and Weyco.

A. Think about it! Explain why Oklahoma's future growth may depend more on manufacturing than on agriculture or mining.

B. Find out what clean air manufacturing is. Why is it desirable?

C. Why is conservation of forests necessary for the future of the lumber industry? Give other reasons for conserving the forests. (Consider Oklahoma's tourist industry. Also, find out why the clearing of Amazon jungles is causing world environmental problems.)

6

EARLY OKLAHOMANS

Native Americans have lived in Oklahoma for thousands of years. Perhaps 600 generations of *prehistoric* people called this region home and made a living here. They hunted animals, gathered wild food, and eventually learned to farm.

The natives got their food, clothing, and shelter from the environment without spoiling or wasting it. They lived in harmony with nature.

Unfortunately, the early people did not leave a written record of their activities. Their story has been pieced together from material remains left at campsites or in caves. Much of the evidence was destroyed, however, before professional *archaeologists* could study it.

1. THE FIRST OKLAHOMANS WERE NOMADIC HUNTERS.

Where did the first Native Americans in Oklahoma come from? There are many theories on their origin. Most scholars agree, however, that many of the early people came from Asia by way of Alaska. The natives wandered south in search of food. They scattered over North America as well as Central and South America.

How do we know about these early Americans? Archaeologists study their *artifacts*. Modern scientific methods are used to date tools, weapons, animal bones, pottery, shelters, and other materials.

Mammoth hunters. The evidence indicates that hunters were killing huge, elephant-like *mammoths* on the plains of western Oklahoma by

9000 B.C. These big game hunters were the first people to live in this area.

The era of the mammoth is sometimes called the *Clovis phase* of Native American *culture*. The name comes from Clovis, New Mexico, where weapon points used for killing mammoths were first found.

Clovis hunters killed mammoths with spears. Beautifully-shaped spearheads, three to six inches long, were fastened to wooden shafts. Craftsmen made the points by pressing flakes from a piece of flint rock with a pointed stone or bone.

Bison hunters. The Clovis culture was followed by the *Folsom culture*. The Folsom people also lived on the High Plains. They depended on a now-extinct *bison*. Folsom hunters are identified by their *projectile points*.

Bison hunters and food gatherers. The *Plainview culture* came after the Clovis and Folsom. The Plainview hunters did more food gathering than their ancestors.

2. THE CLOVIS HUNTERS WERE KILLING MAMMOTHS IN OKLAHOMA AT LEAST 11,000 YEARS AGO.

Oklahoma was different then. The first Native Americans began arriving in this area more than 11,000 years ago. That was near the end of the last *Ice Age*. A glacier which had covered Canada and the northern part of the United States was melting slowly. This huge ice mass never reached as far south as Oklahoma, but the climate here was affected. How?

The first Oklahomans found this area cooler and wetter than it is now. The land was covered with dense vegetation, streams, and natural lakes.

Tall, thick grass provided food for a variety of animals, many of which are now extinct. Hunters killed the giant mammoth, huge bison, *tapir*, a ground *sloth*, small horse, and camel.

Specimens of these animals have been reconstructed from bones found in gravel pits in western and central Oklahoma. A Columbian mammoth and other prehistoric animal skeletons can

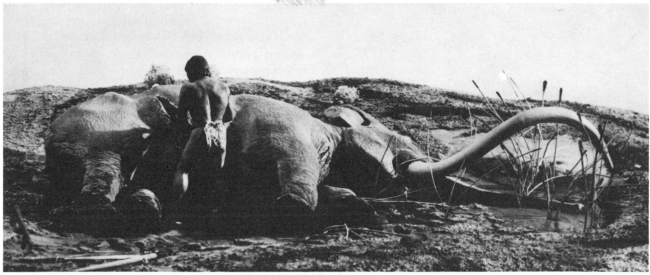

Diorama of an elephant hunter butchering a mammoth. (Arizona State Museum, University of Arizona, Tucson)

be seen at the Oklahoma Museum of Natural History (Stovall Museum) on the University of Oklahoma campus in Norman.

Elephant hunters. The early Clovis people who hunted the mammoth are called "elephant hunters" for good reason. The mammoth looked like an elephant. When full-grown, it stood about thirteen feet at the shoulder and had huge tusks.

The elephant hunters waited for their giant prey at a watering hole and worked together in killing it. The weapon they used was the spear—a wooden shaft attached to spearheads called Clovis points.

About 11,000 years ago, the elephant hunters killed a mammoth at Stecker, southwest of present-day Anadarko. It was an Imperial mammoth which was larger than the Columbian. Bones of the slayed mammoth were discovered at a place now known as the *Domebo site*. Clovis points were dug up with the bones. A scraper was found downstream.

Archaeologists were able to date the Domebo kill site. They measured the amount of radioactivity in wood, bone, and earth material. This method of dating is called the *carbon-14 process*.

The mammoth at Domebo was probably not the first one killed in Oklahoma. A mammoth may have been felled by hunters at Cooperton in Kiowa County as early as 18,000 years ago. Mammoth bones were discovered there. No hunting weapons or tools, however, were found with the bones.

3. AFTER THE MAMMOTH DISAPPEARED, HUNTERS DEPENDED ON THE PREHISTORIC BISON FOR FOOD.

Following the last Ice Age, the climate became drier. With less vegetation to feed on, the mammoths moved farther north and gradually disappeared. The bison then became the most-hunted animal on the plains.

Bison. The bison provided primitive hunters with the ideal form of food. The bison were abundant and easily killed. Unless wounded, they would not stand their ground to fight. Also, they would not scatter like antelope do. For defense the bison relied on numbers. But they did not attack hunters *en masse*. Instead, they gathered into a herd and ran away in a straight line into the wind.

The prehistoric bison became extinct or migrated to Canada by the time the first Europeans came to this area in the 1500s. The bison in Can-

The modern buffalo (bison) has shorter horns than its ancestors.

ada today may be descended from these migrants. Canadian bison have much larger horns than the modern plains buffalo.

Folsom hunters. The Folsom hunters were the first poeple to depend mainly on the bison for food. They came into prominence about 8500 B.C. Folsom projectile points help us identify their campsites. The points, well-made and about two inches long, were named for Folsom, New Mexico, where they were first found. But Folsom points have been discovered in all parts of Oklahoma except the southeast.

Folsom hunters killed bison near waterholes. The hunter tried to spear an animal below and behind the left shoulder. The point had to penetrate the heart, lungs, or spinal cord for a kill.

When the Folsom people butchered a bison, they removed the tail with the hide. They liked the meat in the hump the best.

4. THE PLAINVIEW CULTURE WAS A BRIDGE BETWEEN THE HUNTING AND MIXED HUNTING-GATHERING CULTURES.

Plainview or Plains Culture (7500 B.C. to 4500 B.C.) The *Plainview culture* was a *mixed economy* of hunting and food gathering. It followed the Clovis and Folsom cultures.

Like the earlier hunters, the Plains people were always searching for food. But they made more progress in storing food for later use. They used fiber baskets and storage bags made from animal skins. A crude *metate* (stone) was developed to grind seed into flour.

Bison meat was preserved by drying it in the sun. Dried meat was mixed with berries and animal fat to make *pemmican*. This food was packed in cleaned animal guts, like sausages, or in skin bags.

The best-studied site of the Plainview people is south of Boise City in Cimarron County. Known as the Nall site, it was first noticed during the 1930s "dust bowl" days. Winds eroded the topsoil, exposing artifacts left by the Plains people. Archaeologists found projectile points that were made to kill the huge extinct bison. Several varieties of stone scrapers were uncovered.

5. THE MIXED HUNTING-GATHERING LIFESTYLE LASTED THOUSANDS OF YEARS.

Three stages of economic development in prehistoric Oklahoma. The economic lifestyle of early Oklahomans slowly went through three stages: hunting, hunting-gathering, and farming. Archaeologists studied all three stages at a site on Cedar Creek in Caddo County. They sifted through layers of trash to find clues.

In the top layer, diggers discovered charred corn and beans grown by early farmers. Parts of farm houses, built out of clay and grass, were also found.

The middle layers contained debris left by people who hunted animals and gathered wild foods. The bottom layer had spear points and animal bones left by Folsom hunters.

Beginning of the hunting-gathering stage. By 8000 B.C. the age of almost complete reliance on hunting for food was drawing to a close. Prehistoric people gradually developed a mixed economy based on a combination of hunting and gathering of wild berries, nuts, roots, and seeds.

As we have seen, the Plainview bison hunters were the bridge between the hunting and hunting-gathering cultures. Thousands of years were to pass before the hunter-gatherer became a farmer.

Hunting-gathering people in the Ozarks. Remains of people who lived in Oklahoma near the end of the hunting-gathering stage have been found in caves.

Cave dwellers in the Ozarks hunted with the bow-and-arrow. They fished with bone hooks and sinkers.

Cultural advances were made by the Ozark people. They learned to grow corn and to make pottery.

Kenton caves. Caves near Kenton, at the west end of the Panhandle, were also occupied near the end of the hunting-gathering stage.

The Kenton cave dwellers hunted buffalo, deer, rabbits, and other animals. Hunting weapons found in the caves include the bow-and-arrow, nonreturnable boomerangs, and the *atlatl*. The atlatl was a notched throwing stick used to hurl a spear with great force. It had the effect of lengthening the hunter's arm by two feet.

Killed animals were butchered with stone knives. The skins were cleaned with shell scrapers. Fires for roasting the meat were started with wooden drills.

The Kenton people evidently ate a balanced diet. They ground flour from acorns on metates. Their cooks mixed this flour with berries and baked small cakes. These pastries were shaped like doughnuts for easy storage on a stick or string. Other food was stored in woven-grass baskets and skin bags.

Corn and some beans were found in the caves. These foods would indicate that the people were beginning to farm.

The crafts and arts of the Kenton cave dwellers were also a sign of cultural progress. They wove baskets, rugs, and yucca sandals. They made baby cradles, fur-lined moccasins, bone crochet needles, hairpins, wooden beads, brooms, and many other things. Drawings, known as *petroglyphs*, were carved or painted on the cave walls.

In the 1920s, boy scouts helped "Uncle Billy" Baker dig out some of the Kenton caves. Baker

was the Cimarron County farm agent. His artifacts are now in the No Man's Land Museum at Goodwell.

Archaeologists found other Kenton materials which are now located at the Museum of Natural History, the Woolaroc Museum in Bartlesville, and other scattered places.

Last years of the hunting-gathering stage. Prehistoric people gradually moved away from the caves during the late hunting-gathering stage. Over a period of about three thousand years before A.D. 1500, they began to build homes in the valleys. The human remains of several cultures were covered with silt along Oklahoma's rivers and preserved.

6. THE MOUNDBUILDERS DEVELOPED THE MOST ADVANCED CIVILIZATION IN PREHISTORIC OKLAHOMA.

The moundbuilders were the most advanced prehistoric people in Oklahoma. For more than a thousand years they built villages and farmed in the river valleys west of Fort Smith. The best villages were along the Poteau River and Fourche Maline Creek.

Mural of natives at Spiro Mounds State Park. (Fred Marvel)

45

WPA excavation at Spiro Mounds in 1930s. (OHS)

Farming was the main occupation at Spiro and other mound villages. The farmers planted corn, beans, squash, pumpkins, and sunflowers in the rich valley floodplains. The people also gathered wild pecans, acorns, plums, berries, and edible roots.

The moundbuilders stored surplus food. With food on hand, they had leisure time to work at crafts. The people also developed a religion. They were able to have an orderly *society*.

Spiro golden age. The peak of the Spiro culture was between A.D. 1250 and 1450. After the *golden age*, outsiders began to raid the villages. The raiders killed, robbed, and destroyed. The villages were never the same again.

Sketch of a carved stone human effigy pipe, 9½ inches long, found at Spiro Mounds. (Oklahoma Museum of Natural History, Norman)

Mounds. Mounds were the most unusual thing about the villages. In some places, mounds were built to raise houses above the flood level. Other mounds were built as open air religious shrines and burial places.

The burial mounds contained grave goods that tell the story of an advanced people. The goods include pottery, tools, weapons, blankets, and masks made of cedar or copper. Drawings on concho shells show activities of the people. One drawing, for example, showed a green corn ceremony.

Spiro. Spiro, near the Poteau River in LeFlore County, was the most famous village. The Spiro burial mounds tell us about the people who lived there. Weavers at Spiro made fine cloth. Potters shaped and fired pots. They also made little statues of people and animals. Other craftsmen made good tools, weapons, and farm implements.

The Spiro people traded for some raw materials. Copper came from the area that is now Michigan. *Turquoise* was from mines in New Mexico. Shells were carried from the Gulf of Mexico. Black stones for beads were quarried in Muskogee County. Flint has been traced to Kay County and as far away as Tennessee.

46

ROUNDUP

1. Define archaeologist. Prehistoric people left no written records, so how do we know about them?
2. List Oklahoma's three prehistoric Native American (Indian) cultures and the approximate time each group moved here.
3. In what ways was Oklahoma different when the first Oklahomans arrived? Why were the Clovis people called elephant hunters? Where have kill sites been discovered in Oklahoma?
4. Explain why the bison provided the ideal form of food for Folsom people.
5. Why do we say the Plainview people had a mixed economy? What is pemmican?
6. Name the three stages of economic development in Oklahoma.
7. At which places have remains been found of people who lived in the late hunting-gathering stage? What proof do we have that they may have begun to farm?
8. Make a chart of advances made by Kenton people under the following headings: Weapons, Tools, Food Storage Containers, and Crafts and Arts.
9. Who were the most advanced people in prehistoric Oklahoma? How do we know about them?
10. Make a list of cultural achievements made by the Spiro mound people. Why did they have leisure time for arts and crafts?
A Think about it! What lesson about the environment can we learn from prehistoric people?
B How does an archaeologist use the scientific method—identify a problem, gather information, analyze and test data, list alternative solutions (hypotheses), and reach a conclusion? Explain how the work of an archaeologist and a detective are similar.

7

UNDER THE FLAGS OF SPAIN AND FRANCE

Spain was the first European nation to explore the Americas. In the 1500s, the Spaniards conquered the Aztecs in Mexico and the Incas in Peru. Explorers rode thousands of miles to claim a huge empire for the king of Spain.

The land now in Oklahoma was part of New Spain—at least on paper. Spanish explorers blazed trails through this area in search of gold. But they made no permanent settlements here.

In the 1600s, France entered the race for an *empire*. The first French settlers in America were scattered along the St. Lawrence River in Canada. The main industry of New France was fur trading. The Frenchmen exchanged guns, cloth, tools, brandy, and other goods to the natives for furs. Many of the fur traders lived among the natives and took Indian wives.

The French empire gradually spread across the Great Lakes region. Then, in 1682, Robert La Salle led a small party in canoes down the Mississippi River to its mouth. He claimed the whole Mississippi basin, including Oklahoma, for the king of France.

In the 1700s, the French were trading with the Native Americans in Oklahoma. Most French traders came up the Red and Arkansas rivers. Others arrived overland from the Illinois country.

Let's take a look at the European explorers and their motives—first the Spaniards and then the French.

1. THE SPANISH KING CLAIMED OKLAHOMA AS A PART OF NEW SPAIN FROM 1541 TO 1800.

Oklahoma history begins. Oklahoma was on the *frontier* of the Spanish empire. Spain claimed this area for more than two and a half centuries.

Spanish explorers, soldiers, and priests began crossing Oklahoma in 1541. They described what they saw in diaries. They also wrote letters and reports to the king. These records tell us about the natives and the geography of this region in the 1500s. Thus, the recorded history of Oklahoma area began before the first English colonists landed in Virginia.

Spanish empire. Columbus stumbled on the New World in 1492. Within fifty years, King Carlos of Spain claimed an empire as far north as present Kansas. The Spanish goals in the New World were the 3 g's: gold, glory, and gospel.

With gold in mind, the Spaniards conquered the wealthy Aztecs and Incas. Gold then poured into the king's treasure chests. Mexico City, the Aztec capital, became the base for more conquests. As the Spaniards moved north, they enslaved Indians. The natives were forced to work in mines. They herded cattle on huge Spanish ranches. It is said that the first cowboy was branded before the first cow.

Missionaries were given an important role in New Spain. Their main purpose was to convert the natives to the Roman Catholic religion. The priests also traveled with explorers. They drew maps of new lands. Their diaries were good accounts of what they saw.

Spanish explorers rode thousands of miles in search of gold and glory. They were lured by tales of rich cities to the north. These stories were made up by the Indians. What better way to get rid of the Spaniards? The natives would tell their visitors about riches to be found "somewhere else."

2. SPANISH EXPLORERS AND PRIESTS WERE JUST PASSING THROUGH THE LAND AREA WE NOW CALL OKLAHOMA.

Coronado. Francisco Coronado led an expedition across Oklahoma in 1541. He was kept on the move by clever Indians.

When Coronado left Mexico he was searching for the "seven cities of gold." He was chosen for

Coronado in full armor. (Mural by Gerald Cassidy in the Post Office at Santa Fe)

this job by Viceroy Mendoza, the king's ruler in Mexico. Coronado crossed northern Mexico and Arizona. In New Mexico he found the Zuni villages. These towns were made of mud and stone, not gold. Disappointed, Coronado sent out small groups to explore. One of his captains discovered the Grand Canyon in Arizona.

From Indians along the Rio Grande in New Mexico, he learned about a rich city called Quivira. El Turco, a slave, told the story. He agreed to lead Coronado to Quivira. Coronado took the bait.

In the spring of 1541, the search for phantom gold began again. El Turco eagerly guided the Spaniards across the Texas and Oklahoma pan-

handles. They were amazed by the vast expanse of the High Plains. "Nothing but sky and cows," wrote one diarist. The cows were roving herds of buffalo.

Coronado described the plains Apaches in a letter to King Carlos. "The Indians do not plant," he wrote. "They eat the raw flesh and drink the blood of the cows." Their clothes and "little field tents" were made from the hides.

"They also have dogs," Coronado said. "The dogs carry the tents and poles and other small things." Later, the plains Indians used horses for this purpose. They had never seen horses, however, before the Spanish came.

While on the plains, Coronado's men killed

buffalo and cooked the meat. They built fires with buffalo chips because no wood could be found.

After 77 days of travel, the Spaniards came to Quivira. This village of cone-shaped grass huts was near present-day Wichita, Kansas. The natives were Wichita Indians, a tribe that also lived in Oklahoma. They planted corn along the Arkansas River and hunted buffalo for food. Coronado observed that the Wichitas also had grapes, mulberries, nuts, and prunes.

There was no gold in the village! The only metal was a piece of copper worn by the chief about his neck.

El Turco confessed that he had lied about Quivira. The angry Spaniards strangled him to death. Then they took a shortcut to New Mexico. Some Wichita warriors guided Coronado along the Santa Fe Trail. This route crosses Cimarron County. Coronado was back in Mexico City in 1542.

Coronado was a successful failure! He found no golden cities. But he claimed the Oklahoma area and much of the Southwest for Spain. His letter to the king is important to us. It is the first description we have of western Oklahoma and some of the Native Americans who lived there.

Padilla and Oñate. Father Juan Padilla was a priest who made the trip with Coronado to Quivira. He later returned to work among the Wichitas and other tribes.

Juan de Oñate, governor of New Mexico, led a party to Quivira in 1601. He followed the Canadian and passed the Antelope Hills in western Oklahoma. Like Coronado, he found no wealth. After Oñate's journey, the Spanish paid little attention to the Oklahoma area until the late 1700s.

3. THE FRENCH WERE THE FIRST EUROPEANS TO EXPLORE EASTERN OKLAHOMA.

Oklahoma was a part of New France. LaSalle claimed the whole Mississippi basin for France. His government tried to make good its claim to the heartland of America. French settlers started a colony in Louisiana. In 1718, Jean LeMoyne founded New Orleans. France was ready to compete with Spain for control of the Mississippi basin.

French explorers slowly paddled their way up the rivers that flow into the Mississippi. They went up the Red and Arkansas rivers to Oklahoma. The French hoped to make friends with the natives in this region. They wanted to trade for furs. Another French goal was to open a trade route to the Spanish settlement of Sante Fe in New Mexico.

Two French explorers reached Oklahoma in 1719. One came up the Red River. His full name and title were Jean-Baptiste Benard, Sieur de la Harpe.

The other explorer was Claude Charles du Tisne. He came overland from the Illinois country.

Du Tisne. Du Tisne arrived in the Kansas-Oklahoma region on horseback. He visited the Osages. Du Tisne also traded with the Pawnees for Spanish horses. He raised the French flag over a Pawnee village.

La Harpe. La Harpe had come from France to Louisiana to seek his fortune. He was given a land grant on the Red River and led a small party upstream. The trip took eight weeks because huge *rafts* blocked the river. A raft was caused by uprooted trees and brush packing together like a dam. La Harpe's heavy boats had to be tied to ropes and pulled over the rafts.

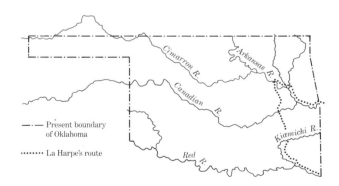

La Harpe's Route

Finally, La Harpe reached his land grant. Caddo Indians helped him build a fort on the Texas side of the river. They cut cypress logs to make the walls. A vegetable garden was planted.

On August 11, 1719, La Harpe led a party on horses into eastern Oklahoma. In three weeks he reached the Wichita villages. They were located near the Arkansas River.

On the way, La Harpe's party camped one night where Idabel is today. They killed deer, two buffalo, and "a very large bear" in the Ouachita Mountains. North of present Hartshorne, the Frenchmen met some Osage warriors carrying tomahawks.

"I advanced toward them with three Frenchmen well-armed," La Harpe later wrote in his journal. The Osages were surprised by this boldness. They offered the peace pipe. La Harpe gave them presents.

Wichita chiefs greeted La Harpe outside their villages. They were mounted on horses with Spanish-style saddles.

"I mounted a beautiful horse that they led out to me," La Harpe said. "We went together to the villages . . . the most delightful location I ever saw."

Each grass, dome-shaped house in the villages had a piece of leather over the door. It showed the tribal coat of arms of the people who lived in the house. Several Caddo-speaking tribes lived in the villages.

A typical Wichita village.

French trading post at the Indian village of Ferdinandina. (OHS)

La Harpe learned about the tribal customs. For several days he sat on a buffalo robe with the chiefs in a circle around him. The chiefs told him about their Apache enemies and the Spanish towns and mines in New Mexico. At mealtime the native women tried to outdo each other bringing smoked meat, corn, and greens.

One day the chiefs painted La Harpe's face blue. They brought him gifts of buffalo hides, rock salt, chunks of tobacco which they had grown, and a little Apache slave. The chiefs said they wanted to be friends with the French. They hoped that French traders would come to supply them with guns and other goods.

La Harpe wanted to leave men at the villages to start a trading post. Two black men in the party were especially popular with the Wichitas. But La Harpe learned that the Indians always left their villages in October to hunt. They didn't return until March to plant corn, beans, squash, and other crops for summer food.

La Harpe went back to his fort and on to New Orleans. He spoke highly of the Oklahoma area as a land of promise and opportunity. La Harpe liked the "good climate, fertile land, and rich minerals."

French traders and fur trappers. Frenchmen began entering Oklahoma in the 1720s to trade for furs along the Arkansas. They traded north of present-day Poteau and in the Three Forks area near Muskogee. A trading post was established at Ferdinandia, near what is now Newkirk. This post has been called the first white

French trapper and trader. (Sketch by Frederic Remington)

settlement in Oklahoma, though it was actually an Indian village.

Once a year the traders loaded bundles of furs and buffalo hides on boats. They sold the cargo in New Orleans and came back with trade goods.

4. THE WICHITAS AND CADDOES WERE MIDDLEMEN IN THE FUR AND HIDE TRADE.

The French traders got along well with the Wichitas and other Indians who spoke the Caddo language. The French depended on these natives to trade with tribes that had furs and buffalo hides. Comanches, for example, brought their buffalo skins to the Wichitas. They went back to the plains with farm crops and French goods.

Comanches. The Comanches were feared by many village tribes. The Comanches were once farmers themselves, but the Spanish horse changed their way of life. They became nomadic buffalo hunters and raiders. Always ready to move with the buffalo herds, the Comanches lived in portable teepees. Heavy loads were moved on drags. These were poles fastened to pack horses.

The Comanches and other Plains tribes were expert horsemen. On horseback they were described as "the best fighting men in the world."

The Wichitas moved to the Red River. Like people today, the Wichitas sometimes moved. Why? Sometimes the soil wore out. Another tribe might raid and burn their villages. That's what happened in the mid-1700s. Osage warriors were attacking the Wichita villages that La Harpe had found so peaceful.

The Wichitas and French traders moved to the Red River. There they built two villages. One was in present Jefferson County. The other was across the river in Texas. The French flag flew over these villages.

The village on the north bank was a fort. A wall of logs protected cone-shaped grass houses. A moat was dug around the village and on both sides of the winding road to the river. Guards were posted at the ford downstream to keep away invaders.

Today we would say that the Wichitas had a "balanced economy." They farmed, growing a variety of crops. They were also traders. Comanches

A Comanche camp. (Sketch by George Catlin)

52

and Kiowas brought buffalo hides, horses, and Apache slaves to the Red River villages to trade for French goods.

Indian war with Spain. A state of war developed between Spanish Texas and the Oklahoma tribes that were allied with the French. Why? The Spanish claimed the land now in Oklahoma. They wanted the trade that the Frenchmen enjoyed with the Indians.

The Spaniards tried to capture or tax French cargo boats going down the Red River. The Wichitas, Caddoes, and Comanches fought back. In 1758, these Indians raided the San Sabá mission in Texas. The next year, they struck again. All of the twenty Spanish soldiers at San Sabá were killed. A large herd of horses and mules were driven away.

Battle at the Red River villages. Diego Ortiz Parrilla, a Spanish military officer, decided to punish the Wichitas and their allies. He put together a strange-looking army of about 500 men. Only a few were trained Spanish soldiers. The rest were mission Indians, "cowboys, tailors, laborers, cigar dealers, hatters, miners, and others." Two priests went along. One of them was a surgeon.

Muskets and swords were the main weapons though bows-and-arrows were used by a small band of Apaches. Parrilla also took some small cannon. A total of 1600 animals were driven along. These included a herd of horses, a pack train, and cattle for food.

Parrilla led this motley army to the Red River in October, 1759. The Spaniards were attacked before they reached the fort. They were no match for the well-armed, disciplined Wichita and Comanche warriors. These Indians attacked Parrilla's army on both flanks. This tactic put the army in a crossfire.

The Spaniards fired about a dozen cannon volleys at the fort. No damage was done. In fact, the Indians inside the fort laughed loudly. They dared the army to attack. But Parrilla's troops retreated. They left muskets, saddles, the cannon, and other equipment on the field of battle.

Parrilla later praised the warriors, especially the Wichita chief. This brave man led his men in the thick of the fight. The chief was easy to see. He was mounted on a beautiful horse and wore a white buckskin jacket. His helmet was made of the same material and adorned with feathers.

The Spanish army was a different story. Parrilla called it a "disgrace." He said the men showed no discipline. There was "a lack of spirit to fight the kind of Indians which have been seen."

The battle of the Red River villages was a victory for the Wichitas and their allies. It has been called Oklahoma's "war of independence from Spanish rule." French traders were happy for the Indian victory, but they did not have long to enjoy it.

5. OKLAHOMA BELONGED TO THE NATIVE AMERICANS, NOT TO SPAIN OR FRANCE.

The end of French and Spanish claims to Oklahoma. France was defeated on three continents by England in the Seven Years War (1756–1763). In America, this struggle was called the French and Indian War.

In 1763, France gave up her claim to land east of the Mississippi River to England. Spain, which had helped France in the war, lost Florida to England. To make up for this loss, Spain was given New Orleans and all of France's land west of the Mississippi. As a result of these treaty terms, the Oklahoma area was claimed only by Spain from 1763 to 1800. Many French fur traders stayed in the West, however.

Indians in Oklahoma paid little attention to these world affairs. This area belonged to the Indian tribes, no matter which outsiders claimed it. The Europeans left their imprint, however. Place names are reminders that the Spanish and French were here. Cimarron, for example, comes from the Spanish. Poteau, Verdigris, Grand, Illinois, and San Bois are some of the French names. Also, some of Oklahoma's Native Americans can trace a line of ancestors back to the French fur traders.

Oklahoma became a part of the United States. Spain sold the Louisiana basin west of the Mississippi River to France in 1800. Three years later, President Thomas Jefferson bought it from Napoleon Bonaparte, the French emperor. This deal is known as the Louisiana Purchase of 1803. It made Oklahoma, except for the Panhandle, a part of the United States. The Panhandle was still claimed as part of the Spanish empire.

ROUNDUP

1. Why can it be said that Oklahoma history began with the Spanish explorers? What were the 3 g's? From what city did the Spanish explore the Southwest?
2. For what city was Coronado searching when he crossed Oklahoma? Describe what he actually found at this place.
3. How did Coronado describe the Apaches? How did his men survive on the plains?
4. Why has Coronado been called a "successful failure?"
5. What rivers did the French use to reach the Oklahoma area? List their two main goals.
6. Where did La Harpe build a fort? Which Indian tribe did he visit near the Arkansas River? How did he describe these villages? How did the Indians treat him?
7. Where did the Comanches live? How did they make a living?
8. Near what river did the Wichitas build new villages? Why can we say they had a "balanced economy?"
9. Why did the Spanish want to attack the Wichita villages? Who led the Spanish army? What has the "battle of the Red River" been called?
10. Explain how the United States got control of present-day Oklahoma.
A. Think about it! Explain how the Spanish introduction of the horse and metals changed the lifestyle of many Indians.
B. Try this! Visit the closest museum that has exhibits on the Wichitas, Caddos, or Comanches and write a report on what you learn. Alternative project: Make a list of items you would expect to find in a museum about these tribes.

8

OKLAHOMA BECOMES PART OF THE UNITED STATES

The Mississippi River was the western boundary of the United States from 1783 to 1803. The thirteen colonies won independence from England in 1783. In the *treaty*, England gave most of the land east of the Mississippi River to the colonies. Florida, New Orleans, and the land west of the Mississippi (including Oklahoma) were still claimed by Spain.

American *pioneers* soon filled up the area between the Appalachian Mountains and the Mississippi. Kentucky became a state in 1792 and Tennessee in 1796. Roads barely existed in this area. The easiest way to take farm products to market was by river to New Orleans. Farmers and *middlemen* loaded flatboats with flour, tobacco, pork, potatoes, whiskey, and other products. In New Orleans the goods were transferred to oceangoing ships.

American leaders wanted to buy New Orleans from Spain. The idea of getting land west of the Mississippi was also in the minds of many Americans.

1. OKLAHOMA WAS PART OF THE LOUISIANA PURCHASE WHICH WAS ADDED TO THE UNITED STATES IN 1803.

In 1800, Spain sold New Orleans and her western lands (Louisiana) to Napoleon Bonaparte of France. But Napoleon was about ready to go to war with England. He needed money.

President Thomas Jefferson sent a *minister* to Paris, France to see if the United States could buy New Orleans. Jefferson didn't want this port city to be controlled by a powerful foreign nation. To everyone's surprise, Napoleon offered to sell all of Louisiana.

The American minister jumped at this opportunity. The Louisiana Purchase Treaty was signed on April 30, 1803. The total price was $15 million—about three cents an acre.

Results of the Louisiana Purchase. Louisiana doubled the size of the United States. It was a vast new area for agriculture and the fur trade. President Jefferson was happy because he wanted farming, not manufacturing, to be America's main industry.

Jefferson also had the idea that eastern Indians should be moved to the Louisiana Purchase lands. White pioneers had an eye on Indian lands in Georgia and other states. Jefferson wanted to give the Indians a "permanent" home in the West. There, he said, they would be free "forever" from pioneer crowding.

Thirteen states, in whole or part, were carved out of the Louisiana Purchase. The first was Louisiana in 1812. The last was Oklahoma in 1907.

Finally, the American spirit was changed by the addition of Louisiana. People began to think that the United States should buy more land. "Why not expand the United States all the way to the Pacific?" they asked.

2. PRESIDENT JEFFERSON SENT EXPEDITIONS TO EXPLORE THE LOUISIANA PURCHASE.

When Jefferson bought Louisiana, he had only a vague idea what this territory was like. He needed good maps so that boundary lines could be worked out with Spain and England.

Lewis and Clark expedition. Jefferson chose his secretary, Meriwether Lewis, and William Clark to lead the first exploring *party*. These men followed the Missouri and other rivers

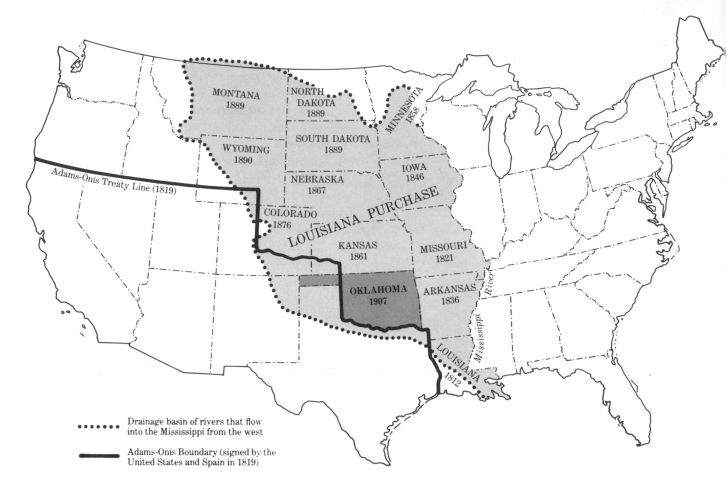

Drainage basin of rivers that flow
into the Mississippi from the west

Adams-Onís Boundary (signed by the
United States and Spain in 1819)

Louisiana Purchase, 1803

to the Pacific Northwest in 1804-1806. They made maps and learned about the geography and Indians.

Lieutenant Zebulon Pike was sent to explore the southwest. Pike was arrested by Spaniards while searching for the source of the Arkansas River in Colorado. He was taken to Mexico, by way of Santa Fe. After a year in captivity, Pike was freed. In his report, he said the "desert" southwest didn't have much of a future.

Captain Richard Sparks was given the job of exploring the Red River in 1806. Sparks moved upstream from the Mississippi until he came to the great raft. He led his party around this huge mass of tangled logs and plant growth.

When Sparks got to the present location of southeast Oklahoma, he was stopped by Spanish soldiers. The officer in charge ordered the Americans to leave Spanish territory. Sparks saw no point in fighting. No one knew where the border was. He went back to New Orleans.

3. TWO OF OKLAHOMA'S BOUNDARIES
    WERE SET BY A TREATY WITH SPAIN
    IN 1819.

The Louisiana Purchase boundaries were indefinite. In 1803, Talleyrand, the French foreign minister, was asked where the boundaries of Louisiana were. He said, "No one knows." A good guess was all the area that drains into the Mississippi from the west.

"You have made a noble bargain for yourselves," Talleyrand told the American minister in Paris. "I suppose you will make the most of it."

56

Talleyrand was right. Eager to expand, the United States later claimed both Texas and the Oregon country.

Adams-Onís Treaty with Spain. In 1819, the United States signed the Adams-Onís Treaty that set the southern boundary. This border zigzagged from the Gulf of Mexico to the Pacific Ocean.

Parts of the boundary line ran along the Red River and the 100th meridian. These are two of Oklahoma's boundaries today.

The northern border with Canada. This border was set where it is today by treaties with England.

4. LIEUTENANT JAMES WILKINSON EXPLORED ALONG THE ARKANSAS RIVER IN 1806.

Exploring the Arkansas River was one of the main goals of the Pike *expedition.* When Pike reached this river in western Kansas, he split his men and supplies. He went upstream. In late October, 1806, Lieutenant James Wilkinson led a small party downstream. His men endured many hardships.

The expedition was in trouble before it reached the present Kansas-Oklahoma line. All the meat and ammunition was lost when a cottonwood canoe overturned. The men had no food and no means of hunting. The weather was cold. Unfriendly Pawnees were nearby.

Good relations with the Osages. Luckily, Wilkinson met some friendly Osage hunters. These natives killed a fresh supply of meat for Wilkinson and asked him to visit Chief Tuttasuggy. The chief was ill at his camp near present Ponca City. Wilkinson rode there by mule to see him on November 30, 1806. This trip was the first entrance of an American explorer into northern Oklahoma.

Bad weather slowed down Wilkinson after he resumed his journey on the Arkansas. The men had to axe their way through the ice-choked river. One canoe ran aground and capsized during a fierce snowstorm. Tired and frostbitten, the Wilkinson party reached the Osage winter camp at Three Forks before Christmas. This area, where the Verdigris and Grand rivers run into the Arkansas, abounded with furbearing animals.

One of Wilkinson's main goals was to make a friendly *alliance* with Chief Big Track and the Osages. That he did. The chief welcomed the Americans and offered them land to build a *trading post.* Big Track's Osages had moved to the Three Corners area from Missouri in 1802 at the urging of Jean Pierre Chouteau, a French fur trader.

After Wilkinson left Three Forks, he went downstream to the Arkansas Post. The 74-day expedition had broken his health. He never returned.

Wilkinson's goals were achieved. First, questions about the Arkansas River were answered. The water level upstream from Three Forks was not dependable. Overland portage was necessary in some places.

Lieutenant Wilkinson also learned the location of Osage settlements. He discovered that friendly relations with this tribe were possible.

In his report, Wilkinson suggested that a fort be built at Three Forks. The army would be needed, he said, to keep peace among the Indians. The Osages resented new tribes, especially the Cherokees and Choctaws, who were beginning to move in from east of the Mississippi.

5. GEORGE C. SIBLEY LIKED WHAT HE SAW OF OKLAHOMA.

George C. Sibley was an *Indian agent* at Fort Osage in Missouri. Though raised an educated gentleman in the east, he loved the western frontier.

A strong patriot, Sibley traveled at his own expense to win the friendship of the Kansa and Pawnee Indians in Kansas. In event of a possible war with Spain over boundaries, he wanted the natives to be on the American side. He gave them flags and medals.

Sibley led two expeditions into Oklahoma. People who read about his journeys gained a good impression of this area.

Buffalo hunter.

Sibley was the first white man to visit the Great Salt Plains in Alfalfa County. Sibley first touched Oklahoma soil in June, 1811. He visited Chief Pawhuska (White Hair) of the Osages near present Blackwell. Then he traveled west to the Great Salt Plains. Atop a hill (near Jet) his party saw "thousands of bushels" of pure salt. This salt was "sweated up" by water flowing through salt beds not far from the surface.

Sibley realized that salt was a valuable item in trade. In pioneer days it was used to preserve meat and to soften hides.

In the gypsum hill country, Sibley spotted a huge buffalo herd that stampeded. The rumbling of their hoofs sounded like thunder. Sibley chased after the herd, firing his two pistols at them with no effect. An Osage boy showed him how to hunt, killing two buffalo with only two arrows.

Sibley returned to Missouri and wrote about the wonders he had seen. The interest he created in the Great Salt Plains lasted a long time. As late as 1843, Nathan Boone led a military expedition to the plains. A son of the famous Daniel Boone, he was an officer at Fort Gibson. Unfortunately, salt mining was never developed extensively. In later times, however, farmers and ranchers hauled chunks of salt crust in wagons to their cattle. Today the Great Salt Plains Reservoir provides a refuge for waterfowl.

Sibley marked the Santa Fe Trail. In 1825, Sibley returned to a different part of Oklahoma. He was one of three survey commissioners appointed to mark a road to Santa Fe. The survey party was guided by two famous mountain men: "Old Bill" Williams and Joseph R. Walker.

Sibley's party followed the Cimarron River

Historical marker north of Boise City, Cimarron County. (Fred Marvel)

into what is now the Oklahoma Panhandle. The men camped at Flag Springs, north of present Boise City. From this camp they pointed their wagon tongues at the Rabbit Ears Mounds. This *landmark* is in New Mexico. Sibley kept a journal of the Santa Fe Trail survey. It contains one of the earliest descriptions of the Oklahoma Panhandle.

6. MAJOR STEPHEN H. LONG LED TWO MILITARY EXPEDITIONS INTO OKLAHOMA.

Major Long founded Fort Smith. In 1817, white settlers in Arkansas appealed to the War Department for military protection. The settlers feared they would be caught in the middle of a war between the Osages and the Western Cherokees. This conflict developed as the Cherokees began moving to Arkansas from the east. They were attracted to the wild game, climate, and soil of the land north of the Arkansas River. The Cherokees often hunted on land claimed by the Osages in what is now northeast Oklahoma. That led to attacks on hunting parties and eventually open warfare between the tribes.

The War Department sent Major Long to build a fort between the hostile tribes. He picked a site for Fort Smith and also explored along the Kiamichi and Poteau rivers. Fort Smith was built at Belle Point where the Poteau empties into the Arkansas River. This site was a low cliff with ferns and flowers. A stockade of pointed logs was built around the houses for soldiers.

At the time it was built, Fort Smith was the westernmost fort in the nation. It became the gateway for American trappers and traders going west. Fort Smith was also the supply depot for forts that were built later in Oklahoma.

Major Long followed the wrong river across Oklahoma. Long's second expedition in 1820 turned out to be unusual. The Department of War sent him to find the headwaters of the Arkansas and Red rivers and trace these rivers to the American settlements. Long divided his men in the Colorado Rockies, sending Captain John R. Bell down the Arkansas.

The source of the Red River was harder to find. Long located a creek to follow downstream, not knowing where it would lead. Comanches along the way assured him it was the Red River. Like the Spanish, the Comanches called any river with red color, Rio Colorado (red). But Long's party was actually on the Canadian, one of many "red" rivers.

Long labelled the plains country as the "Great American Desert." Before the Long party reached the Arkansas, the men camped for awhile at the Canadian Falls. They took time to talk about where they had been.

Stephen H. Long.

59

Edwin James, a botanist in the Long party, expressed the general feeling. James described the plains country as a "sandy waste." He said it was suitable for only "nomad native hunters." The plains had no timber, no navigable streams, and little water.

On Long's map, the plains country was named the "Great American Desert." This description helped delay settlement of the plains region. The label was used on maps and in schoolbooks for half a century.

What Long didn't foresee, of course, was that scientific dry farming and irrigation would change the dry plains into a livable place.

Long's expedition in 1820 was not a complete failure. Scientists who were with him wrote about the vegetation and Native American customs. An artist made the first sketches of plant and animal life of the plains. Long's report also contained the first description of central Oklahoma. Finally, the Long and Bell expeditions drew attention to the lush, fertile lands in eastern Oklahoma.

Captain John R. Bell explored the Arkansas in 1820. By the time Bell's party reached Oklahoma, they were short of food. As luck would have it, they found an Indian field where the Arkansas flows into Kay County. The men gorged themselves on watermelon and corn.

Downstream the Osages gave Bell a "fat buck" for another feast. The smokers in Bell's party had run out of tobacco and were happy to smoke the peace pipe with the son of Clermont, chief of the Osages.

Bell was able to get supplies at Hugh Glenn's trading post on the Verdigris. The men also went up the Illinois River a few miles to visit Mark and Richard Bean. These men had a farm and a saltworks. Bell then went on to Fort Smith and waited for Major Long's party.

7. THE THREE FORKS AREA WAS THE CRADLE OF OKLAHOMA HISTORY.

Fur trappers, hunters, and traders were the first pioneers in Oklahoma. They started coming to the Three Forks area even before Oklahoma became a part of the United States in 1803.

Trappers came this way for the furs of the beaver, otter, muskrat, and other animals. Hunters gathered the skins of deer, bear, and the buffalo. Traders bought furs and skins from both the whites and Indians.

Three Forks was an attractive place. People came to the Three Forks region (near Muskogee) for many reasons. The area was rich in furbearing animals. The climate was mild. Salt springs were nearby. The Arkansas River was a good trade route to markets downstream.

Also, the Osage Trace ran to Three Forks. It was a network of overland trade trails to Missouri. Later, the Osage Trace was part of the Texas Road. This road connected Missouri to Texas. Highway 69 and the M-K-T Railroad were built almost parallel to the old Texas Road.

President Jefferson had a good word for Three Forks in his 1806 message to Congress. He said Three Forks had a future as a trading center. For the first time, a place in present Oklahoma was mentioned in an official presidential document.

Chouteau family. Many of the early traders, such as the Chouteau family in St. Louis, were of French ancestry. The Chouteaus traded with the Osages in Missouri when that region was claimed by France and Spain.

Chouteau trade items came from France or England by way of New Orleans or Montreal. The Osages wanted steel traps, rifles, blankets, knives, axes, kettles, calico cloth, ribbons, and cheap jewelry. The natives bartered furs for these goods.

In 1802, Jean Pierre Chouteau persuaded Chief Big Track and several thousand Osages to move to the Three Forks area. Chouteau started a trading post at Grand Saline on the Grand River. Now called Salina, this place is known as the first "permanent" white settlement in Oklahoma. Each year on October 10, Chouteau's birthday, Salina celebrates Oklahoma Historical Day.

In 1817, Colonel Auguste Pierre Chouteau, the founder's son, came to Grand Saline. He became the leading merchant in Oklahoma. Colonel

Colonel A. P. Chouteau. (Sketch by Vincent Lackey, OHS)

Chouteau built a large log house that was called "La Saline." He lived there with his Osage wife, children, Indian servants, and slaves.

Colonel Chouteau built a race track to entertain friends and visitors. In 1832, Chouteau escorted Washington Irving, the famous writer, from St. Louis to Oklahoma. Irving described his visit at La Saline in his book *A Tour of the Prairies.*

In the early 1820s, Chouteau bought a trading house on the Verdigris from Henry Barbour and George Brand, who was married to a Cherokee. After taking over the business, Chouteau added a small shipyard. He hired carpenters to build *keelboats,* 50 to 80 feet long. These boats carried Chouteau's fur to New Orleans. In 1824, the peak year, nearly 39,000 pounds of furs were shipped downstream.

Before his death in 1838, Colonel Chouteau began building a chain of trading posts. One post was on the Canadian near Purcell. Chouteau also built the first trading post in Kiowa country. It was located on Cache Creek near the present site of Fort Sill. Chouteau became a great favorite of the Kiowas, Wichitas, and Comanches.

Descendants of the Chouteau pioneers still live in Oklahoma. Lovely Yvonne Chouteau, the world-famous ballerina, is a sixth generation Oklahoman.

Joseph Bogy and the Indian war. Bogy was the first trader to start a post at Three Points. In 1806, he brought a large boatload of goods up the Arkansas. His crew built a post where the town of Okay is located today.

Bogy's post was attacked in January, 1807, by Choctaw warriors led by Chief Pushmataha. The warriors took all the goods, furs, and guns. Bogy's own boats were used to haul away the loot. The chief said the warriors attacked because Bogy was trading with their enemies, the Osages.

Bogy continued to trade with the Indians at Three Points, however, for many years.

Nathaniel Pryor was one of the most romantic traders at Three Forks. Pryor had led an exciting life. He was a sergeant with the Lewis and Clark expedition. Then came service as a lieutenant in the War of 1812.

In 1819, Pryor was given a license by the governor of Arkansas to trade with the Osages. He built a trading store on the Verdigris River and lived there with his Osage wife.

Pryor spent much time with the Osages at Clermont's town (Claremore). At the time of his death in 1831, he was working as the Indian sub-agent for the Osages. The city of Pryor is named after him.

Hugh Glenn was another pioneer in the Three Forks area. Glenn, a former Cincinnati banker, and Nathaniel Pryor were business partners for a while. In 1821, Glenn joined Jacob Fowler in a trade expedition to Santa Fe. The Glenn-Fowler party was in Santa Fe when news

Choteau's trading post on the Grand River.

arrived that Mexico had won independence from Spain.

Oklahoma's first mission and school. Pryor helped Epaphrus Chapman, a Presbyterian, pick a site for Oklahoma's first *mission.* Called the Union Mission, it was located near the Grand River south of Chouteau. The mission was sponsored by the United Foreign Missionary Society.

The first missionaries were nineteen men and women who survived a ten-month trip from New York in 1820. They opened a school the following year with four French-Osage pupils. The children learned English and helped with farm chores at the mission.

The missionaries had reasons to be discouraged. A flood washed away their crops. They worried about the safety of the children because the Osages and Cherokees were at war. Chief Clermont, the Osage leader, gave them some hope. "My people will soon see the superior advantages of your way of living," he told them.

In 1835, Reverend Samuel A. Worcester, who had worked among the Cherokees in Georgia, arrived at Union Mission. He set up Oklahoma's first printing press. Among other things, Worcester published *The Child's Book,* a primer for Indian children. It was the first book printed in Oklahoma.

Sam Houston. A former governor of Tennessee, Houston lived among the Cherokees at Three Forks for three years. He took Tiana Rogers, a Cherokee, for his wife. They lived at Wigwam Neosho, a trading post near Fort Gibson.

In 1832, Houston left Tiana at this post with two slaves. He moved on to Texas and glory. Houston became president of the Lone Star Republic. He sent runners to Tiana, urging her to join him in Texas. She refused. Tiana wanted to stay with her people. Her relatives included ancestors of the famous Will Rogers.

The Bean saltworks. Salt springs were one of the main attractions of the Three Forks area. Long before white settlers came, Indians took the Osage Trail from Missouri to a salt spring near

Sam Houston.

present Mazie in Mayes County. Eventually two white men ran a saltworks there. In 1819, however, one of the partners killed and scalped the other.

Mark and Richard Bean bought the salt kettles and hauled them by boat to a site on the Illinois River. They started a *saltworks* there to supply Fort Smith and white settlements along the Arkansas River. The Beans got a bushel of salt from every 55 gallons of salt water boiled in the kettles. Boats were built to ship the salt downstream. The Beans also planted Indian corn and raised cattle.

In 1828, the U.S. government gave the land in northeast Oklahoma to the Cherokees. By treaty the government gave the Cherokees the right to decide which white settlers could stay on Indian land. The Beans were not among the chosen. They were forced to give up their saltworks and move. The works were taken over by Walter Webber. He was a wealthy, part-Cherokee trader and black slaveowner from Arkansas. Webbers Falls is named after him.

Like other white settlers on Cherokee land, the Beans were each given a 320 acre farm in Arkansas. Nearly thirty years later, they were paid almost $15,000 by the U.S. government for their equipment at the saltworks.

ROUNDUP

1. Explain why the United States bought Louisiana (including the Oklahoma area) in 1803 from France rather than from Spain.
2. List four results of the Louisiana Purchase.
3. Outline the early American exploration history of Oklahoma. List each explorer, routes followed, contact with other people, main events, goals, and results.
4. For what reasons is the Three Forks area called the "cradle of Oklahoma history?"
5. List the achievements of the Chouteau family in Oklahoma's early history.
6. Tell why each of the following pioneers was important: Bogy, Pryor, Glenn, Chapman, Clermont, Worcester, Houston, Bean family, and Webber.
A. Think about it! Look up the meaning of "manifest destiny" and explain what this belief had to do with Oklahoma.
B. Try this! Draw a map showing the routes of American explorers in the Oklahoma area.
C. Make a crossword puzzle, or a seek and find puzzle, using names of people and places in this chapter.

9

REMOVAL OF THE FIVE CIVILIZED TRIBES

Many new faces appeared on the Oklahoma scene after this area became part of the United States in 1803.

White settlements grew up along the Red and Arkansas rivers. These settlements were a part of Arkansas after the U.S. Congress established that territory in 1819. The Arkansas territorial legislature created two counties in 1820. Miller County was in the southeast corner of present-day Oklahoma. Crawford County included what is now northeast Oklahoma. Later, Lovely County was carved out of the part of Crawford County lying north of the Arkansas River.

The U.S. Army built posts to protect the white settlements. Fort Smith was established in 1817. Soldiers moved into Fort Gibson and Fort Towson in 1824.

Then came the *Five Civilized Tribes*—Cherokees, Creeks, Choctaws, Chickasaws, and Seminoles. President Andrew Jackson relocated these tribes in Indian Territory (Oklahoma) after Congress passed the Indian Removal Act in 1830. Jackson wanted to remove all tribes then living east of the Mississippi River. He ordered federal troops to remove any tribal members who refused to go.

1. WESTERN CHEROKEES SETTLED FIRST IN ARKANSAS AND THEN REPLACED THE OSAGE TRIBE IN NORTHEASTERN OKLAHOMA.

In the early 1800s, a few Cherokees had moved voluntarily from Georgia to Arkansas.

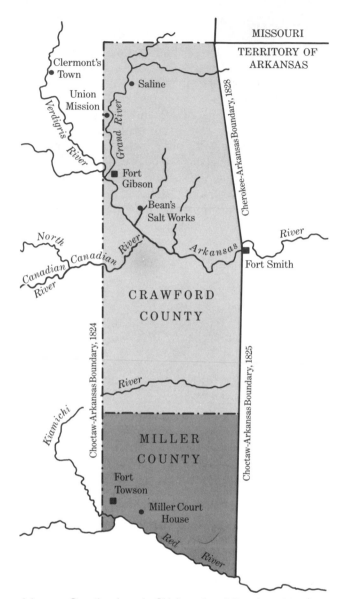

Arkansas Counties (now in Oklahoma) and Creation of Present Stateline

They became known as Western Cherokees. Cherokee hunters often fought with the Osages. Each tribe accused the other of stealing horses.

Lovely's Purchase. In 1816, Major William Lovely, a federal Indian agent, made an effort to keep the Osages and Western Cherokees apart. He brought their leaders together at the mouth of the Verdigris River. Lovely promised that the federal government would pay all claims of whites and Cherokees for damages caused by Osage raids. The Osage chiefs accepted these

64

President Andrew Jackson.

terms. They agreed to give up a large area north of the Arkansas River and east of the Verdigris as a Cherokee hunting ground. Osage warriors, however, continued to ambush and kill Cherokee hunting parties. The Cherokees got revenge.

Battle of Claremore Mound. In 1817, a large Cherokee force attacked Clermont's town (Claremore). The attack came during the "Strawberry Moon," the season of the wild strawberries. Clermont and his Osage warriors were away on a hunting expedition. The Cherokees, however, killed many women, children, and old men at the village. This massacre is called the "Battle of Claremore Mound."

The federal government tried to bring order to the northeast Oklahoma area. Troops arrived to establish Fort Smith and then Fort Gibson. Finally, the Osage chiefs decided to move their followers to present-day Kansas. (In 1872, the tribe returned to a reservation, now Osage County, in Indian Territory.)

Treaty of 1828—the Western Cherokees moved to Oklahoma. By the 1820s, white settlers in Arkansas wanted the Cherokees to move farther west. The Indians were ready. In 1828, Cherokee chiefs signed a treaty that gave them the Lovely Purchase lands as a "permanent home." This new space was to "remain theirs forever" and "never be included in any territory or state."

The Western Cherokee pioneers settled west of Fort Smith. They built homes in the valleys of the Arkansas, Sallisaw, Illinois, and Grand rivers. The Cherokees were disappointed to find Creeks already farming rich bottom land along the Verdigris River.

As it turned out, the 1828 treaty was important for another reason. It set one part of the Arkansas state line where it is today. The boundary started at a point on the Arkansas River 100 paces west of Fort Smith. It ran north in a "direct line to the southwest corner of Missouri." This treaty provision explains the jog in Oklahoma's eastern boundary.

Sequoyah. An unusual provision of the 1828 treaty directed the U.S. government to give $500 to George Guess, better known as Sequoyah. This grant was a reward for his invention of the Cherokee *syllabary*. He was also given a salt spring on Lee's Creek to replace the one he gave up in Arkansas. Sequoyah's cabin can still be seen near Sallisaw.

While in Arkansas, Sequoyah had completed a twelve-year study of the Cherokee language. He

Sequoyah with his Cherokee syllabary. (Smithsonian Institution)

knew no English but got his idea for a syllabary from the white man's books—"talking leaves," he called them.

Sequoyah returned east for a while to explain his invention. The Eastern Cherokee council adopted the syllabary system. Before long, the Eastern and Western Cherokees were corresponding in their own language. Anyone who memorized the sound symbols could read and write Cherokee.

White settlers moved to the Territory of Arkansas. Once Lovely County was given to the Cherokees, the white settlers had to leave. Congress allowed each head of a household over 21 to select 320 acres in Arkansas.

A typical Cherokee farm home.

2. THE EASTERN CHEROKEES WERE FORCED TO MOVE WEST.

The Cherokees once occupied the beautiful hills of Georgia and nearby states. Early travelers in the South were impressed with the Cherokee people. The Cherokees had adopted the lifestyle of their white neighbors. They were prosperous farmers. A few of them had large plantations with slaves. Some Cherokees owned grain or lumber mills.

Cherokee children attended mission schools. A tribal newspaper, *The Cherokee Phoenix,* was printed in both English and Cherokee.

The Georgia government put pressure on the Cherokees to leave. The Georgia legislature abolished Cherokee government and took away civil rights. No Cherokee could sue or be a witness in a Georgia court. When gold was discovered on their land, the Cherokees had no legal way to keep white prospectors off their farms.

The legislature took a big chunk of Cherokee land. This land was surveyed and divided into ten counties. It was sold by state lottery. White planters took over the estates of Chief John Ross and other Cherokee leaders.

A mission school was turned into a saloon. The Cherokee newspaper was shut down. Why? Because it opposed the removal of the tribe to Indian Territory.

Eastern Cherokees were divided on the question of removal. The Cherokees were tired of being mistreated. One faction, led by a wealthy slaveowner named Major Ridge, wanted to move. In 1835, Ridge and other leaders of like mind met with federal officials at New Echota, Georgia. They signed a removal treaty.

By the treaty terms, the tribe gave up eight million acres for $5 million. The Eastern Cherokees had two years to move to Indian Territory. There they would share land with the Western Cherokees.

To move or not to move—that question divided Eastern Cherokees. Only about two thousand tribal members moved voluntarily. They were mainly mixed bloods.

Forced removal and the "Trail of Tears." Two years after the treaty was signed, General Winfield Scott led troops to the Cherokee Nation. His soldiers seized the Indian families in their homes and fields. Farm buildings were burned.

The Cherokees were herded into fenced camps like prisoners. When 17,000 had been gathered, removal to Indian Territory began. Summer heat and sickness killed many of the first groups to leave. Cherokees who went later suffered from cold weather, hunger, and disease. They had only the clothes they were wearing when taken from their homes. Hundreds of people died and were buried along the trail. Survivors arrived in Indian Territory broken in health and spirit. Ever after, the Cherokees called

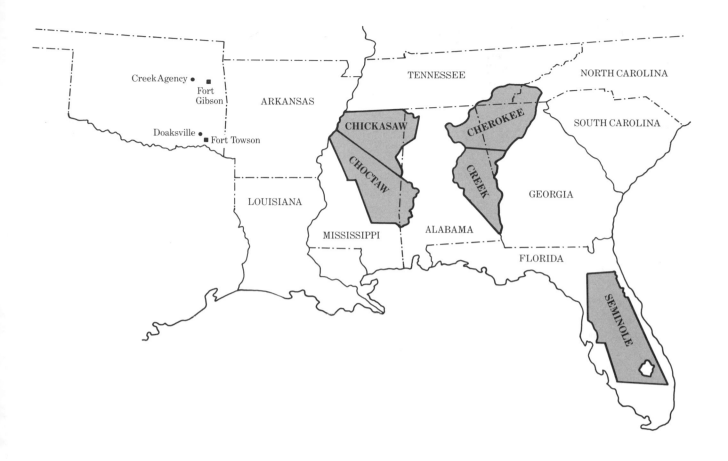

Homelands of the Five Civilized Tribes

the journey *nuna dat suhn'yi,* the "trail where they cried."

One small group of Cherokees escaped General Scott's roundup and fled to North Carolina.

3. THE CHEROKEES ADJUSTED WELL TO INDIAN TERRITORY.

The Cherokees were divided into factions but were able to form a government. Cherokees who were forced to move from Georgia did not forgive the treaty signers. Major Ridge, his son John Ridge, and Elias Boudinot, were murdered. Stand Watie, another removal leader, arrived at Park Hill shortly after his brother, Boudinot, was killed. Facing an unfriendly crowd, he said, "I will give ten thousand dollars for the

names of the men who did this." No one spoke up. The murders made the hostile groups even more bitter.

In 1839, however, the Cherokees were able to hold a convention at Tahlequah. They adopted a constitution modeled after the U.S. Constitution. The principal chief and assistant chief of the Cherokee Nation were like the president and vice president. The Cherokee National Council was a two-house legislature. The judicial branch of government had a supreme court and lower courts.

John Ross, leader of the anti-removal Cherokees, was elected principal chief.

The Cherokees adapted quickly to their new homeland. Many of the mixed bloods lived like country gentlemen. They owned large plantations with slaves. Their mansions had thick

67

Cherokees on the Trail of Tears. (Painting by Robert Lindneux, Woolaroc Museum, Bartlesville, Oklahoma)

Chief John Ross. (Woolaroc Museum, painting by Robert Lindneux)

carpets, a grand piano, and expensive china. As many as forty guests could stay comfortably at Rose Cottage, John Ross's mansion near Tahlequah.

The full blood Cherokees usually lived in log cabins in wooded areas. Each cabin had a fireplace for heat and cooking. Chairs, benches, and bedsteads were homemade. "Straw ticks" were used as mattresses to sleep on. The women spun wool and cotton thread. They wove cloth on hand looms.

Cherokee farmers planted corn as a staple food. Their apple, pear, peach, and apricot trees grew from root stock carried from Georgia. The farmers owned a few cattle, horses, hogs, and sheep.

The Cherokees started a public school system. Rural elementary schools were taught mainly by Cherokee teachers. Two seminaries for

Chief Pushmataha. (Smithsonian Institution, painting by C. B. King)

higher education had teachers from Yale and other eastern colleges. The seminaries, opened in 1851, were located on Chief Ross's estate at Park Hill.

A newspaper, the *Cherokee Advocate,* was printed partly in English and partly in Cherokee.

4. THE CHOCTAWS WERE REMOVED TO SOUTHERN OKLAHOMA.

The Choctaws once lived on the rich black delta land in Mississippi and in Alabama. Their fertile farms were the envy of land hungry frontiersmen.

Choctaws followed the same pattern of removal as the Cherokees. They were pressured many ways to leave their homeland. White intruders took part of their land and stole livestock. Law officers gave the Choctaw farmers no protection. The Mississippi legislature abolished tribal government. Federal officials ignored treaties. They talked to tribal leaders about moving west.

Choctaw removal to Indian Territory. In 1820, General Andrew Jackson met with Chief Pushmataha and other Choctaw leaders at Doak's Stand, Mississippi. Jackson persuaded the Choctaws to give up a third of their land. In re-turn, he promised them a vast tract of land between the Red and Canadian rivers. This land in Indian Territory would be theirs, he said, "as long as grass grows and the water runs." No more than a fourth of the Choctaws, however, moved voluntarily.

In 1830, Chief Greenwood LeFlore and other leaders signed the Treaty of Dancing Rabbit Creek. They gave up all Choctaw land east of the Mississippi River—about ten million acres. The federal government promised that their land in Indian Territory would never be included "within the limits of a state."

The Choctaw journey to Indian Territory was another "trail of tears." Many Choctaws were caught in the freezing blizzard of 1831–1832. They were ill-prepared for the trip. The government had issued only one blanket to each family. Muddy roads, a lack of food, smallpox, and an epidemic of cholera added to their miseries.

Miller County—early white settlers in southeast Oklahoma. The Red River country was the too-much promised land. White farmers were raising crops there at the time of the first Choctaw treaty. In 1820, the Arkansas territorial legislature included the settlers in Miller County. The county seat was Miller Courthouse at the mouth of the Kiamichi River. The U.S. Army built Fort Towson to protect the settlers.

Arkansas boundary line. Both the Choctaw Nation and the Territory of Arkansas claimed what is now the southeast corner of Oklahoma. The dispute was settled by a treaty signed in 1825.

The Arkansas boundary was moved east, about where it is today. It was to begin "100 paces west of old Fort Smith and thence due south to the Red River." Actually, the Arkansas surveyors were four miles west of due south when they reached the Red River. (The false survey line is still the state boundary today.)

White settlers were removed from Choctaw lands. The 1825 boundary line treaty had one immediate result. The federal government forced about 2,500 white settlers in Miller County to leave.

County Sheriff Claybourne Wright's records reveal that the settlers had 6,000 acres in crops.

Robert M. Jones. (OHS)

They owned 55,000 cattle and 8,500 horses. A cotton gin and two flour mills were in operation.

Most of the settlers moved to Texas. About 300 families, however, went to live along the Arkansas River in Lovely County. As we have seen, they had to move again when this area was given to the Cherokees.

Amazing Choctaw progress in Indian Territory. In the 1830s, 1840s, and 1850s, the Choctaws had an amazing record of achievement. They shipped cotton, corn, and pecans down the Red River to market. Their cotton gins, flour mills, lumber mills, and a salt works were busy. Choctaw merchants were selling goods in the towns of Doaksville, Eagletown, Perryville, and Skullyville.

The richest Choctaw was Robert M. Jones. He had at least five plantations along the Red River. He owned hundreds of slaves. Jones also operated several steamboats and a large store at Doaksville.

Choctaw government, schools, and newspaper. The Choctaws adopted the first written constitution in Oklahoma. It provided for three branches of government.

The executive branch consisted of a chief elected in each of three, later four, districts. The Choctaw National Council was a legislature with members from each district. Judges on the national court were elected. Trial by jury was guaranteed in the bill of rights. An 1850 revision of the constitution created counties, each county with a county court.

The first Choctaw national capital was at Nanih Wayah, near Tuskahoma. In 1850, it was moved to Doaksville.

The Choctaws opened both day and boarding schools. Missionaries ran some of the schools. Adults could attend "Saturday and Sunday neighborhood" schools. An academy for boys and a seminary for girls provided higher education.

The *Choctaw Telegraph,* printed partly in Choctaw and partly in English, began publication at Doaksville in 1848.

5. THE CREEKS WERE DIVIDED ON THE QUESTION OF REMOVAL TO INDIAN TERRITORY.

The Creeks were divided into two main groups. *Upper Creeks* lived in northern Alabama. They were full bloods with Indian names. They opposed removal to Indian Territory.

Many of the *Lower Creeks* along the Georgia-Alabama line were mixed bloods. Their chief, William McIntosh, had a Scot father and a Creek mother. McIntosh believed the Creeks should move. They could still get something for their lands, he said.

Chief McIntosh's Lower Creeks moved to Indian Territory. In 1825, McIntosh signed the Treaty of Indian Springs. He traded Creek land in Georgia for land in Indian Territory. The Creek National Council had reason to oppose this action. For years the Creek lands had been shrinking as white settlers moved in. The council members condemned McIntosh to death. They set fire to his house. He was shot trying to escape the flames.

Chilly McIntosh, son of the murdered chief, led the first party of Lower Creeks to Indian Territory. In 1828, this group arrived at Fort Gibson. They were aboard two *keelboats* pulled by a steamboat.

The Lower Creeks settled on rich bottom land on the west side of the Verdigris River. Coweta and Tulsey Town (Tulsa) were early Creek settlements. The famous Creek Council Oak is known

Chief William McIntosh. (Smithsonian Institution)

6. THE CHICKASAWS WERE THE WEALTHIEST TRIBE BUT ONE OF THE LAST TO RECOVER FROM FORCED REMOVAL.

By the early 1800s, the Chickasaws were living on family-centered farms in northern Mississippi and Alabama. A few well-to-do mixed bloods owned large cotton plantations and slaves. Some members of the tribe ran trading posts and other businesses. In general, the Chickasaw Nation resembled most white American frontier communities in the Old South.

Removal to Indian Territory. Like the other civilized tribes, the Chickasaws were forced to leave their homeland. The Chickasaws, however, got more for their property. Their farms were sold to white settlers. The money from these land sales went into a tribal fund. Then the federal government paid *annuities* to the Chickasaw people from this fund.

The Chickasaws bought land in Indian Territory from their relatives, the Choctaw tribe. They had plenty of time to move their personal property, livestock, and slaves. Pitman Colbert, a wealthy Chickasaw trader, put his gold in kegs. He hauled it in a special wagon pulled by six mules. On one occasion, the Chickasaws had 7,000 horses at Memphis waiting for transportation across the Mississippi River.

as Tulsa's "first city hall." Roley McIntosh, William's half-brother was the first Creek principal chief in Indian Territory.

The "Creek War" led to the forced removal of all Creeks to Indian Territory. In 1832, Opothleyahola and other Creek leaders signed away all Creek lands east of the Mississippi River. The treaty allowed some Creeks to stay in Alabama. But lawless whites and the Alabama courts began taking their farms away.

Angry Creek warriors fought back. They raided white settlements. They burned houses, barns, and wagons. The War Department sent General Winfield Scott to put down this "Creek War." His soldiers rounded up 15,000 Creeks, both rebels and peaceful Indians. About two thousand hostiles were shackled in chains. The Creeks were moved to Indian Territory over another trail of tears. Hundreds died from the cold, disease, and bad food. One large group drowned in the Mississippi River when an unsafe steamboat sank. Survivors of the westward journey camped near Fort Gibson in the spring, 1837.

The Upper Creeks settled between the Canadian and North Canadian rivers. North Fork Town (near Eufaula) was a major settlement.

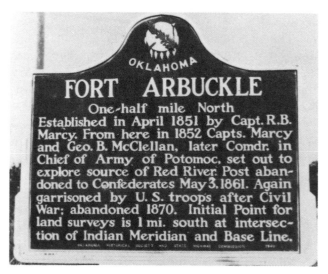

OKLAHOMA

FORT ARBUCKLE

One-half mile North
Established in April 1851 by Capt. R.B. Marcy. From here in 1852 Capts. Marcy and Geo. B. McClellan, later Comdr. in Chief of Army of Potomoc, set out to explore source of Red River. Post abandoned to Confederates May 3, 1861. Again garrisoned by U.S. troops after Civil War; abandoned 1870. Initial Point for land surveys is 1 mi. south at intersection of Indian Meridian and Base Line.

OKLAHOMA HISTORICAL SOCIETY AND STATE HIGHWAY COMMISSION 1949

Historical marker west of Davis.

Fort Arbuckle. (Harper's Weekly, March 16, 1861)

Indian horse race. (Sketch by Frederic Remington)

Like the other tribes, however, the Chickasaws suffered hardships on the journey to Indian Territory. Many people died from disease, bad weather, and spoiled government food.

New military posts made it possible for the Chickasaw Nation to develop. The Chickasaw District was in south-central Oklahoma. At first, the Chickasaws were afraid to occupy their new land. Why? The Plains tribes (Comanches, Kiowas, and Kickapoos) were hostile to newcomers in the area.

The Chickasaws lived in tents near the Choctaw towns and Fort Coffee until new forts were built. In 1842, General (later President) Zachary Taylor established Fort Washita. Another post, Fort Arbuckle (near Davis), was started in 1851.

With the protection of these forts, Chickasaws scattered across their land. Most of them lived in cabins on small farms. They planted corn and vegetables for food. Their favorite pastimes were dances, Indian ball games, and horse races.

The Chickasaws soon became famous as stockraisers. A "Chickasaw horse" was the most desired animal in Indian Territory. The Arbuckles region (now known as "Hereford heaven") provided good grazing land.

Wealthy Chickasaw planters settled on fertile land in the Red River Valley south of Fort Washita. The Colbert, Love, and other families kept three cotton gins busy. They also grew corn for the army.

Chickasaw government after 1855. For awhile the Chickasaws shared a government with the Choctaw tribe. In 1855, the tribes separated. The Chickasaws wrote their own constitution. This document provided for a two-house legislature, a court system, and a governor. Cyrus Harris was elected the first governor.

Tishomingo, named for a Chickasaw warrior chief, was the capital. In the 1890s, the Chickasaws built a stone capitol to house their government. This building served as the Johnston County courthouse after Oklahoma became a state in 1907. This county was named for Douglas H. Johnston, a Chickasaw governor.

7. THE SEMINOLES OF FLORIDA WERE THE SMALLEST AND THE LAST OF THE FIVE CIVILIZED TRIBES TO MOVE WEST.

The word "Seminole" is a Creek word that means "runaway" or "a strayed people." The Sem-

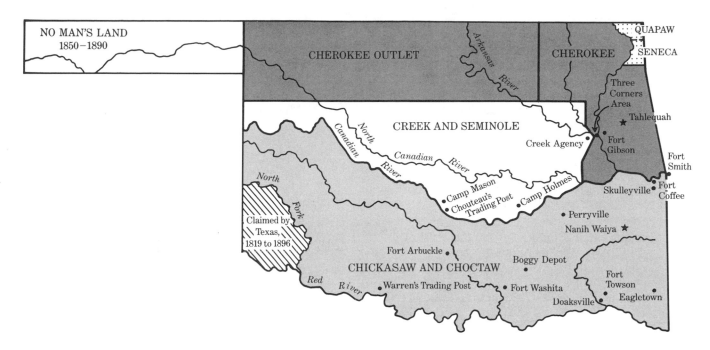

Indian Territory Before 1855

inole tribe was made up of people from several tribes in Georgia—Creeks, Ocanee, Yamassee, and others. The Seminoles were divided into bands named after chiefs. Osceola, who was part Scot, was the most famous chief. A few Seminoles owned black slaves.

Seminoles once farmed rich lands along the west coast of Florida. But their lifestyle changed after the United States bought Florida from Spain in 1819. White settlers moved in and the Seminoles were forced into the swamplands away from the coast.

Seminole War. In 1832, federal commissioners persuaded some Seminole leaders to sign a removal treaty. The tribe was to live on Creek lands in Indian Territory. Many Seminoles, however, refused to go west. These rebels attacked U.S. troops sent to remove them. Runaway black slaves, who had fled to Florida, helped the Seminoles against the soldiers.

For seven years, the U.S. Army burned Indian towns, killed cattle, and chased the scattered Seminoles into the Florida Everglades. The na-

tives and their black allies survived on fish, game, and flour from swamp roots.

Soldiers used bloodhounds to seek out the Seminoles. As the Indians were captured, they were shipped by boat to New Orleans and upriver to Fort Coffee or Fort Gibson in Indian Territory. About 3,000 were removed. The Seminole War cost the lives of 1,500 soldiers. An unknown number of Seminoles were killed.

Seminoles in Indian Territory. At first, the federal government assigned the Seminoles to live among the Creeks. They lived in the Canadian Valley and then along the Little River (south of Wewoka).

Finally, in 1856, the Seminoles were separated from the Creeks. Their new land stretched from present Pottawatomie County to northwest Oklahoma.

The Seminole removal from Florida brought to a close one of the darkest periods of American history—the uprooting of the Five Civilized Tribes. The "trail of tears" era will never be forgotten.

ROUNDUP

1. List the names of the Five Civilized Tribes. What power did the Indian Removal Act give the President?

2. Who were the Western Cherokees? Why did the federal government buy Lovely's Purchase from the Osages? What were the results of the Battle of Claremore Mound and the Treaty of 1828?

3. Why is Sequoyah honored (only one of four Oklahomans) with a special mural portrait at the State Capitol?

4. Briefly tell the story of Eastern Cherokee civilization, their forced removal, the "trail of tears," and their adjustment to life in northeast Oklahoma.

5. Identify each of the following: Chief Pushmataha, Greenwood LeFlore, Miller County, Robert M. Jones, the main Choctaw towns, and the Choctaw National Council.

6. Who were the Lower Creeks? Why was Chief McIntosh killed? Why was the Creek War fought? Where did the two Creek groups settle in Indian Territory?

7. Why did the Chickasaws delay moving to their land in Indian Territory? How did the federal government help? Describe the Chickasaw government that was formed in 1855.

8. Why was the Seminole War fought? At what places did the Seminoles settle in Indian Territory?

A. Think about it! A New Jersey senator, who opposed Jackson's Indian removal policy, asked, "Do the obligations of justice change with the color of skin?" What did he mean? Explain how his thought has meaning today.

B. "The Trail of Tears national historic trail (east of Tahlequah) should remind us of the way the Indians were treated during the early part of our country's history." Explain this statement.

C. Evaluate this statement by a Cherokee leader: "We're trying to educate our young to be in the mainstream, but we don't want them to forget their own culture. We think its possible to do both."

10

CIVIL WAR: A TURNING POINT

The Indian Territory made economic progress in the 1830s, 1840s, and 1850s. The Five Civilized Tribes farmed the fertile river valleys. They had a surplus of cotton, grain, and hides. They shipped these products to market by steamboat down the Arkansas and Red rivers.

Signs of social progress were everywhere. Most of the tribes had a constitution. An elected chief and a council did the governing. In 1832, the Cherokee Council passed the first public school law in Oklahoma. Books and newspapers were published in the Cherokee, Creek, and Choctaw languages. The tribes had every reason to be proud.

The Civil War, 1861–1865, interrupted progress. Armies and outlaw gangs laid waste to the Indian Territory. Farms were stripped of cattle, horses, and grain. Fields went unplowed as people fled to safer places. Some Union (North) sympathizers went to Kansas. Confederate (South) refugees found a haven in the Red River country or in Texas.

In 1861, all the Five Civilized Tribes signed treaties to support the South. Many Indians, however, remained loyal to the Union. They fought against their fellow tribesmen.

After the war, the tribes were punished for helping the South. The federal government took away their lands in what is now western Oklahoma. Plains tribes and other Indians were resettled there.

1. THE FIVE CIVILIZED TRIBES JOINED THE SOUTH, THOUGH MANY INDIANS REMAINED LOYAL TO THE UNION.

The Five Civilized Tribes still had strong ties to the Old South. It was the home of their ancestors. The location of Indian Territory was another reason for the tribes to join the South in the Civil War. Two neighbors, Arkansas and Texas, *seceded* from the Union.

Federal forts abandoned. The federal government lost its chance to hold on to Indian Territory. The War Department had been protecting peaceful tribes from hostile Plains Indians. But, in 1861, all troops were withdrawn from the seven forts in or near Indian Territory. Forts Smith, Gibson, Towson, Wayne, Washita, Arbuckle, and Cobb were abandoned.

The South was quick to move in. A large force of Texans rode into Fort Arbuckle the day after United States troops left. The Texans caught up with the *rearguard* of the departing cavalry near what is now Pauls Valley. On May 5, 1861, a small skirmish was fought. This was the first encounter between armed forces of the North and South in Indian Territory.

Treaties with the South. Confederate President Jefferson Davis sent Albert Pike to make treaties with the Indians. Pike, an Arkansas lawyer, promised arms and *annuities*. He got all the Five Civilized Tribes and some others to sign treaties.

The Choctaws had the strongest ties with the Old South. Armstrong Academy (east of Durant) became the Confederate capital in Indian Territory. The Cherokees were the last to sign a treaty. Chief John Ross wanted to be neutral in the war, even though he was a slaveowner. But his rival, Stand Watie, went ahead and organized a Cherokee regiment to fight for the South.

2. PRO-UNION CREEKS AND OTHER INDIANS FOUGHT THREE BATTLES WHILE FLEEING TO SAFETY IN KANSAS.

Chief Opothleyahola was against the Confederate treaty signed by other Creek leaders. About half the Creeks supported him. They gathered at his plantation with their wagons, livestock, and slaves. These Creeks were joined in camp by pro-North Indians from several other tribes.

Opothleyahola. (Smithsonian Institution)

Douglas H. Cooper.

Opothleyahola and his followers began moving to a safe haven in Kansas. They had to fight three battles on the way. The score was two wins for the Union and one for the Confederates.

Union victories at Round Mountain and Caving Banks. Two Confederate military units trailed the fleeing pro-Union Indians. One group, Colonel William Quayle's Texas cavalry, rode into an ambush. The soldiers were attacked by Opothleyahola's warriors near the mouth of the Cimarron River. The fight that followed is known as the "Battle of Round Mountain." It is called "the first battle of the Civil War in Oklahoma." The Texas cavalry was forced to retreat. The Texans were delayed further when the Creek warriors set fire to tall grass. This action created a smoke screen so the warriors could move on.

About three weeks later, the "Battle of Caving Banks" was fought. Opothleyahola's followers took a defensive stand in heavy timber along Bird Creek. Colonel Douglas Cooper's mounted Confederate Indians left their horses to attack on foot.

The brother versus brother nature of the Civil War came to reality in this battle. Creeks fought Creeks in hand-to-hand combat. After awhile, Cooper's Confederates ran low on ammunition. They retreated to Fort Gibson and Tulsey Town (Tulsa). Opothleyahola's warriors moved north to catch up with their families.

Battle of Chus-te-nah-lah—a Confederate victory. The Confederates again caught up with Opothleyahola northwest of modern Tulsa. The chief's warriors took cover in a high grove of blackjacks. Then the Confederates charged uphill. Rebel yells filled the air.

"The sharp report of the rifle came from every tree and rock until the summit of the hill was gained and we mingled with the enemy," said Colonel James McIntosh, a Creek Confederate.

Several hundred Union Indians were killed or captured as they fled north. The survivors reached Kansas. There, they suffered terribly from cold weather. Army surgeons amputated more than a hundred limbs. The Union Army was slow in providing blankets, clothing, tents, and food.

3. TWO UNION FORCES INVADED CHEROKEE COUNTRY IN 1862–1863.

Indian expedition from Kansas. Pro-Union Creeks, Seminoles, and Cherokees

Stand Watie.

organized an invasion from Kansas. They met and defeated Stand Watie's Cherokee cavalry. Tahlequah and Fort Gibson fell with little opposition.

Chief John Ross was captured at his Park Hill home. An old man, Ross was soon freed. He moved to Philadelphia and switched sides. He worked for the Union until the end of the war.

Union withdrawal caused chaos. The "Indian Expedition" soon returned to Kansas. Stand Watie's Confederate troops were then free to dash through the countryside. The raiders destroyed anything they couldn't ride, eat, carry, or drive away. The Cherokee Nation was in chaos.

William C. Quantrill and his Missouri gang of Southern sympathizers added to the confusion. They burned and pillaged along the Texas Road in Indian Territory. Jesse James, a member of the gang, was injured in a raid near Fort Gibson. He recovered, only to become a famous train robber.

Other *guerrilla* gangs, both white and Indian, also made hit-and-run raids on Indian communities.

General James G. Blunt made Fort Gibson (Blunt) the Union headquarters. Blunt's Union soldiers invaded Indian Territory from Arkansas. They recaptured Tahlequah and Fort Gibson. Intending to stay awhile, they rebuilt Gibson. It was renamed Fort Blunt.

The fort soon became a busy place. Cherokee farm families, frightened by Watie's raids, came to the fort for safety. About six thousand natives and three thousand soldiers were crowded into a small area. The Cherokees were half-starved, ill-clothed, and sick wth dysentery. The nearest supply point was Fort Scott, Kansas, 165 miles away. Cheers went up when a wagon train got through Watie's Confederate raiding parties.

Battle of Honey Springs—the most important Civil War battle in Indian Territory. General Blunt, with a month's provisions on hand, decided to attack the Confederates at Honey Springs (south of Muskogee near Oktaha). Blunt took three thousand men across the Arkansas River in hastily-built boats.

On July 17, 1863, Blunt's Union army defeated Cooper's larger Confederate Indian force near Honey Springs. The Union soldiers had superior weapons and artillery. The big guns forced the Confederates to retreat from heavy timber. Some untrained Confederates threw their guns away. They had been issued rotten gunpowder that would not ignite.

The Union side lost seventeen killed and sixty wounded who were taken to Fort Blunt in

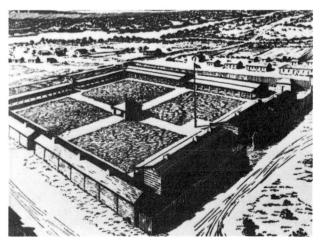
Fort Gibson.

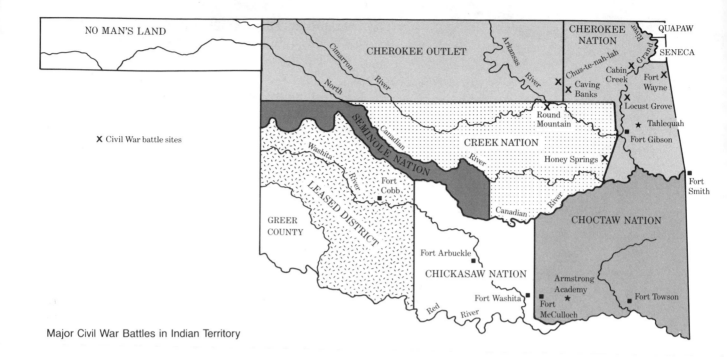

Major Civil War Battles in Indian Territory

army ambulances. About 150 Confederate dead were buried. Merciful Union surgeons and nurses looked after the Confederate wounded. They had to amputate the legs of seven soldiers.

The battle at Honey Springs marked the doom of the Confederate cause in Indian Territory. During the rest of the war, the Union held Fort Blunt and Fort Smith. Confederate troops occupied the southern forts: Washita, Arbuckle, Towson, and McCulloch. Guerrilla bands provided most of the action.

Honey Springs was significant for another reason too. It was one of the first Civil War battles in which black soldiers had a chance to fight. General Blunt praised the Kansas First Colored Volunteers for their "coolness and bravery" under fire.

4. STAND WATIE WAS THE MOST ACTIVE AND AGGRESSIVE LEADER IN THE INDIAN TERRITORY.

General Watie kept the pressure on the Union. The year 1864 was a good one for him. He captured a large steamboat, the *J. R. Williams.* This boat was moving up the Arkansas River

with supplies for Fort Blunt. The cargo included hundreds of barrels of flour and tons of bacon, sugar, blankets, boots, and cloth. The Confederate Indian troops took part of this loot to their destitute families.

Later in the year, General Watie pulled off his greatest exploit. He captured a large Union wagon train at Cabin Creek crossing. (This creek empties into the Grand River south of Vinita.) The goods, wagons, horses, and mules were valued at well over a million dollars. This victory at Cabin Creek made it possible for Watie to feed, clothe, and arm his ragged, hungry regiment.

Today, Watie's picture hangs in Battle Abbey. This is a shrine of Confederate heroes at Richmond, Virginia. Watie was the only Indian in the war to achieve the rank of general.

5. THE CIVIL WAR LEFT INDIAN TERRITORY IN RUINS.

The Civil War ended in 1865. By that time, the Indian nations lay in waste. Houses and barns had been burned. Fields were covered with weeds. Fences were down. Thousands of cattle had been rounded up by rustlers and driven to

Steamboats on the Arkansas River. (OHS)

The Seminoles then bought a 200,000 acre tract from the Creek Nation. This land became the Seminole Nation. A council house was built at Wewoka, the capital. Years later, many Seminoles discovered that the government surveyors made an error in the boundary. They were living in Creek country. To solve the problem, the Seminoles bought more Creek land at a dollar an acre. The enlarged area was organized as Seminole County when Oklahoma became a state.

Choctaws and Chickasaws—the name "Oklahoma" suggested. The Choctaws and Chickasaws signed a joint treaty, giving up the Leased District. They were paid only $300,000 for this vast area in southwest Oklahoma.

This treaty also contained a plan for an all-Indian "Territory of Oklahoma." Allen Wright, a Choctaw who signed the 1866 treaty, suggested the name. It comes from "Okla Homa." These Choctaw words mean "Red People." The plan was

Kansas. Churches and schools had almost ceased to exist.

One Cherokee leader wrote that half his people had no animals or plows to cultivate the soil. "I have known one solitary plow and horse to pass from farm to farm under loan for a whole season," he said. Some Indians had to use sharpened sticks to plant seeds.

6. THE FIVE CIVILIZED TRIBES WERE FORCED TO SIGN NEW TREATIES THAT GREATLY CHANGED THE INDIAN TERRITORY.

The tribes were punished for joining the South in rebellion. In 1866, tribal leaders signed treaties in Washington, D.C. They had to give up the western part of Indian Territory. The federal government planned to settle Plains Indians and northern tribes in this area.

Creeks and Seminoles were punished the most. The Creeks had to give up 3,250,000 acres in western Oklahoma for thirty cents an acre. The Seminoles surrendered all their land. They were paid only fifteen cents an acre.

Allen Wright. (OHS)

79

never carried out. But the name was later used for the Territory of Oklahoma (1890) and the forty-sixth state (1907).

Cherokee treaty terms. The Cherokees got slightly more liberal terms. Why? One reason is that Chief John Ross switched to the Union side during the Civil War.

By the treaty in 1866, the Cherokees had to give up the *Cherokee Neutral Lands* in southeast Kansas. They also ceded the *Cherokee Strip*. This area was a narrow ribbon of land lying north of the present Oklahoma-Kansas line. These lands were sold at auction. The proceeds were turned over to the Cherokee Nation.

The treaty also gave the federal government the right to settle other Indian tribes in the *Cherokee Outlet* (often called the Cherokee Strip). In 1893, the government paid the Cherokees $1.25 an acre for six and a half million acres left in the Outlet. Land not occupied by tribes was opened to settlement. Later, the Outlet area was divided into twelve counties and parts of counties in northern Oklahoma.

Other treaty concessions made by the Native Americans. Giving up land was not the only punishment forced on the Indian Nations. Each tribe was to grant right-of-ways for railroad lines across Indian Territory. Also, the Indians had to free their black slaves and give them equal rights. In addition, the treaties provided that United States courts could be established to handle cases involving non-Indians.

The Indian Territory changed rapidly after the Civil War. Members of the Five Tribes replanted weed-grown fields and acquired herds of cattle. Each tribe rebuilt ruined school buildings and established a public education system. Indian children went to neighborhood day primary schools taught by native teachers. Advanced students attended boarding schools (seminaries and academies). Gradually the tribes also took over the support of mission schools. A large number of the Indians learned to read and write both their native language and English. Many Indian settlements had a church—usually Presbyterian, Methodist, or Baptist—served by a native pastor.

But the Indian Territory had lost its protected isolation. By the 1870s, Texas cowboys were driving cattle across Indian lands to Dodge City, Abilene, and other shipping points. Coal was being dug by white miners in the McAlester area. Then came railroads and new towns along the tracks.

Native Americans quickly became involved in the white lifestyle. Indian farmers discovered they could rent their land to white or black tenants. They hired non-Indian skilled laborers. Grasslands were leased to Texas cattlemen. Intermarriage, not a new idea to the Five Civilized Tribes, became common after the Civil War. The white population in Indian Territory rose rapidly as newcomers were encouraged to settle here.

The first federal census of the Five Tribes area was made in 1890. It showed a population of more than 109,000 whites, nearly 19,000 blacks, and only 50,000 Indians.

ROUNDUP

1. What were the signs of progress in Indian Territory before the Civil War? In what ways did the war interrupt progress?
2. Why did the Five Tribes support the South in the war? What promises were made to the Indians for their support?
3. List the three battles which the pro-Union natives fought en route to Kansas. Which side won each? Identify Opothleyahola, Col. Douglas Cooper, and Col. James McIntosh.
4. What problems did Union troops have in holding on to Fort Gibson (Blunt)?
5. Why was the Battle of Honey Springs the most important Civil War conflict in Indian Territory?
6. Give examples of Stand Watie's guerrilla activities.
7. How were the Five Tribes punished for siding with the South?
A. Think about it! How might the history of Oklahoma be different if the Five Tribes had stayed in the Union? Would Oklahoma have remained an Indian territory? Would it have been admitted into the Union as an Indian state? Or would it be much as it is today?

11

PLAINS INDIANS AND RESERVATIONS IN INDIAN TERRITORY

Buffalo skin tepee used by Plains Indians.

For centuries, scattered native tribes moved freely over the vast open spaces of the Great Plains. This area was a sea of grass where the buffalo roamed. Daily life for the Plains Indians centered around the huge herds that grazed between Texas and Canada.

The buffalo provided about everything the Plains people needed except water for drinking and wood for tepee poles. The women roasted buffalo meat over a fire fueled by *buffalo chips*. Some of the meat was dried in the sun to make *jerky*. Hides were stretched, scraped, and cured to make clothing, bedding, moccasins, ropes, tepees, shields, and drums. The buffalo bones and horns were used for tools and utensils.

Plains Indians were skilled horsemen. They were good buffalo hunters and also excelled at warfare. The warriors fought other tribes and white settlers to hold on to their hunting grounds. They fought the U.S. Army to keep from going on *reservations*. The Plains tribes—Arapaho, Cheyenne, Comanche, Kiowa, Apache, and many others—refused to settle down to farm or raise cattle until the buffalo disappeared.

The buffalo hunter and warrior became the *stereotype* for all Indians. Why? People the world over have been thrilled by stories and movies about the Plains Indians.

The hunter-warrior way of life, however, went the way of the buffalo. By 1870, white hunters armed with high-caliber repeating rifles were killing half a million buffalo a year. They supplied eastern tanners with tons of hides to make shoes, harness, belting, and many other things. The buffalo carcasses were left to rot on the plains.

New railroads in Kansas provided cheap transportation to markets. Railroad companies encouraged the slaughter of buffalo in other ways too. They hired "Buffalo Bill" Cody and other hunters to furnish meat for track construction crews. The railroads also sponsored hunting *excursions* for eastern and European "sportsmen." These men shot buffalo from train windows.

By the mid-1880s, at least ten million buffalo had been killed. The Smithsonian Institute in Washington, D.C. had trouble finding a few buffalo to preserve. All the huge herds had vanished, leaving only piles of weathered bones to be gathered up for fertilizer.

Meanwhile, white ranchers and farmers filled up the empty grasslands. Just as Indians had been pushed across the continent, now they were

Bill Tilghman (age 17 at left) and Jim Elder in buffalo hunting gear, 1873. (OHS)

confined to limited reservations. In the years following the Civil War, more than two dozen tribes were moved to the Indian Territory. A chain of military posts was established to keep wilder tribes on their reservations.

1. THE CHEYENNE AND ARAPAHO TRIBES WERE TWO OF THE FIRST TRIBES PUT ON A RESERVATION.

In 1851, the Cheyennes and Arapahoes agreed to live on a reservation in the Colorado foothills. But gold was discovered there and thousands of miners rushed into the hills. The tribes were given poorer land along Sand Creek in eastern Colorado. At first, the Cheyennes and Arapahoes refused to go to the new reservation. Warriors began raiding mining camps.

Finally, in 1864, Chief Black Kettle and his Cheyennes agreed to live at Sand Creek. A band of Arapahoes soon joined them.

Sand Creek Massacre. On November 29, 1864, Colonel J. M. Chivington ordered the Colorado volunteer *militia* to attack the village. "I have come to kill Indians," he said.

Surprised, Black Kettle raised both the American flag and a white flag of truce. But the attack went on. An estimated 450 Indian men, women, and children were slaughtered. News of this massacre spread across the country. Most people were horrified.

Cheyenne and Arapaho braves took to the warpath again. They raided ranches and mail stations in Colorado. They cut telegraph lines. They destroyed *emigrant* wagon trains. They fought battles with soldiers.

Two wrongs, of course, do not make a right. Something had to be done to bring peace to the plains.

2. THE SOUTHERN PLAINS TRIBES WERE PUT ON RESERVATIONS IN INDIAN TERRITORY.

Peace commission from Washington, D.C. After reading a report on the Sand Creek massacre, Congress sent a *commission* to make peace with the Plains tribes still at war with the United States.

The peace commission decided to put these tribes on "small, out-of-the way reservations." They would be separated from westward-moving pioneer farmers and from the major routes of travel.

Native Americans who lived or hunted in the central plains area of Kansas and Nebraska were to be removed. Some would be sent to Dakota Territory. Others would be given a reservation in what is now Oklahoma. Thousands of square miles of land in Kansas and Nebraska would then be opened to settlers for farming.

Medicine Lodge Treaties (1867). The peace commissioners met with leaders of the Southern Plains tribes at Medicine Lodge Creek in Kansas. Treaties were signed that marked a change in United States Indian policy. The Great Plains area was no longer to be "one big reservation." Tribes were to be "concentrated on limited reservations."

The peace commission gave the Cheyennes and Arapahoes a reservation in the western part of Indian Territory. The Kiowas, Comanches, and

Council at Medicine Lodge. (Harper's Weekly)

Kiowa-Apaches were to live in what is now southwestern Oklahoma. Their reservation stretched from present Anadarko on the north to the Red River on the south.

Satanta, a Kiowa chief who was known as the "orator of the plains," expressed the feeling of most Plains Indians. He said the Indians did not want to settle on reservations and become farmers.

"I love to roam over the wide prairie," Satanta said, "and when I do, I feel free and happy. But when we settle down we grow pale and die."

The peace commission permitted the southern Plains Indians to hunt buffalo off their reservations, but only as far north as the Arkansas River. In return, the Indians pledged not to interfere with railroad building, wagon trains, white settlements, or cattle herds. They agreed to "never kill or scalp white men."

3. THE U.S. ARMY BUILT FORTS IN WESTERN OKLAHOMA TO KEEP PLAINS TRIBES ON THE RESERVATIONS.

Indian warfare. Assigning the Indians to reservations was one thing. Getting them to live there was another. Many young warriors would not give up their nomadic life and stay on the reservation.

By the fall of 1868, warfare was in full swing. Warriors of the Plains tribes had been supplied with new guns by soft-hearted Indian agents. Chief Black Kettle and other chiefs led raids into Kansas and Colorado.

Camp Supply and Colonel George A. Custer. General Philip Sheridan, a famous Civil War officer, was ordered to wage relentless warfare against Indian raiders. In November, 1868, he established Camp Supply as a military base. Supply was located where the Beaver and Wolf creeks join to form the North Canadian River.

Colonel George A. Custer was placed in command of troops at Camp Supply. Custer was colorful. At West Point he was a discipline problem and graduated at the bottom of his class. A showman, he rose fast in rank during the Civil War. After the war he lost his command for a year when convicted of cruel treatment to deserters and overmarching his troops. A vain person, Custer promoted his image as an Indian fighter. He wore buckskin clothing and let his hair grow long.

Battle of Washita. Shortly after arriving at Camp Supply, Custer led his troops south. His scouts followed a fresh Indian trail in foot-deep snow.

Chief Satanta. (Smithsonian Institution)

Camp (Fort) Supply.

General George Armstrong Custer. (National Archives)

At daybreak, November 26, 1868, Custer attacked a Cheyenne and Arapaho camp on the Washita River near the present town of Cheyenne. Several hundred warriors and some women and children were caught by surprise. Custer's troops killed more than a hundred Indians. Chief Black Kettle and his wife were shot in the back as they tried to escape across the Washita. The soldiers burned the camp and the people's store of goods. Among the soldiers killed in the charge on the Indian camp was Captain Louis Hamilton. He was the grandson of the famous Alexander Hamilton, the first U.S. Secretary of the Treasury.

Indian survivors of Custer's attack fled downstream to warn other camps. They were chased by Major Joel H. Elliot with more than a dozen soldiers. This military detachment was surrounded and killed by the fleeing warriors. In retaliation, Custer ordered his men to shoot Black Kettle's entire herd of about 800 horses.

Aftermath of the battle. The "Battle of Washita" was the most important fight between the Plains Indians and soldiers in Oklahoma. (A diorama of the Indian campsite before Custer at-

tacked can be seen at the Black Kettle Museum in Cheyenne.)

News of the *atrocity* angered even the peaceful tribes. Leaders of the Five Civilized Tribes signed a document protesting Custer's attack and sent it to Washington, D.C. The Plains tribes felt a hatred for the white man that was not satisfied until Custer and part of his army lost their lives in the Battle of the Little Big Horn in Montana in 1876.

New forts in western Oklahoma. After the Battle of Washita, General Sheridan led troops to a camp near old Fort Cobb. This post had been burned during the Civil War. The army rounded up the Kiowas and forced them to live near the fort so they could be watched.

Fort Cobb remained the chief military post in this area until Fort Sill, called Camp Wichita at first, was laid out in 1869.

General Sheridan persuaded some Cheyennes

Big Tree. (Smithsonian Institution)

and Arapahoes to move near Camp Supply. In 1874, Fort Reno was established across the North Canadian River from the Cheyenne-Arapaho Agency at Darlington. Oklahoma's first telephone line was strung between Fort Reno and Fort Sill in 1879.

4. THE SOUTHERN PLAINS INDIANS WERE NOT READY TO SETTLE DOWN ON RESERVATIONS.

The Cheyennes, Arapahoes, Kiowas, and Comanches were not content with reservation life. They wanted to roam freely over the plains.

During the 1870s, small bands of warriors often slipped away from the reservations on moonlit nights to raid ranches in Texas. They stole horses and sometimes killed settlers. The raiders usually got back before they were missed by the United States agents in charge of the reservations.

Kiowa leaders of a raiding party were arrested and convicted. In May, 1871, a party of Kiowas slipped away. Led by Satanta, Satank, and Big Tree, the Kiowa raiders destroyed a wagon train in Texas and killed the white drivers. The leaders of this raid were arrested when they came to Fort Sill.

General William Sherman ordered these men put in chains and sent to Jacksboro, Texas for trial. On the way, Satank was shot dead trying to escape. The other two were tried, found guilty, and sentenced to be hanged. The Texas governor *commuted* their sentences to life imprisonment. Satanta and Big Tree were later freed on parole providing the Kiowas and Comanches remained on their reservation at peace.

Reasons for Indian hostilities. In 1874, the Kiowas, Comanches, and Arapahoes held a council near Camp Supply. They were greatly alarmed because white hunters were rapidly killing off the buffalo. These whites took only the hides, leaving the carcasses to rot.

The Indians were also angry because gangs of whites were raiding their horse herds. The thieves sold the horses to innocent buyers at Fort Dodge and other places in Kansas or Texas.

Illegal traders were another problem. Whiskey peddlers, especially, were the scum of the frontier. They traded whiskey for buffalo robes that the Indians needed to barter for food, sugar, coffee, and cloth. On one occasion, Cheyenne women went on a slowdown strike because their menfolk were trading too many robes for booze.

Battle at Adobe Walls in Texas. Concerned about the rapid killing of buffalo and the theft of their horses, the Plains Indians took action. They began sending out war parties in all directions. Only the Arapahoes, near the agency at Darlington, remained at peace.

At daybreak, June 27, 1874, a war party—mainly Cheyennes, Comanches, and Kiowas—attacked white hunters and cowboys at Adobe Walls. This place was a trading post on the Canadian River in the Texas Panhandle. Adobe Walls was near one of the best buffalo hunting grounds.

Several hundred warriors in full war paint charged the post. The hunters and cowboys, armed with big buffalo guns and Sharps rifles, fired at the Indians through holes poked in the thick adobe walls. The attackers were forced to retreat, but they killed all the horses and cattle at the post before riding away.

Quanah Parker, chief of the Quahadi Comanches, established his reputation as a leader in this battle. His band would be the last group of Indians to surrender and settle on a reservation.

Chief Quanah Parker. (Smithsonian Institution)

Which Native Americans are shown in this mural by Maynard Dixon? (National Archives)

A memorial monument now marks the site of the Battle of Adobe Walls.

The Hennessey tragedy. On July 3, 1874, a Cheyenne war party under Crazy Mule attacked Pat Hennessey's three-wagon train on the Chisholm Trail. The wagons were hauling sugar and coffee from Wichita, Kansas to the Kiowa-Comanche agency. Hennessey was tied to a wagon wheel and burned. His wagon drivers were killed. The town of Hennessey in Kingfisher County was later built near the massacre site.

Red River War (1874–1875). In August, 1874, Colonel (later General) Nelson A. Miles launched a military campaign against the southern Plains tribes. He searched the area between the Cimarron and Red rivers. His orders were to "attack all Indians who are, or have been, hostile during the present year wherever found."

On August 30, Miles defeated a large body of Cheyennes, Kiowas, and Comanches. With cavalry on the flanks and artillery and infantry in the center, he drove the Indians across the Red River.

During the fall and winter, 1874, smaller skirmishes were fought, mainly with the Cheyennes. The army's strategy was to keep the Indians moving and under pressure. Villages were destroyed and horses captured. Several of the engagements took place in the Texas Panhandle. All these fights between the army and Plains Indians are known in military records as the Red River War.

End of the Plains wars (1875). By the late summer, 1875, most of the warriors had surrendered. The army took away horses and weapons from the Plains tribes.

The warrior chiefs were arrested. Satanta, the Kiowa chief who had broken parole, was sent back to prison in Texas. Seventy-two raider chiefs were put in irons and sent to a military prison at Fort Marion, Florida. Disarmed, dismounted, and their leaders gone, the Plains tribes had no choice but to settle down.

Buffalo hunts, the warpath, and the thrill of horse raids were all in the past. Government rations, schools, Christian religions, farming—the white man's way—were in the future.

5. MANY PEACEFUL TRIBES WERE MOVED TO LANDS GIVEN UP BY THE FIVE CIVILIZED NATIONS AFTER THE CIVIL WAR.

More than two dozen tribes were moved to Oklahoma following the Civil War. Most of these tribes were removed peacefully from reservations in Kansas and elsewhere.

About 15,000 Native Americans eventually

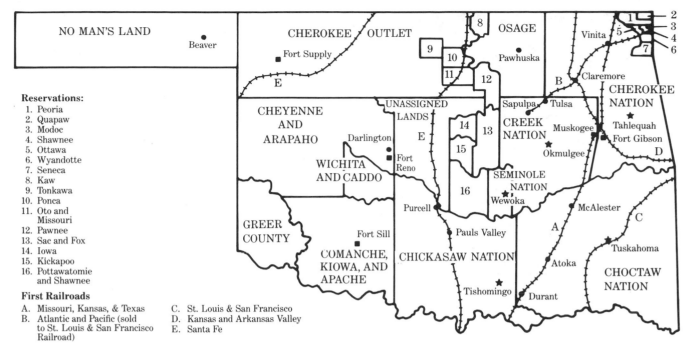

Reservations:
1. Peoria
2. Quapaw
3. Modoc
4. Shawnee
5. Ottawa
6. Wyandotte
7. Seneca
8. Kaw
9. Tonkawa
10. Ponca
11. Oto and Missouri
12. Pawnee
13. Sac and Fox
14. Iowa
15. Kickapoo
16. Pottawatomie and Shawnee

First Railroads
A. Missouri, Kansas, & Texas
B. Atlantic and Pacific (sold to St. Louis & San Francisco Railroad)
C. St. Louis & San Francisco
D. Kansas and Arkansas Valley
E. Santa Fe

Indian Territory Before 1889

lived on reservations west of the Five Civilized Tribes. In most cases the newcomers were concentrated in settlements along the streams. Most of their land was unoccupied and was visited only by hunters.

President Grant's peace policy. President Ulysses S. Grant (1869–1877) adopted a new Indian policy. It was based on kindness and moral persuasion—not military force. The Native Americans were put on reservations, given rations, and supervised by agents of the federal government. Many of the Indian agents were Quakers. The Quaker church (Society of Friends) was known for its peaceful relations with Indians.

Seven Indian agencies were established in Indian Territory. Each agency was in charge of one or more reservations.

Osage Agency. This agency supervised the Osage and Kaw reservations from headquarters at Pawhuska.

The Osage reservation was a rough, hilly, grass-covered area that is now Osage County. The Osages bought it from the Cherokee Nation in 1872 after selling their reservation in Kansas to the federal government. The first Quaker agent, Isaac T. Gibson, lived in a log cabin on Agency Hill in Pawhuska. Soon, stone buildings were constructed for a school, doctor's office, and the first newspaper—*The Indian Herald*. The Osages became rich when oil was discovered on their land.

The Kaw (Kansas) Indians moved to land in the northwest corner of the Osage reservation in 1873. The Kaws and Osages are related by language and culture.

Ponca Agency. This agency was located near present Ponca City. It had responsibility for four reservations. They were the Ponca, Otoe and Missouri, Pawnee, and Tonkawa.

The Poncas were a Siouan tribe from South Dakota and Nebraska. Before coming to Indian Territory, the Otoe tribe had split into two bands because of a quarrel between two chiefs. One band became known as the Missouris.

The small Tonkawa tribe from Texas was given the Nez Perces reservation in 1885. The Nez Perces, led by Chief Joseph, had been moved to Indian Territory but were allowed to return to their homeland in Idaho and Washington.

Jim Thorpe

izens in Oklahoma and the nation. The famous athlete Jim Thorpe was born on the Sac and Fox reservation. William Jones, the well-known anthropology scholar, was also a member of the tribe. Keokuk, Iowa is named after the best-known Sac and Fox chief.

The Pottawatomie and Shawnee were separate tribes which shared a reservation east of present-day Oklahoma City. Two other Shawnee groups also lived in Indian Territory.

Cheyenne and Arapaho Agency. This agency was at Darlington, north of Fort Reno. It was named after Brinton Darlington, the first Quaker agent.

The Kiowa and Comanche Agency was in charge of two reservations. The Kiowas, Comanches, and a few Kiowa-Apaches were on the largest reservation. Geronimo and his Chiricahua Apaches were also permitted to live there. The Apaches were brought to Fort Sill as prisoners of war in 1894. Geronimo had surrendered in Arizona eight years earlier. He was exiled to Florida and then to Alabama before being settled permanently in Oklahoma.

The Wichitas, Caddoes, and several smaller tribes were on a separate reservation. They had their own supervision—the Wichita Agency at Anadarko—until 1879. In that year, the Kiowa-Comanche Agency was moved from Fort Sill and consolidated with the agency at Anadarko.

Union Agency. In 1874, the Five Civilized Tribes were combined under the Union Agency at Muskogee. A separate agent for each tribe was replaced by a single agent. He was called the Commissioner to the Five Civilized Tribes. This commissioner had an important job. He took care of nearly all relations between the five tribes and the federal government.

Each nation, of course, had its own government and capital. Tahlequah was the Cherokee capital. The others were Okmulgee for the Creeks, Wewoka for the Seminoles, Tuskahoma for the Choctaws, and Tishomingo in the Chickasaw Nation.

Neosho Agency. This agency supervised seven small reservations in the northeast corner of present Oklahoma.

Sac and Fox Agency. This agency was established near what is now the town of Stroud in Lincoln County. The four reservations under its direction were on lands formerly owned by the Creeks.

The Iowas were a Siouan tribe. The Sac and Fox, Kickapoo, and Shawnee-Pottawatomie were of Algonquin stock. They once lived east of the Mississippi.

The Sac (Sauk) and Fox were once two independent tribes. But they have long been allied and are classed as one tribe. The Sac and Fox were among the most conservative Indians in Oklahoma. They wore blankets and tribal costume longer than most natives. Though reluctant to adopt the white man's customs, the Sac and Fox eventually produced some outstanding cit-

The Seneca, Shawnee, and Quapaw were given lands there before the Civil War.

The Ottawa and Miami tribes shared a reservation. The others belonged to the Peorias, Wyandottes, and Modocs.

Agencies combined. All the reservations were abolished before Oklahoma became a state in 1907. The Native Americans were allotted private farms. The remaining reservation land was opened to white settlement. In brief, many tribes were forced to move to Indian Territory. Then, after a few years, they were dispossessed of their reservations.

The seven agencies continued serving the tribes. In 1947, they were combined into three. The Neosho Agency was added to the Union Agency at Muskogee. The Osage Agency, minus the Kaw Reservation, remained at Pawhuska. All the other agencies were combined into the Kiowa-Comanche Agency at Anadarko.

ROUNDUP

1. Describe the lifestyle of the Plains tribes that made these people the stereotype of all Indians.
2. What happened to the huge herds of buffalo? Why were the Plains tribes put on reservations?
3. In what way did the federal government's Indian policy change as a result of the Medicine Lodge treaties? How did Chief Satanta feel about reservations?
4. Why was Camp Supply built? Identify Black Kettle and Col. George A. Custer.
5. What happened at the Battle of Washita? Which new forts were established after this battle? Why?
6. Why were several Kiowa leaders sent in chains to Texas for trial? What complaints did the Plains tribes have against white intruders? Who was Quanah Parker?
7. What was the Red River War? Who was Col. Nelson A. Miles? What were the results of the war?
8. Make a chart of the Indian agencies in Indian Territory and the tribes that were served by each.
A. Think about it! "The Indians are not one people. They are many peoples, as different from each other as, say, the Italians and the Germans." Explain this statement.
B. Expand on this observation: "Today, traditional Indian tribal life is fading, so everything that represents the Indian has become precious."
C. Try this! All but a few American Indian tribes live far from their original homes. Find out the names of all the tribes in Oklahoma (67 according to one expert) and the places from which they came.

12

CATTLE, COAL, AND THE FIRST RAILROADS

Indian Territory experienced great economic changes between the end of the Civil War in 1865 and the first land opening in 1889.

The *range cattle industry* developed rapidly. By the 1880s, Oklahoma was part of the vast "cow country" that stretched from Texas to Montana. *Open ranges* in the Great Plains area were filled with *Longhorns*. These animals had multiplied in the wild in Texas during the war.

Beginning in 1886, Texans drove millions of cattle to *railheads* in Kansas. Buyers loaded the cattle on railroad cars for shipment to eastern markets or feeding areas.

Cowboys who rode herd along the trails spread the word about rich grazing lands in Indian Territory. Texas *drovers* began lingering here for weeks at a time to fatten their cattle. Before long, ranchers were raising cattle on the *public domain* and on the Indian reservations.

Railroads were a major cause for economic change in Indian Territory. Good rail transportation made coal mining profitable in the Choctaw Nation. As tracks crisscrossed this area, many new towns were started. Lumbering developed in southeastern Oklahoma to supply the needs of the railroads and the towns.

1. **WESTERN OKLAHOMA WAS PART OF THE OPEN RANGE CATTLE INDUSTRY THAT STRETCHED FROM TEXAS TO MONTANA.**

Ranching on the open range was a frontier industry. As Americans moved west, cattle raisers went ahead of the farmers. Livestock was pastured on unoccupied land beyond the farms and towns.

The Great Plains became "cow country" after the Civil War ended in 1865. The amount of public land used by ranchers reached a peak by the mid-1880s. Millions of cattle were grazing the open range where the buffalo once roamed.

The open range cattle industry had its origin in Texas. That state had been ranch country since the Spaniards introduced cattle there in the 1500s. A mild climate, cheap land, and large ranches were favorable to cattle raising. Herds multiplied rapidly, especially during the Civil War when Texans were away fighting for the Confederate States.

After the war, fat cattle in Texas sold for as little as five dollars a head. Prices were much higher in the eastern and northern states where four years of war had greatly reduced the number of cattle. Out of this situation came the famous trail drives. Texans rounded up large herds and drove them north.

In the twenty years following the Civil War, ten million head of cattle were driven north from Texas. Many were shipped to market from railheads in Kansas. Others were put out to graze on ranges as far north as Montana.

The western part of Indian Territory was suitable for range cattle. This region was covered with a thick coat of grass. The land was only thinly-populated with Native Americans. Stockmen were attracted to the huge Cheyenne-Arapaho and Kiowa-Comanche reservations and the Cherokee Outlet. Pastures were also found on the smaller reservations.

Before 1880, cattlemen were running stock on three large blocks of the public domain. The cattle company of Ikard and Harrold alone had sixty thousand head in *Greer County*. This area, be-

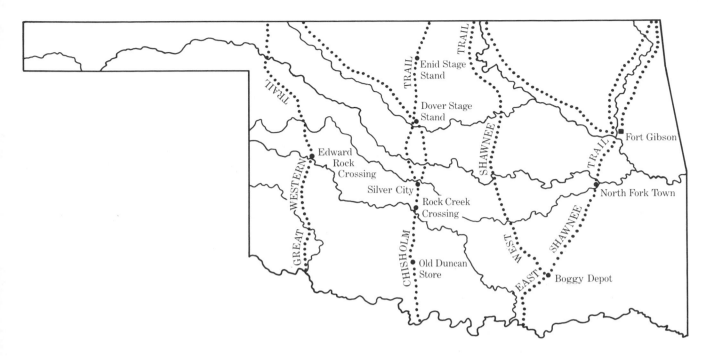

Cattle Trails in Indian Territory

tween the two forks of the Red River, was claimed by Texas. (In 1896, the U.S. Supreme Court made Greer County a part of the Oklahoma Territory.)

Another area used by cattlemen was *No Man's Land,* now the Panhandle of Oklahoma. This land was included in the Territory of Oklahoma that was organized in 1890.

Cattle also grazed on the *Unassigned Lands* in the center of present Oklahoma. These lands were opened to white settlement by the land run of 1889.

2. FOUR MAIN CATTLE TRAILS WERE ESTABLISHED ACROSS INDIAN TERRITORY.

Texas cattle were driven across Indian Territory to railheads in Kansas and to northern ranges. Each main trail had branches and offshoots.

East Shawnee and West Shawnee trails. The first Texas herds were driven north in 1866. They followed the old Texas Road in what is now eastern Oklahoma. The trail ran about 750 miles from San Antonio, Texas to Sedalia, Missouri. Known as the East Shawnee Trail, it crossed the Red River below the mouth of the Washita. The trail ran by Boggy Depot and Fort Gibson to Baxter Springs, Kansas.

A branch, the West Shawnee Trail, ran north from Boggy Depot by the present sites of Shawnee and Cushing to Junction City, Kansas.

The first drovers faced problems. Many of the 260,000 cattle that headed north in 1866 never reached a profitable market. Cattle often strayed from the herd in the hilly, forested areas in what is now Oklahoma. Cowboys were *bushwhacked* by outlaw gangs that drove off cattle and horses. Eventually, some of the tribes taxed the drovers for grass eaten by cattle along the trail.

Armed farmers tried to stop Texas cattle from entering Kansas and Missouri. The Longhorns, though immune to "Texas fever," spread this disease through ticks. A few Texas drovers were beaten or killed. Some of their herds were stampeded. Discouraged, the Texans sometimes sold their cattle for any price they could get and returned home.

Chisholm Trail and Abilene, Kansas. The drovers were forced to enter Kansas west of the farm settlements. In 1867, Joseph G. McCoy established the town of Abilene on the Kansas Pacific Railroad. McCoy, a cattle dealer and feeder from Illinois, built *stockyards* and a hotel named Drover's Cottage. He sent riders south to tell Texans about his new town.

Part of the trail to Abilene was blazed in 1865 by Jesse Chisholm for his supply wagons. He was a part-Cherokee trader at Wichita, Kansas. The main Chisholm Trail ran along the present route of the Rock Island Railroad and Highway 81. This highway is appropriately marked with the spreading Longhorn symbol. Present towns along the trail are Waurika, Duncan, Rush Springs, El Reno, Dover, Kingfisher, Pond Creek, and Enid. Museums and markers in some of these towns show the fame of the Chisholm Trail.

Abilene was the leading cowtown for several years. Other towns sprang up as Kansas settlers moved west.

The Western Trail and Dodge City, Kansas. The Western Trail crossed the Red River at Doan's Store. It passed through the Kiowa-Comanche and Cheyenne-Arapaho reservations en route to Dodge City and Ogalalla, Nebraska. The present-day towns of Altus, Elk City, Fort Supply, and Buffalo are on or near the old Western Trail. Stream crossings on this trail were safer than the "steep bank fords" on the Shawnee trails.

By 1875, Dodge City was the "cow capital of the world." The end of the trail, it was a wild place from early spring to late fall. Cowboys let off steam at saloons, gambling halls, and dance palaces. The rowdy element made Dodge City a living hell for peaceful residents.

Dodge City's first jail was a deep well where drunks were kept until sober enough to leave town. Other cowboys were not so lucky. They died of "lead poisoning" and were buried in Boot Hill

Stampede of Texas longhorns. (Sketch by Frederic Remington)

Cemetery with their boots on. Gunslingers were hired to keep law and order. Dodge City had Bat Masterson and Wyatt Earp, just as Abilene had Wild Bill Hickok.

Contrary to the impression given by some western films, many cowboys were peaceful and saved their wages. To these men, Dodge City meant a bath, haircut, shave, new clothes, and a room at the Dodge House or the Great Western Hotel.

Panhandle trails to the northwest. An offshoot of the Western Trail ran west of present Laverne, Oklahoma through the Panhandle to pastures in Colorado or Wyoming. In present Cimarron County this trail joined with the Potter-Bacon Trail that ran north across the Texas Panhandle.

Technique of trail driving. Drovers left Texas along about March. With spring grass all the way, cattle could make the 750 to 1,000 mile walk to northern shipping points in two or three months.

A typical herd of 2,500 cattle required ten or

Every trail driver had an assigned job to keep the herd moving. (Sketch by Frederic Remington)

twelve men with four to six horses each. The cowboy furnished his own saddle and bedding. Cattle herd owners supplied the horses.

After a herd was rounded up in Texas, the cattle were passed through a chute and given a "road brand." During the first few days on the trail, they were pushed fast to lessen the danger of stampede. When the animals were "trail broken," the pace slowed to ten or twelve miles a day. A stop was made early in the afternoon for the cattle to water and graze "at ease."

Usually a herd was "strung out" for a mile along the trail. The cattle selected their own places in the column. The "lead steer" and other aggressive animals moved out first. Two of the most experienced cowboys worked as "points" to keep the herd on course.

The "swing riders" were back a distance where the herd widened out. They kept the cattle from wandering sidewise. The "flank riders" were still further back.

Several "drag riders" brought up the rear. They were usually the young "greenhorn" cowboys. Their patience was tested by the slow, lame, and lazy cattle that fell behind the herd. A drag rider kept the animals moving by stinging them with a buckskin "popper" fastened to the end of his rope. He pulled a neckerchief over his mouth and nose for protection against dust stirred up by the herd.

A cook drove the chuck wagon well ahead of the herd. A *wrangler* followed him with a *remuda* of horses. Each cowboy changed horses frequently. The "trail boss" was in charge of the whole operation. He laid out the trail to be followed, located water, and picked out camp sites. The trail boss was paid $125 a month. The "hands" got $25 to $40 a month.

End of the trail drives. By the mid 1880s, the "northern drive" had outlived its usefulness. Why? Reasons include Kansas quarantine laws, the full stocking of northern ranges, and the building of north-south railroads.

Some railheads in Indian Territory became important shipping points. Purcell grew up after the Santa Fe railroad arrived from the north in 1887. Purcell was located in the Chickasaw Nation where branches of the Chisholm Trail and the California Road crossed the South Canadian River. Texas cattle were fattened along Beef Creek and then driven to Purcell for shipment. Purcell was "dry," but cowboys could reach the Sand Bar Saloon that was built on stilts in the middle of the river by foot bridge. This saloon was supplied by a distillery at Lexington which was located in the Unassigned Lands. Several times the saloon was washed downstream and rebuilt.

3. SOME MEMBERS OF THE FIVE CIVILIZED TRIBES WERE WELL-TO-DO STOCKRAISERS.

Before they were removed to Oklahoma, the Five Civilized Tribes owned large herds of cattle. Their knowledge of stockraising got them off to a new start in Indian Territory. The tribes prospered during the 1840s and 1850s.

The Civil War put an end to the short-lived boom in eastern Oklahoma's cattle industry. Before the war, for example, several wealthy Seminoles owned herds of ten to twenty thousand head each. A few years after the war, a livestock census set the total number of all Seminole cattle at only four thousand head.

The tribes did not regain their pre-war prosperity. They had the land but not the capital to get into the range cattle industry on a large scale. Some individual Indians prospered, however.

A few wealthy Native Americans owned large herds. Under an ancient Indian custom, any tribal member could have as much available land as he kept in use. A few wealthy tribal citizens got control of much of the land. Most of these men had other businesses too. They owned stores and had investments in banks, mines, or real estate.

Chief Wilson Nathaniel Jones, a Choctaw full blood, fenced 17,000 acres. Jones ran a herd of five thousand cattle. He owned a cotton gin and several stores. His interests also included coal mines.

Sixty-one wealthy Creeks held more than a million acres, about a third of the Creek lands. Frederick B. Severs, a Creek by adoption, enclosed large pastures for his cattle and horses. He also owned most of the town of Okmulgee and businesses in Muskogee.

Tribal businessmen like Jones and Severs developed farms as well as ranches. Most of the labor was done by white or black tenants who had residency permits.

A change in government policy eventually put an end to most large ranches in Indian Territory. To make room for white settlers, each tribal citizen was allotted an individual farm. Surplus reservation land was returned to the public domain.

4. THE RANGE CATTLE INDUSTRY LARGELY ENDED WITH THE BREAKUP OF RESERVATIONS AND THE OPENING OF OKLAHOMA FOR SETTLEMENT.

By the 1880s, white cattlemen were occupying most of the grasslands in western Oklahoma. But ranching on the reservations and public domain was short-lived. The federal government cancelled leases with the tribes and opened up surplus reservation land to homesteaders. Land not on reservations was also settled.

The range cattle industry and the northern drive only lasted about two decades on the Great Plains. The cowboy, a symbol of this era, caught people's imagination. He was romanticized into America's greatest folk hero. Fiction writers and Hollywood producers of western films saw to that.

Cheyenne-Arapaho grazing leases. Cattlemen grazed their herds on the lands of friendly Indians for several years before the federal government permitted leases. In 1883, seven white ranchers leased more than three million acres on

Cheyenne camp with meat drying on racks. (Smithsonian Institution)

the Cheyenne-Arapaho reservation for two cents an acre. The native leaders demanded payment in silver. Accordingly, the ranchers packed in silver dollars on horseback from Caldwell, Kansas to make payments.

The largest spread was the million acre ranch of the Cheyenne and Arapaho Cattle Company from Texas. The C and A foreman, Edward Fenlon, hired about forty line riders.

At roundup time, the ranches worked together. Cowboys were on the range from sunup to sunset with only two meals. They cut out cattle, roped calves, and branded. At night the men slept on the ground and did night herding. Cowboy work was hard and took endurance.

Some Cheyennes and Arapahoes opposed the leasing of reservation lands. They cut fences, burned dry grass, and killed cattle for beef when hungry. The reservation was in turmoil. In 1885, President Grover Cleveland ordered the white ranchers to remove all their cattle—about 210,000 head—from the reservation.

In 1887, Congress passed the Dawes Allotment Act. This law ended tribal ownership of common reservation lands in Indian Territory. After each tribal member took individual land, the surplus area was opened to settlement by outsiders. The Cheyenne-Arapaho land opening was in 1892.

Cherokee Strip Livestock Association. Ranchers were quick to pasture cattle on the Cherokee Outlet. Texas drovers lingered to fatten their herds. Kansas ranchers let their cattle stray across the border. The Cherokee council at Tahlequah levied a grazing fee, but was not able to collect much money.

In 1883, cattlemen who used the Outlet formed the Cherokee Strip Livestock Association. This group leased the Outlet from the Cherokee Nation for $100,000 a year. The first semi-annual payment in silver was hauled by wagon to Tahlequah.

The Cherokee Strip Livestock Association divided the Outlet into about a hundred ranges. Each member rancher fenced his range, built corrals and cowboy camps, and adopted a brand. The Association ran more than 300,000 cattle in the Outlet. The lease was renewed in 1888.

Two years later, however, President Benjamin Harrison ordered all cattle removed from the Outlet. Then the federal government bought this area for $1.40 an acre. In 1893, the Cherokee Outlet was opened to white settlement.

5. THE 101 RANCH BECAME A SUCCESSFUL AGRIBUSINESS AND WAS FAMOUS FOR ITS WILD WEST SHOW.

The 101 Ranch survived the breakup of Indian reservations and the opening of Oklahoma to settlement.

Colonel George W. Miller, a Kentuckian, founded the 101 Ranch in 1879 after operating a cattle spread in the Miami area. Miller leased Indian grasslands near present-day Ponca City for Texas Longhorns. The largest size of the ranch at one time was about 110,000 acres, mostly leased land.

Agribusiness. Miller died in 1903. His three sons expanded the ranch, turning the cattle operation into an *agribusiness*. The Miller brothers experimented with crossbreeding and raised horses, hogs, and other animals as well as cattle.

About 15,000 acres were planted in cereal

Advertisement for Miller's Wild West Show.

crops. Most of the grain, except the wheat, was fed to livestock. Wheat and seed corn were sold for good profits. The drought-resistant White Wonder hybrid corn was developed. Stored in an elevator on the ranch, White Wonder corn was popular with farmers in Oklahoma and Texas.

A wide variety of vegetables, fruits, and nuts were produced and sold at the 101 market. The Millers eliminated middlemen by processing their products on the ranch. They operated a meat packing plant, tannery, harness and saddle shop, creamery, department store, ranch cafe, gasoline refinery, and filling station. Oil and gas were a source of ranch income in the 1920s.

Wild West Show. The Miller economic record was impressive. Their fame, however, came from the 101 Ranch Wild West Show. The first show was performed in 1904 for a national convention of editors meeting at Guthrie. The show included war dances by Ponca Indians from whom George Miller had leased his first grazing land. Cowboy roping and a buffalo hunt featuring Geronimo gave the show a frontier flavor.

"Bulldogging," now called steer wrestling, became a featured event. Bill Pickett, a famous black cowboy, developed a technique of biting a Longhorn's upper lip and holding on like a bulldog. At one time, Will Rogers worked as a hazer for Pickett.

Gradually the Millers drifted away from the romantic attraction of cowboys as the main theme. A circus became a major part of the show.

Both the show and the 101 Ranch were hit hard by the 1930s depression. The 101 was sold at auction.

6. COAL MINING ATTRACTED MANY WHITES AND BLACKS TO INDIAN TERRITORY IN THE 1870s.

Blacksmiths had mined coal in southeastern Oklahoma before the Civil War. They picked away at coal outcrops to get fuel for their forges.

Commercial coal mining began when railroads provided a market and transportation in the 1870s.

James J. McAlester developed the first mines. A Confederate Colonel, McAlester settled at Fort Smith after the Civil War. He found out about coal deposits in Indian Territory accidentally. He read the notebook of a geologist who had explored the coal area.

Bill Pickett. (OHS)

96

J. J. McAlester. (OHS)

Keeping his information secret, McAlester moved to Bucklucksey, also known as "Cross Roads," in the Choctaw Nation. In 1870, he opened a store in a tent where the California Trail crossed the heavily-traveled Texas Trail.

McAlester married a Chickasaw girl. This marriage gave him citizenship in both the Chickasaw and Choctaw Nations. He could also mine "the rock that burns" on Indian land. Mr. Mac, as people called him, mined some coal at Krebs and hauled it by wagon to Parsons, Kansas. There he helped persuade the M-K-T (Missouri, Kansas, and Texas) railroad to build a line through Bucklucksey. The M-K-T renamed the town McAlester.

McAlester and the Choctaws. The Choctaw government claimed McAlester's coal revenues, but he refused to turn over his profits. Coleman Cole, the principal Choctaw chief was furious. A full blood, Cole sensed the danger of letting white men take over Indian coal and other resources. The chief put McAlester in jail and sentenced him to death.

McAlester bribed the jailers and escaped from Choctaw troops who were known as the "Light Horse." Later, a large number of his white friends met with Chief Cole. They threatened to hang the chief's hide on a fence if he harmed a hair on McAlester's head. A compromise was reached by the two sides. McAlester could resume his mining. The Choctaw Nation would receive half the coal profits.

Coal was important to the railroads. After 1872, coal mining and the railroads grew hand in hand. Within fifteen years, eight mines in the Choctaw Nation produced nearly 700,000 tons of coal a year. The M-K-T railroad depended more on coal shipments than on Texas cattle.

Non-Indian workers. The growth of mining, railroads, and the cattle industry set the stage for other changes in Indian Territory. This area had been set aside as a haven for Native Americans. But a flood of whites and blacks came in the 1870s. These newcomers worked in the mines, laid railroad tracks, became tenant farmers for Indian landlords, and built towns.

European ethnic groups and Mexicans. Company agents went to eastern states and Europe to recruit miners. Workers from the British Isles, especially the Welsh, were the largest group. Italians were the biggest non-English speaking nationality. They settled in Krebs, Henryetta, and other places. Little communities of Poles, Lithuanians, Czechs, Russians, and other immigrants began to dot the McAlester area. Mexicans sometimes came as railroad workers and stayed to work in the mines.

The foreign-born ethnic groups usually lived in poorly-built company houses in one section of town. The women and girls did the shopping but did not mix much outside their national group. At first, the immigrants spoke mainly their own language and held on to their customs and religion. Entertainment came from church functions, ethnic festivals, dances, playing musical instruments, and singing songs from the "old country."

The 1890 census revealed that Native Americans made up only 28 percent of the population in Indian Territory. By 1907, the year Oklahoma became a state, only nine percent of the people were Native Americans. Chief Cole turned out to be quite a prophet.

7. THE COMING OF THE RAILROADS SPELLED DOOM FOR THE INDIAN NATIONS.

Before the Civil War, the Army surveyed possible railroad routes to connect California to the rest of the nation. In 1853, an expedition led by Lieutenant Amiel Whipple mapped a route west of Fort Smith across Indian Territory. (Whipple's journals are now kept at the Oklahoma Historical Society in Oklahoma City.)

No railroads were built in present Oklahoma until after the Civil War. In 1866, the Five Civilized Tribes were forced to offer land for two railroad right-of-ways. One would run north and south and the other east and west.

First railroad in Oklahoma. Three companies competed for the right to build the north-south line. The award was to go to the first company that completed a good railroad in Kansas to the northern boundary of the Indian Territory in the Neosho Valley. The Missouri, Kansas, and Texas, better known as the "Katy" or M-K-T, won the race.

The M-K-T stockholders included some of the wealthiest men in the country—J. P. Morgan and John D. Rockefeller, for examples. Parsons, Kansas and Denison, Texas were named after two other investors.

Congress promised land to the M-K-T. The land grant was to extend for several miles on both sides of the track through Indian Territory. This nearly two million acre grant was only on paper, however, because the Cherokees and other tribes had to consent. They refused to give up any land except for the right-of-way. The M-K-T filed a claim in the federal courts but lost.

Construction problems. The M-K-T began laying track at Chetopa, Kansas in March, 1871. The line was built along the Texas Road used by cattle drovers and wagon freighters. Progress was slow, partly because railroad ties were hard to get. Individual Cherokees had fenced in the best timber trees. The M-K-T had to deal with each of these people separately.

Another problem was illness. Half the workmen, many of them veterans of the Civil War, fell sick. They had malarial fever, dysentery, typhoid, and chills.

Disorder at Muskogee and other terminus towns. On Christmas Day, 1871, a locomotive named the "General Grant" crossed the Arkansas River over an 840-foot bridge. The site of present Muskogee was reached by New Year's Day.

Muskogee was a lawless tent city while it was the southern *terminus* of the Katy line. Whiskey peddlers, gamblers, thieves, and other frontier bad men swarmed into town. They hoped to take easy money from the hard working track layers and bridge builders. Murders and other crimes were a daily occurrence.

The same kind of disorder followed the railroad south to Eufaula, McAlester, and other towns. Finally, a detachment of soldiers was sent to Choctaw country to round up rowdy camp followers and remove them from Indian Territory.

The M-K-T line was completed to the Red River by the end of 1872. The first passenger train crossed Indian Territory from Kansas to Denison, Texas on Christmas Eve.

Switches and water tanks. Some new towns like Durant grew up at lonesome switches along the M-K-T line. These switches put trains on sidings so other trains could pass on the single track. They were built about every ten miles. Cattle and freight were loaded at these places.

In the early days, locomotives were smaller and pulled fewer cars than modern engines. The old coal-burning steam locomotives made frequent stops at water tanks. Small villages that sprung up near these watering stops were called "tank towns."

The Frisco line and Vinita. The first east-west railroad in Indian Territory was started by the Atlantic and Pacific. In 1871, the A and P built a line from Missouri across the Shawnee and Wyandotte reservations to the Katy line at Vinita.

The M-K-T wanted the junction to be at Big Cabin and, for awhile, Katy trains did not stop until they were some distance past Vinita. This inconvenience for passengers was soon remedied. The A and P blocked the crossing with a freight train each time a Katy passenger train was due to arrive. The M-K-T finally gave in and built a station at Vinita. This town was Oklahoma's "first great railroad center."

The St. Louis and San Francisco Railroad took over the A and P line in Indian Territory. In the 1880's, the "Frisco line," as it was then called, was extended to Tulsa and Sapulpa.

Railroads speeded the breakup of Indian nations. Railroads ended the isolation of Native Americans. White and black people followed the rails into Indian Territory. They came as storekeepers, miners, farm tenants, millers, or railroad workers. The existence of the Indians as free, self-governing people was threatened. The opening of the Indian Territory to settlement was not long in coming.

The Santa Fe line opened up central Oklahoma to settlement. By the summer of 1887, Santa Fe freight and passenger trains were rolling through Indian Territory between Kansas and Texas. The U.S. Congress had authorized this line and provided a one hundred feet wide right-of-way.

Two Santa Fe affiliate companies built the railroad. The Southern Kansas Railway laid a track south of Arkansas City, Kansas to Purcell in Indian Territory. At the same time, the Gulf Colorado and Santa Fe extended its service across Texas and the Red River to Purcell. This

This M-K-T diamond stack locomotive was used in the 1870s.

town, on the South Canadian River, was named for a Santa Fe official. It was to become an important railroad town.

A race developed to see which company could reach Purcell first. Subcontractors and thousands of workers were hired to make a level grade. They used mule-pulled scrapers to move dirt. Track crews followed, laying rails at record speeds. The men often were delayed at rivers, however, while wooden trestle bridges were built. A bridge across the Cimarron River was 975 feet long. High waters held up construction on the South Canadian bridge.

The race to Purcell ended in a dead heat. Both companies arrived on April 26, 1887. The last spike, a silver one, was driven to celebrate the completion of the railroad.

Many of the men who worked on the Santa Fe line were *Boomers* (people who wanted Indian Territory opened to settlement). They especially wanted to settle the Unassigned Lands. These lands, in central Oklahoma, had not been assigned to any tribe. The Boomers believed that a railroad through this area would open the door to settlers. Both the Boomers and the Santa Fe company were pleased when the federal government opened the Unassigned Lands—Oklahoma's first land run—on April 22, 1889.

Cattle being loaded for shipment. Railroads brought an end to the trail drive.

ROUNDUP

1. Define open range, public domain, drover, and railhead.

2. What years were the heyday of the cattle trail drives? Which public domain areas were used by cattlemen?

3. List the four main cattle trails across Indian Territory. What problems did drovers encounter here? Name the main railheads in Kansas. Identify Joseph G. McCoy and Jesse Chisholm.

4. Describe a trail drive.

5. Name two prominent Native American cattlemen and list their enterprises.

6. Which Indian reservations provided large areas of leased grazing land for cattlemen? How were the lease payments made? Identify the Cherokee Strip Livestock Association.

7. Why was James J. McAlester important in Oklahoma history? For what reasons did coal mining and railroads grow hand in hand? How did these industries change the population of Indian Territory?

8. List the ethnic groups that were attracted to Indian Territory by the coalfields. What did the 1890 census reveal about the population of Indian Territory?

9. Which company built the first railroad in what is now Oklahoma? What problems did the builders encounter? Define tank towns.

10. Describe Muskogee in 1871.

11. Which company built the "Frisco line?" Where did this line connect with the M-K-T?

12. What was unusual about the construction of the Santa Fe line across Indian Territory? What important event resulted from the building of this railroad?

A. Think about it! "Frontier ranching and cowboys are part of Oklahoma's rich heritage." Explain how the spirit of the pioneer cattle industry is kept alive today.

B. "The growth of Oklahoma has always depended on good transportation." Explain this idea and give historical examples of transportation that prove the point.

C. Try this! European immigrants left their social and cultural imprint in several communities. So did Hispanic people. Choose an ethnic group and find out why they came to Oklahoma, where they settled, and their contributions. (See the "Suggested Readings" in the appendix.)

13

BOOMERS, SOONERS, AND LAND OPENINGS IN WESTERN OKLAHOMA

Elias C. Boudinot, Jr.

All of present-day Oklahoma, except the Panhandle, was promised to Native Americans. Indian Territory was to be theirs "as long as the grass grows and the water runs." The tribes did not want their lands opened to settlement by other people.

White cattlemen who leased Indian grasslands also opposed the opening of Indian Territory to settlement. They knew that homesteaders would plow up the grassy prairies.

Pioneers who wanted to farm in Oklahoma had two questions: Why should Native Americans control land they do not use or need? Why should cattlemen be allowed where farmers are kept out?

As we shall see, the promised land rights of the natives were swept aside. The tribal members were forced to take individual allotments, usually 160 acres. Then, their surplus reservation land was opened to settlement.

1. LAND-HUNGRY BOOMERS PUT PRESSURE ON THE GOVERNMENT TO OPEN LAND IN INDIAN TERRITORY FOR SETTLEMENT.

Elias C. Boudinot wrote a newspaper article in 1879 that aroused popular support for land openings. Boudinot was a Cherokee lawyer who differed from most other Cherokees on the issue of settlement. Boudinot had been influenced by *lobbyists* for the M-K-T and other railroad companies. The railroads would have more business if settlers occupied empty lands in Indian Territory.

Boudinot described the fertile land and mild climate of the "Unassigned Lands." He said this area, also called "Oklahoma District," should be opened. It contained about two million acres in the heart of Indian Territory. (This land is now divided into the counties of Payne, Logan, Oklahoma, Cleveland, Canadian, and Kingfisher.) After reading his article, many people wrote to Boudinot for maps and details.

Hundreds of homeseekers began gathering in southern Kansas. Known as the *Boomers,* they would try again and again to settle in Indian Territory.

David L. Payne led the Boomer movement in the early 1880s. He was a Union Army veteran and a Kansas legislator. Payne once worked as a doorkeeper for Congress in Washington, D.C. While there, he met Boudinot and learned about the lands in Indian Territory.

Payne gave leadership to the scattered Boomer groups in Kansas. He visited their camps and gave speeches. "Go forth and possess the

David L. Payne.

Payne was planning his ninth colony attempt when he died at Wellington, Kansas in 1884. One of his assistants, William L. Couch, became the new leader.

Buffalo soldiers. The 9th Cavalry had the thankless job of keeping Boomers out of Indian Territory. The 9th and the 10th Cavalry, as well as the 24th and 25th Infantry, were black regiments that were organized after the Civil War. The black troopers were called "buffalo soldiers" by the Plains Indians. Why? They had short, curly hair and wore buffalo skin coats. The officers, including Colonel Edward Hatch who commanded the 9th Cavalry, were white.

All the black regiments did duty in Indian Territory at one time or another. They were assigned to Fort Sill, Fort Reno, Fort Supply, and other posts in Indian Territory, Texas, and Kansas. Their job was to keep the Plains Indians peaceful. Several black units fought in the Red River War and other battles to subdue hostile

Promised Land," he urged. Payne published a newspaper, the *Oklahoma War Chief,* to keep his Boomer followers informed. He got financial backing from railroad companies. Merchants in Wichita and other towns gave money. Payne also charged the Boomers for a membership certificate.

In April, 1880, Payne led about two dozen Boomers across the Cherokee Outlet to the Unassigned Lands. They camped on the Canadian River near the future site of Oklahoma City. Payne built a stockade and surveyed a town. One Boomer, who brought a wagon load of booze and cigars, started a saloon. The colony was short-lived, however. Federal soldiers from Fort Reno escorted the Boomers back to Kansas.

A short time later, Payne was arrested in Indian Territory. He was taken to Fort Smith for trial. Judge Isaac Parker fined him a thousand dollars for *trespassing* on Indian lands. The court never collected this fine, however.

After another attempt to colonize in Indian Territory, Payne was tried again. This time, a federal judge in Topeka, Kansas found him innocent. The judge said the Oklahoma District was *public domain.* This court decision encouraged the Boomer movement. Payne continued to lead colonies to Indian Territory.

Buffalo soldiers escorting Boomers out of Indian Territory. (Sketch by Frederic Remington)

102

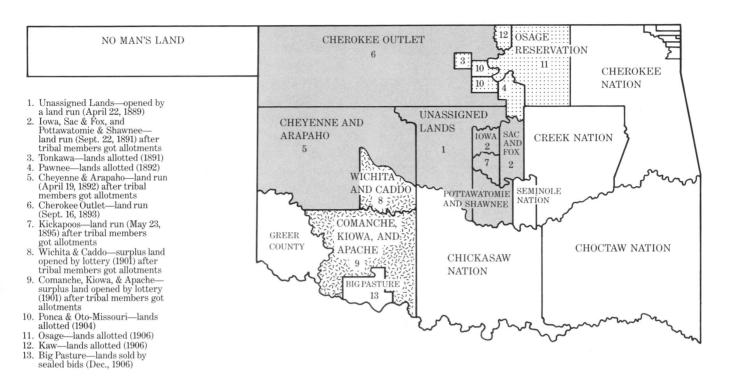

NO MAN'S LAND

CHEROKEE OUTLET
6

12 OSAGE
RESERVATION

3
10
10
4
11

CHEROKEE
NATION

1. Unassigned Lands—opened by a land run (April 22, 1889)
2. Iowa, Sac & Fox, and Pottawatomie & Shawnee—land run (Sept. 22, 1891) after tribal members got allotments
3. Tonkawa—lands allotted (1891)
4. Pawnee—lands allotted (1892)
5. Cheyenne & Arapaho—land run (April 19, 1892) after tribal members got allotments
6. Cherokee Outlet—land run (Sept. 16, 1893)
7. Kickapoos—land run (May 23, 1895) after tribal members got allotments
8. Wichita & Caddo—surplus land opened by lottery (1901) after tribal members got allotments
9. Comanche, Kiowa, & Apache—surplus land opened by lottery (1901) after tribal members got allotments
10. Ponca & Oto-Missouri—lands allotted (1904)
11. Osage—lands allotted (1906)
12. Kaw—lands allotted (1906)
13. Big Pasture—lands sold by sealed bids (Dec., 1906)

CHEYENNE AND ARAPAHO
5

UNASSIGNED LANDS
1

IOWA
2

SAC AND FOX
2

CREEK NATION

WICHITA AND CADDO
8

7

POTTAWATOMIE AND SHAWNEE

SEMINOLE NATION

GREER COUNTY

COMANCHE, KIOWA, AND APACHE
9

CHICKASAW NATION

CHOCTAW NATION

BIG PASTURE
13

Breakup of Indian Reservations in Western Oklahoma

natives. The cavalry regiments also did duty in Arizona rounding up Geronimo's Apaches.

During the 1880s, the 9th Cavalry was busy arresting and ejecting Boomers. As the Boomers became more stubborn, the troopers sometimes had to bind them hand and foot and then toss them in wagons "as if they were sacks of shelled corn." Payne hated the determined buffalo soldiers. In *War Chief* articles, he called them "Yellow Legs" and worse names.

Many sketches of the buffalo soldiers were drawn by Frederic Remington, the great artist of the frontier West. Rising above the race prejudice that was so common at the time, Remington said the buffalo soldiers were not only good fighters but also "charming men with whom to serve."

Stillwater colony. Couch, Payne's successor, led several hundred Boomers to a camp on Stillwater Creek. The men were armed with shotguns and rifles. To protect the colony, they also built earthworks.

In January, 1885, Colonel Hatch arrived with troops from Fort Reno. To avoid bloodshed, Hatch ordered his men to encircle the Boomer camp. This tactic worked. Supplies from Kansas were cut off. When the settlers ran out of food, they loaded their wagons and returned home with a military escort.

Later in 1885, the disagreeable task of driving Boomers from the "Promised Land" ended for Hatch and the buffalo soldiers. The 9th Cavalry headquarters was transferred to Wyoming. About the same time, the 10th Cavalry marched down the Southern Pacific Railroad tracks from Texas for the final Geronimo campaign in Arizona.

Boomer success with Congress. Newspapers all over the country reported on Boomer activities. Stories also described the beauty and soil fertility of the Oklahoma District in exaggerated terms. This publicity helped Western congressmen who wanted the Indian Territory opened to settlement.

The first Boomer victory in Washington, D.C. came in 1885. Congress paid the Creeks and

TOWNSHIP NUMBERING SYSTEM

-------------------- 6 miles --------------------

6	5	4	3	2	1
7	8	9	10	11	12
18	17	16	15	14	13
19	20	21	22	23	24
30	29	28	27	26	25
31	32	33	34	35	36

(left margin: 6 miles)

A township contains 36 sections.

A SECTION IS A SQUARE MILE

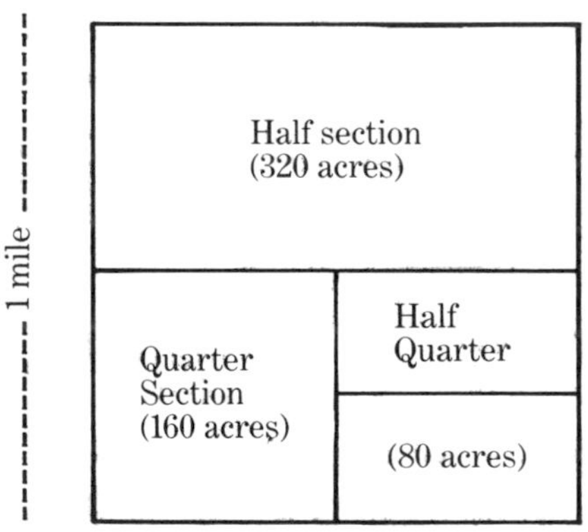

------------ 1 mile -----------

(left margin: 1 mile)

Half section (320 acres)	
Quarter Section (160 acres)	Half Quarter
	(80 acres)

Each section contains 640 acres
which can be subdivided.

Seminoles for their claims to the Unassigned Lands which they owned before the Civil War. Pleasant Porter of the Creeks and John F. Brown of the Seminoles agreed to a price of $1.25 an acre for their claims. The lands then became a part of the public domain.

2. THE FIRST GREAT LAND OPENING IN OKLAHOMA WAS IN 1889.

President Benjamin Harrison announced that the Oklahoma District would be opened for settlement at 12 o'clock noon, April 22, 1889.

Survey. The land area to be settled was located in central Oklahoma. It was about fifty miles long from north to south and thirty miles wide from east to west. It had been divided into *townships* six miles square when most of the Indian Territory was surveyed in the 1870s.

Each square mile *section* of 640 acres was split into *quarter sections* containing 160 acres. The corners were marked by stones or dirt mounds. Sections 16 and 36 in each township were reserved for the benefit of public schools.

Rules for the 1889 land run. The Oklahoma District was opened to settlers on a first-come, first-served basis. Homeseekers were to start at the same time from the district's borders.

A man or woman twenty-one years of age could stake a claim to 160 acres if he/she didn't own that much land elsewhere. A small fee was paid to register the homestead at a land office. A deed to the free land was granted after five years of continuous residence.

Townsites in the Oklahoma District were limited to 320 acres. Land offices were located at two of these places. Guthrie was on the Santa Fe railroad. Kingfisher was a stage stop on the Chisholm Trail.

April 22, 1889! By the morning of the land run, at least fifty thousand homeseekers were massed along the borders of the Oklahoma District. The largest number were along the northern line. They crosssed the Cherokee Outlet from Kansas to get there. The southern line was along the Canadian River.

Every kind of horse, wagon, and buggy was pressed into use. Some people even lined up on foot or on a bicycle. Fifteen crowded trains from Arkansas City, Kansas waited with full steam at the northern line. Other trains were ready to chug north from Purcell on the Canadian.

Exactly at 12 o'clock noon, army buglers sounded the signal. Soldiers fired their carbines.

The 1889 land run begins! (Part of mural at State Capitol by Charles Banks Wilson)

The cannons boomed. The mad race was on. Wild yells, thundering hoofs, and clattering wheels echoed over hills and plains. Ear-piercing blasts from the train whistles added excitement. Many people coming from the south waited in line at fords on the Canadian River. They risked quicksands at some places to get across the river.

The most successful racers had picked out a quarter section or town lot in advance. They knew the quickest route to get there. All the good farm land and town lots were settled the first day. More than nine thousand homestead farms were occupied.

Most of the newcomers, however, were attracted to towns that sprang to life on the day of the run. Born grown were Oklahoma City, Edmond, Guthrie, Kingfisher, and Norman. Within a

few weeks, Stillwater, El Reno, and other towns were also laid out in central Oklahoma.

Many of the best quarter sections or lots had more than one claimant. Disputes were sometimes settled on the spot with a coin flip. Another solution was to divide the tract. Unfortunately, a few people resorted to bloodshed to get a claim.

Sooners. Not everyone followed the rules. *Sooners* were people who sneaked in before the land run officially started. They hid in wooded areas or ravines. On April 22, the Sooners came out of hiding and boldly staked claims where they pleased. At first, the Sooners were called "Moonshiners" because they slipped in early by the light of the moon.

There are many Sooner stories. One is told about two legal riders who raced ahead of the mob to the land they wanted. To their disgust, however, they found a Sooner already living there. He was plowing the sod behind a yoke of oxen. A new garden had onions several inches high. The Sooner explained that his oxen were the fastest animals in the world. The soil was so rich, he said, that the onions sprouted a few minutes after planting. The tired riders were not amused.

Sooners, of course, risked a prison term for *perjury*. When filing a claim at a land office, homesteaders had to swear they did not enter the land run area before starting time.

Today the word "Sooner" has lost its original evil meaning. Oklahomans now accept the name with pride. They would sooner be here than anywhere else. The success of the University of Oklahoma Sooners on the football field also helped to make the term popular.

3. IN THE OKLAHOMA DISTRICT, TOWNS DEVELOPED BEFORE THE FARMS.

Oklahoma came into being with a bang. Several towns sprang into existence almost immediately in 1889. There was no "growing up" process.

By contrast, towns in other states usually grew slowly. They often began with a general store at a country crossroads.

Oklahoma City in 1889. (Oklahoma City Chamber of Commerce)

Guthrie. Before the 1889 land run, Guthrie was a little station house on the Santa Fe railroad. An estimated fifteen thousand people arrived on the day of the run. Several hundred Sooners were already there. They laid out a town and claimed the best lots.

Limited by law to a 320-acre townsite, Guthrie was soon fully occupied. By nightfall, three other townsites were also filled by late arrivals. These towns were named East Guthrie, Capitol Hill, and West Guthrie.

The towns were a beehive of activity. Merchants displayed goods in the backs of wagons. Peddlers sold muddy water from Cottonwood Creek by the dipper. Doctors and lawyers raised flimsy tents and hung out their shingles. Carpenters nailed together false front stores from pre-cut lumber. Families put up tents or built lean-to shacks with branches and brush. Thirsty teamsters stopped by open-air saloons for a cup of washtub gin. Long lines formed at the land office.

Clever people found interesting ways to make a living. A blacksmith with no business became a dentist. He advertised by stringing tooth extractions, like popcorn, and hanging them on the front of his tent. Three other men pooled their money, $8.31, and opened a bank. Some pioneers who came to Guthrie by wagon went into the freighting business.

"Button Mary" was up at sunrise with threaded needle in hand and her carpenter's apron bulging with buttons. When Mary found a man with a missing button she sewed one on. She charged a dime for the repair. Customers who didn't pay remembered the jab of her needle.

A man named Henry Ives dug a deep hole in his lot, surrounded it with foliage, and put up a sign: "Rest Room, 10 cents." The price was lowered to a nickel when rivals got the same idea. Ives made enough money from this enterprise to open a harness repair shop.

Not everyone was able to adjust to the new towns. A day after the run, trains were full of passengers returning home. Some people didn't get the lot or homestead they wanted. Others were discouraged by the ankle-deep red dust, the high price of food, and the lack of water. By 1890, the population of Guthrie was 5,883. By comparison, Oklahoma City had only 4,151 people at the time.

Oklahoma City. On the morning of April 22, 1889, the site of present Oklahoma City consisted of a Santa Fe railway depot, a water tank, and a few shacks. By sundown, it was a bustling tent city with at least ten thousand new residents.

As in Guthrie, the first town settlers were Sooners. A moment after 12 o'clock, members of the Seminole Land and Improvement Company of

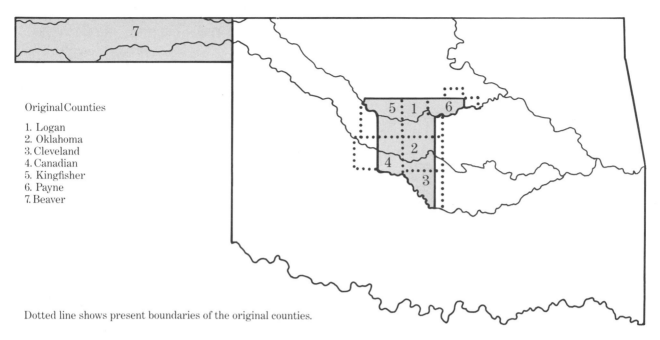

Original Counties

1. Logan
2. Oklahoma
3. Cleveland
4. Canadian
5. Kingfisher
6. Payne
7. Beaver

Dotted line shows present boundaries of the original counties.

Counties of the Territory of Oklahoma, 1890

Topeka, Kansas stepped from the railroad right-of-way. They immediately began surveying a townsite. The railroad tracks, which did not run true north and south, were used as a guide for the survey. Blocks and lots were staked out north of Main Street. This street was perpendicular to the railroad and hence did not run true west and east.

The first legal settlers were organized in Colony, Kansas as the Oklahoma Town Company. The Colony people raced to the site of present Oklahoma City in light, one-horse buggies from a point on the Canadian River west of Purcell. They arrived after one o'clock and were naturally surprised to see a town survey already underway.

The Colony company went ahead with a survey south of the Seminole Company's townsite. They surveyed Reno Avenue, the first true east-west street in Oklahoma City. A compromise had to be worked out when the Colony surveyors were stopped by armed Seminole Company men at Main Street. The two groups agreed that north-south streets would jog between Main and Grand. Blocks between these streets were not square.

Norman. The original townsite of Norman, like Oklahoma City, did not follow the true com-pass directions. Surveyed by railroad civil engineers, it is known as "Santa Fe Norman" today. Streets in this older section of town now bend into the true north-south and east-west streets in the outlying areas.

The Santa Fe surveyors were at work when the first land run train arrived at the Norman switch station from Purcell. They left peacefully, however, after members of a legal townsite company stepped off the train.

Tom R. Waggoner, formerly a chief clerk for the Santa Fe railroad at Purcell, was elected mayor of Norman. Waggoner later served in the territorial legislature at Guthrie. His main achievement was to get the University of Oklahoma for Norman.

4. THE OKLAHOMA DISTRICT HAD NO OFFICIAL GOVERNMENT UNTIL THE TERRITORY OF OKLAHOMA WAS CREATED IN 1890.

Congress neglected to provide any kind of government for the Oklahoma District. Nothing was done to correct this oversight for more than a year. The only authorities at first were the United States marshals and federal troops.

Bill Tilghman. (OHS)

The *Organic Act* combined the Panhandle and the Oklahoma District to make up the Territory of Oklahoma. The law provided for both territorial and local government. Guthrie was designated the territorial capital. There were to be seven counties. The counties were later named Oklahoma, Canadian, Cleveland, Kingfisher, Logan, Payne, and Beaver (all of the Panhandle then).

5. THE TERRITORY OF OKLAHOMA WAS GRADUALLY INCREASED IN SIZE.

The Dawes Act of 1887. This act paved the way for settlement of many surplus Indian lands. It provided for the *allotment* of reservation lands in *severalty*. What does that mean?

Tribal ownership of reservations would end. Each Native American family would get a 160-acre farm and learn to live like white farmers. Native Americans, however, were not permitted to sell or lease their lands for twenty-five years. Most of them, especially the full bloods, were opposed to the Dawes Act. They were not ready to become independent farmers.

At first, the Dawes Act did not apply to the Five Civilized Tribes and the Osages in what is now eastern Oklahoma. Several smaller tribes in northeastern Indian Territory were also exempted.

Jerome Commission. In 1889, the President appointed a three-member commission to talk to tribes in what is now western Oklahoma.

Named after its chairman, David H. Jerome, this commission signed agreements with most of the tribes living west of the Five Civilized Tribes. The western tribes agreed to take allotments. They gave up their surplus reservation lands to the United States for settlement.

Run! Run! Run! Run! During the years 1891 to 1895, four runs were authorized on surplus reservation lands in western Oklahoma.

On September 22, 1891, about twenty thousand people raced to claim some seven thousand quarter sections east of Oklahoma City. Surplus Iowa, Sac and Fox, and Shawnee-Pottawatomie lands were occupied in one afternoon. Town lots at Tecumseh and Chandler also were staked and claimed. Lawman Bill Tilghman took part in the

No counties existed the first year. There were no laws, no sheriff, no taxes, no roads, and no public schools.

Chaos in the Oklahoma City government. Strong leaders in the towns set up temporary governments. In Oklahoma City, a mayor, council, and other officers were elected in May, 1889. Controlled by the Seminole Land Company, the council passed ordinances (laws) to "legalize" the claims of company members to town lots. The *"Seminole"* mayor was William L. Couch, former Boomer leader.

Members of the Colony company opposed the Couch government which called them "Kickers." The Colony people changed this label to *"Kickapoos."* In November, the Kickapoos elected Dr. J. A. Beale as mayor. Beale angered the Seminoles by removing two of their councilmen. The city was on the verge of a civil war when United States Marshal R. A. Walker of Kansas stepped in. He and his deputies took over the temporary government of Oklahoma City. They were assisted by federal troops.

Organic Act. Finally, Congress passed the Organic Act. President Harrison signed this bill on May 2, 1890. This date is celebrated each year on Land Pioneer Day in Guymon.

Iowa, Sac and Fox run. He was a former buffalo hunter, Dodge City marshal, and deputy U.S. marshal. Tilghman was to serve as Lincoln County sheriff. Chandler's city park is named after him.

On April 19, 1892, surplus Cheyenne-Arapaho reservation lands were opened. About twenty-five thousand people raced to the best farm land. Six new counties were added to the Territory of Oklahoma from the Cheyenne-Arapaho reservation. They were Blaine, Custer, Day, Dewey, Roger Mills, and Washita. Day County was later abolished.

Cherokee Outlet Run. September 16, 1893! The *Cherokee Outlet,* as well as some surplus Pawnee and Tonkawa lands, were opened for settlement—about six million acres in all. An estimated 100,000 men, women, and children made the run for farms and town lots.

Not all the forty thousand quarter sections were settled immediately. Some land in the western part of the Outlet went unclaimed for several years. The soil there was thin and the rainfall uncertain.

Four sections in each township were reserved—two for the benefit of public schools, one for higher education, and one for public buildings.

The Cherokee Outlet's dramatic opening was one of the greatest events in Oklahoma history. It is commemorated by annual "Cherokee Strip Celebrations," museums, and restored old buildings in towns like Perry.

One of Oklahoma's instant cities, Perry grew from a station agent's house to a tented city of many thousand people by sundown. Water was scarce, so the Blue Bell, Hell's Half Acre, and a hundred other saloons did a big business.

Fred E. Sutton was the first settler at Perry. Before the race he went to Oklahoma City and bought a white mustang that had never been saddled or ridden. Sutton broke the horse and raced him eighteen miles a day at full speed for two weeks. He then stood in line for forty-eight hours to register for the land run. Sutton stayed awake the night before the race because thieves were looking for good mounts to steal.

At 12 o'clock noon, Sutton darted from the northern boundary of the Cherokee Outlet. He was crowded into the middle of an old freight wagon trail. In the left rut was a big, burly man wearing a six-shooter and mounted on a beautiful paint pony. To Sutton's right was an 18-year-old woman dressed in black tights and riding a coal black racehorse. After a few miles, Sutton's mustang surged ahead of the pack.

Both Sutton and his horse were singed by a grass fire set by Sooners. Sutton bought two pints of water for two dollars from one Sooner. The man who sold it to him pointed his gun and said, "This is my land, and the sooner you are off of it the longer you will live."

A few hundred yards from his goal, Sutton came to a deep gully about ten feet wide. The tired mustang tried to leap over but broke both loins and could not move his hind parts. Sutton ran the rest of the way on foot to claim the first town lot in Wharton which was later renamed Perry.

"I stuck my flag and ran to the land office and made my filing," he said, "after which I watched Wharton grow from a station agent's house to a tented city of 10,000 people in six hours."

Many badmen drifted into Perry. A good law officer was needed to control them. Bill Tilghman was hired for that purpose. Tilghman's chief assets were a pleasant smile, a cheery voice, a sawed-off Winchester, a pair of silver-mounted 45s, and a fast draw.

More lands added to the Territory of Oklahoma. The smallest and last run in Oklahoma was the Kickapoo opening in 1895. The Kickapoo lands were added to Lincoln County.

Greer County. In 1896, the United States Supreme Court decided that the South Fork of the Red River, not the North Fork, was the northern boundary of Texas. The next year, Congress attached Greer County, the land between the forks, to the Territory of Oklahoma.

Residents of Greer County were allowed to file a homestead claim to 160 acres. They could buy another quarter section for one dollar an acre. The rest of the county was opened to homesteaders, but the land was occupied gradually.

Some reservation lands were opened by lottery. The next land addition to the Territory of Oklahoma came in 1901. Surplus lands on the Wichita-Caddo and the Kiowa-Comanche-Apache reservations were opened to settlement by *lottery*.

Each tribal member was allotted 160 acres. In addition, four pastures containing 480,000 acres were set aside for the common use of tribes. Most of this land was in "Big Pasture" south of Lawton.

As in the Cherokee Outlet, four sections in each township were set aside for schools and public buildings. The Fort Sill Military Reservation and the Wichita Mountain Forest Reserve were also withdrawn from settlement.

The remaining land, thirteen thousand quarter sections, was opened to homesteaders by lottery. Nearly 170,000 people registered for the drawing. Winners filed for claims in the order in which their names were drawn from two huge boxes.

Most of the new lands were organized into three counties: Caddo, Comanche, and Kiowa. The towns of Anadarko, Lawton, and Hobart were chosen as county seats. These cities came into existence in almost a day. Lots were surveyed at the townsites and sold at auction for cash. The auction money was used to help the new county governments build roads, bridges, and courthouses.

Pasture lands sold. In 1906, President Theodore Roosevelt signed a bill to open the pasture lands. Allotments were first made to Kiowa, Comanche, Wichita, and Caddo children born after the 1901 land lottery. The remaining land was sold to the highest bidders among qualified homesteaders. About five million dollars was raised for the benefit of the tribes who owned the lands.

Osage and other reservations. The remaining Native Americans west of the Five Civilized Tribes agreed to give up their reservations. Members of each tribe divided their lands. These areas were then added to counties in the Territory of Oklahoma.

The Ponca, Otoe-Missouri, and Kaw (Kansas) reservations were allotted by 1904.

Two years later, Congress passed the Osage Allotment Act. The Osages were not limited to 160 acres each. Every tribal member got approximately 657 acres—three 160 acre tracts plus an equal share of the remaining lands.

Congress also permitted the Osages to keep sub-soil mineral rights for the benefit of the whole tribe. The discovery of oil brought great wealth to the Osages.

Expansion of the Territory of Oklahoma. In less than two decades, the Territory of Oklahoma had expanded to include all of the western and north-central parts of the present state. In 1907, this territory would be combined with the Indian Territory (then the eastern past of the present state) to form the State of Oklahoma.

ROUNDUP

1. Identify: Elias C. Boudinot, Unassigned Lands, Boomers, and David L. Payne.
2. Near which rivers did Payne and Crouch try to start colonies? Why were the Boomer colonies short-lived? How did Congress clear the way for the first land run?
3. When was the first land run in Oklahoma? List the rules of the land run. In which two cities did people board trains for the land run?
4. Who were the "Sooners?" What is a more popular meaning of the word today?
5. Briefly describe Guthrie or Oklahoma City in 1889.
6. Who were the "Seminole" and "Kickapoo" groups in Oklahoma City?
7. List the main provisions of the Organic Act.
8. Explain how the Dawes Act of 1887 resulted in the breakup of the Indian reservations and nations.
9. List the land runs between 1891 and 1895 and the later land lotteries.
10. How did Greer County become part of Oklahoma?
11. In what ways did the Osage Allotment Act differ from the Dawes Act?
A. Think about it! "The Run of 1889 into Oklahoma lands was one of the most unique social phenomenons of American history." Give data that supports this conclusion. (For further reading, see Stan Hoig's book that is listed in the appendix.)

14

TERRITORY OF OKLAHOMA, 1890–1907: PIONEER LIFE

Between the land run of 1889 and statehood in 1907, homeseekers changed the appearance of western and central Oklahoma. The wilderness was turned into a checkerboard of farms and ranches. Pioneer homes dotted the landscape. The first houses were built from the materials at hand—usually logs or sod.

The early years were hard times. Drought worked against the settlers when they desperately needed cash crops. Hundreds of discouraged people left their homesteads. Survivors struggled to exist. Then came rains, good crops, and better times. Farmers built new frame houses and barns. They traded at dozens of small towns that sprung up along the railroads and trails.

The sod house frontier of western Oklahoma had organized government beginning in 1890. Congress passed the Organic Act that year. This law established the *Territory of Oklahoma* with the capital at Guthrie. As Indian reservations were opened to settlement, new counties were created. The county brought government closer to the farming areas and small towns.

The eastern part of present Oklahoma was still called *Indian Territory*. This area was occupied by the Five Civilized Tribes and some smaller tribes in the northeast corner. In a strict sense, the Indian Territory was not a *territory*. It did not have territorial government with a governor and legislature. Each tribe was self-governing with chiefs and a council.

1. PIONEER SETTLERS IN OKLAHOMA STRUGGLED TO PROVIDE THEIR FAMILIES WITH FOOD, SHELTER, CLOTHING, WATER, AND FUEL.

Food. Most '89ers arrived too late to plant crops the first year. They usually had some *staples*—flour, dried beans, sugar, and Arbuckle coffee—to tide them over for awhile. Their cows, pigs, and chickens provided food.

Families gathered wild fruits. The wild sand plum made good pies, jellies, and canned fruit. Some plums were spread on flour sacks in the sun and dried for winter use. The pioneers also shot wild game for food.

When meat supplies ran low, there was gravy made from bacon grease, flour, salt, and milk or water. Women made yeast to leaven dough for homemade bread. Bread pudding with raisins was a special treat. Butter was churned from cream. As soon as they could, the settlers planted gardens and canned the vegetables for winter.

Gradually, general stores opened at central locations in rural areas. They sold staple foods in bulk from barrels or boxes. Dried fruit was a popular item. Everybody came to the corner store to buy groceries, pick up mail, and hear the latest local gossip.

Shelter. Housing was an immediate concern to early settlers. They lived in tents or covered wagons until permanent houses were built.

In wooded areas, pioneers put up log cabins. Logs were sometimes split into boards to shingle the roof. On the plains, where few trees were found, the *dugout* or *sod house* (soddy) were more common. All these houses showed how Oklahoma's pioneers adapted to a new land.

The dugout house was a covered hole in the ground. Some were dug into a hillside. The roof was made of cottonwood or hackberry logs topped with straw or sod. A dugout variation had sod walls above a three or four foot excavation. The walls usually measured twelve to eighteen feet in length. Some pioneers plastered the interior

A dugout along the banks of the Canadian River. (Harper's Weekly)

Pioneer Woman statue in Ponca City. Governor Holloway spoke at the dedication in 1930.

walls. They used gypsum mud, a clay and ashes mixture, or a lime and sand mortar. Many of these prairie shelters were built without a square, plumb, nail, or money.

Dugouts were cool in summer and warm in winter. But there were drawbacks. Floors were hard-packed dirt. Fleas, chiggers, bedbugs, flies, centipedes, mosquitos, and snakes were uninvited visitors. Some of the mosquitoes spread malaria or sleeping sickness. Rats burrowed into the walls. When it rained, water poured down the rat tunnels. Mud and water often dripped through the roof.

Sod houses were built above ground with blocks of sod held together by long buffalo grass roots. Sticky clay mud was used between the foot-wide blocks. If the sod house had a gable roof, a ridge pole in the center supported poles or lumber covered with tar paper and sod. Corn flowers or weeds often grew on the roof.

"My Little Old Shanty" was a popular song in those days. The chorus went like this:

"Oh, the hinges are of leather, and the windows have no glass,

The boards, they let the howling blizzard in,

You can hear the hungry coyote as he sneaks up through the grass

To my little old sod shanty on the claim."

At best, the early houses were dark, crowded, and poorly ventilated. Pioneer women did their best to make their homes comfortable. They braided carpets from rags and pasted newspapers on the walls. Furniture was simple—a stove, a table, a few stiff chairs, and a couple of bedsteads or homemade bunks. Every home had a wash stand with a large pail of water, a tin dipper or gourd, and a wash basin. Mattresses were straw-filled ticks. Lighting came from candles or kerosene lamps. Flowers planted in old coffee cans added a decorative touch.

An original sod house is preserved north of Cleo Springs. Open to visitors, it is a two-room soddy built by a homesteader in 1894.

Clothing. Most settlers had very plain clothes. Women made their own floor-length, full-skirted, long-sleeved blue calico dresses. They wore high top shoes, cotton stockings, and a calico sunbonnet outdoors.

Children were often seen in oversized garments handed down from older brothers and sisters. Men wore overalls, a *flannel* shirt, and a wide-brimmed hat. Most clothes were loaded with patches.

Water. Good drinking water was scarce on the plains. Homesteaders dug wells of the "old oaken bucket" type. A bucket was fastened to each end of a rope that was pulled through a pulley. Water in some areas was undrinkable because of gypsum or other minerals. Many pioneers had to depend on cisterns to catch rainwater. During dry spells, water was hauled in barrels by wagon from the closest stream.

Invention of the windmill was a godsend to plains farmers. The ever-present wind was harnessed to pump water. Whirring blades and a noisy pump shaft broke the monotony of stillness in wide-open spaces.

Fuel. Some areas had plenty of wood to burn. Settlers on the plains, however, used dried buffalo and cow chips for fuel. These chips were called *prairie coal.* They burned quickly, made a lot of smoke, and left a bulky ash. But the chips made a hot fire, had no odor, and left no soot. They kept a sod house warm if the winter was mild. Pioneers cooked their food on chip fires.

Beaver, Oklahoma is known as the "Cow Chip Capital of the World." Pioneers are honored by the annual Cimarron Territory Celebration. A featured event is the cow chip throwing contest. The origin of this "Organic Olympics" goes back to the early days. Children were sent out to gather chips. They made the job fun by seeing who could stand the farthest away from the wagon and still toss the chip in the bed.

Some settlers also burned corn cobs, sunflower stalks, or twisted strands of hay.

2. FARM LIFE WAS A LOT OF WORK AND SOME PLAY.

Farm chores. All members of a farm family shared in doing the daily *chores* and seasonal work.

Milking cows was a chore that young people could do. It was not a fun job. Hungry calves had to be dragged away. At "fly-time" the cows constantly switched their tails and stamped their feet. In cold weather the milker's hands got numb. Nothing was more exasperating than to have a cow kick over a bucketful of foamy white milk.

Farm animals had to be fed and watered. Carrying water in buckets from a well to troughs was a wearisome chore.

Few people enjoyed the task of *churning* butter. The churner pushed a heavy *dasher* up and down in soured cream until butter fat clung together in a mass. The dasher was a round stick fastened to crossed pieces of wood. Sometimes a churner made the dasher beat time to songs so time would go faster.

Children in some areas chopped cotton to thin the stalks and cut weeds. Picking cotton by hand was another hard job. The picker's hands got rough and sore. He or she also dragged a heavy sack of cotton day after day. That was a drudgery.

Farm girls helped their mothers prepare large amounts of food for wheat threshing crews. Children also gathered vegetables, some to be canned for winter use.

These jobs and many other farm chores helped young people develop character and self-reliance.

Social Activities. Early settlers welcomed social contact. Neighbors and friends got together for chicken dinners, watermelon feasts, and visiting. Sunday schools were started in homes and in schoolhouses. An itinerant preacher on horseback might come by to deliver a sermon. He also married young couples and visited the sick. The preacher often spent the night in a settler's home.

The rural schoolhouse was the center of many social activities. Group singing and music by fiddle, banjo, and guitar players attracted a crowd. Spelling bees, recitations, plays, and debates were sometimes on the program at the one-room school.

Square dances were popular in pioneer days. Fiddlers played such tunes as "Turkey in the Straw," "Cotton-eyed Joe," "Golden Slippers," and "Arkansas Traveler." Many church people did not approve of dancing, but took part in other social events.

Box suppers were held to raise money for

Time out! Pioneer farmers worked hard.

community Christmas parties and for other purposes. Each box was auctioned to the highest bidder. A man usually found out which box was brought by his favorite lady. He tried to outbid rivals so he could eat supper with her. Money was also raised by ice cream socials and cakewalks.

3. PIONEER FARMERS WENT THROUGH A CYCLE OF HARD TIMES AND GOOD TIMES.

The drought of 1890 was severe. The year started with frequent rains. "I never saw such prospects for a good harvest," said a farmer near Ingalls east of Stillwater. Then April and May went by without a drop of rain. Green fields turned brown. Hundreds of homesteaders, their hopes shattered, loaded their wagons and left Oklahoma.

Relief for those who stayed came in several forms. Congress voted funds to provide food for the needy. Boxcars filled with flour, cornmeal, and cured meat were shipped to Oklahoma and distributed by local boards. Many people were too proud to accept this charity. But farmers were happy to get wheat seed at cost and on credit from the Santa Fe and Rock Island railroads.

Year of the turnip. Rains came in September. Many farmers planted turnips. This root crop could be raised before the first frost. Tons of turnips, some as big as wash pans, were harvested. Turnips were served three times a day. Farm wives did their best to make them tasty. Turnips were also fed to cows, chickens, and hogs. Oldtimers said that milk, eggs, and pork tasted like turnips.

The story is told about the experience of a cowboy who rode into Perkins for a weekend fling. He stopped at the saloon and then went to a local restaurant. Finding only turnips listed on the menu, he left in disgust. Before bedtime he went by the livery barn to check on his horse. The animal was snorting and swinging his head up and down over a feed box full of raw turnips.

"Dagnab it, Red," the cowboy said to his horse, "they can feed me them things, but they are not going to make you eat them." He saddled up and rode fifteen miles back to the ranch in the dark.

Good times finally came. Drought gripped the plains for awhile. Year after year, farmers went into debt to plant cash crops, especially wheat, cotton, and corn. Farm families struggled to survive. Then the rains came.

One farmer near Blackwell, who had three bad years before his first good wheat harvest in 1897, said, "I paid my debts, bought the family much needed wearing apparel, bought lumber and built two rooms to my house and many other things, including five head of cows and twenty calves...From that time on I always raised plenty."

4. THE MAIN CASH CROPS IN THE OKLAHOMA TERRITORY WERE WHEAT, COTTON, AND CORN.

Wheat. By 1900, the Territory of Oklahoma was producing twenty million bushels of wheat a year on a million and a half acres. Garfield and Kay counties were the biggest producers. The Miller 101 Ranch alone had five thousand acres in wheat. At harvest time, Miller's two dozen *self-*

A frame house, new buggy, and wheat shocks were signs of prosperity for this farm family in the Cherokee Outlet. (W. S. Prettyman photo)

binders, each pulled by three to five horses, cut a swath 150 feet wide.

Cotton. A few acres of cotton were planted in Cleveland and Canadian counties shortly after the 1889 land rush. Cotton quickly emerged as an important cash crop. Merchants in Ardmore, El Reno, and other towns encouraged cotton production. Prizes were offered for the first bale of the season and the largest load delivered to a gin.

Experts at the Oklahoma Agricultural Experiment Station near Guthrie gave advice on how to cultivate cotton and the best varieties to plant. In 1900, Alfred Smith, a black farmer near Oklahoma City, won first and second prizes for his cotton at the Paris Exposition.

By the time of statehood the Territory of Oklahoma had about three hundred cotton gins. Cotton was shipped to textile factories in New England, western Europe, and Japan.

Corn. Most farmers in the Oklahoma Territory planted some corn. About a third of all farm acreage was in corn fields at the time of statehood in 1907.

5. TOWNS IN THE TERRITORY OF OKLAHOMA DEPENDED ON AGRICULTURE.

Some cities and towns in Oklahoma were born "full grown." Guthrie, Oklahoma City, Lawton, Hobart, and Perry were instant cities. These and other urban places grew up after western Oklahoma was opened to white settlement.

Each town has its own interesting local history. In some ways, however, the early settlements in the Territory of Oklahoma were much alike. They were farming communities. Many were located on a railroad.

Residential area. In pioneer days, life was simpler than it is today. People were more self-sufficient. Town lots were large enough for a barn to shelter a cow and horses, a chicken house, fruit trees, and a garden. Water came from a hand-dug well or cistern, or from a town pump in the business district. Coal oil lamps provided lighting. Bread was baked at home.

Business district. Every town had a small business district. At first most of the stores were in tents or wood frame buildings. The general store sold groceries, hardware, cloth, and almost anything a family needed. The post office might be in one corner.

The first specialized stores sometimes had more than one line of goods. The furniture dealer often sold caskets as a sideline and doubled as the undertaker. William C. Grimes, a Republican Party leader in territorial days, ran this type of business in Kingfisher.

At least one saloon was usually located in towns of the Oklahoma Territory. By law the saloons were open to view. People passing could see drunks at the huge oak or walnut-stained bar.

Country store at Curtis, early 1900s. (Part of mural by Paul Laune at Plains Indians and Pioneers Museum, Woodward)

115

Farm families came to town on Saturday to shop and socialize.

The strong odor of booze and tobacco was ever floating out to the street. The saloons were town loafing places and the headquarters for some politicians.

Other businesses might be a small hotel, a bank, or maybe a weekly newspaper. A flour mill or cotton gin could be seen in some towns. A wagon-yard provided a campground for travelers.

Saturday was a big business day. Farm families came to town. Their wagons were loaded with eggs, cream, homemade butter, garden produce, or grain. They sold these items and picked up "store bought" goods. The local blacksmith, barber, and doctor did more business than usual. After the farm families finished their trading and visiting, they returned home to do evening chores.

Schools and social life in the towns. Sunday was a day of rest. Stores were closed. Church services were held in the schoolhouse until churches were built. The preacher delivered "hell-fire and damnation" sermons. Relatives and friends got together on Sunday to feast and visit.

Most of the pioneers preferred religions that are informal in ritual and fellowship. The fundamentalist Baptist, Methodist, and various "Christian" denominations had the most believers. The Lutheran and Mennonite faiths were popular with German pioneers. The more formal Roman Catholic religion had several thousand followers. A small number of Jewish people also came here.

The schoolhouse was usually the first public building in a town. In the beginning, it was a one-room school where one teacher taught all subjects in all grades. The schoolhouse was also the town gathering place for entertainment and social life.

By the time of statehood, the Territory of Oklahoma had been divided into three thousand districts, but not all of them had schools. School terms were short, lasting only a few months, until the community became more prosperous.

European ethnic settlers. The population of Oklahoma Territory consisted mainly of American-born whites, Indian and black minorities, and foreign-born immigrants.

The Germans were the largest foreign group. About five thousand of them were Russian Germans. Their relatives had lived for a century in Russia before coming to America. The town of Korn (later Corn) in Washita County was a typical Russian German farming community. Even today, the Mennonite church, Corn Bible Academy, German supper fund raisers, and a grain elevator tell us much about the culture.

British immigrants (English, Scots, Welsh, and Irish) were the second largest in number. They scattered over the territory, assimilating quickly. On the other hand, about 2500 Czechs concentrated mainly in the Prague and Yukon areas. Americanized descendants of the Czech pioneers celebrate their heritage at annual Kolache festivals. These events, enjoyed by visitors too, feature colorful "old country" costumes, parades, street dancing, and kolache (fruit roll) eating. Catholics revere the small Infant Jesus of Prague statue. It was brought here after World War II when the Russians occupied Czechoslovakia.

Population contrast between territorial days and today. Oklahoma has changed gradually from a *rural* to an *urban* area. Less than four percent of the population in the Oklahoma Territory lived in town and cities in 1890.

The census of 1900 listed fifty-one *incorporated towns* and *cities* in the Territory of Oklahoma. The largest were Oklahoma City (10,037), Guthrie (10,006), Enid (3,444), El Reno (3,381), and Perry (3,351). All were railroad and agricultural centers.

Today, 70 percent of Oklahomans live in urban areas. Agriculture is still an important industry. Most cities now depend, however, on a diversified economy. Factories, tourism, and other industries provide jobs.

ROUNDUP

1. How did the Territory of Oklahoma differ from Indian Territory?
2. Explain the difference between a frontier general store and a modern specialized store.
3. What were advantages and disadvantages of a pioneer dugout? How were the homes usually furnished by pioneer women?
4. What problems did many pioneers face in providing water and fuel for their families?
5. Imagine you are a teenager on a farm in territorial days. List some of your possible chores.
6. List ten pioneer social activities.
7. What farm improvements did pioneers make when good times came?
8. Describe a typical town in the Territory of Oklahoma.
A. Think about it! Study a picture of the "Pioneer Woman Statue" in Ponca City. Describe how the sculpture caught the confidence, religious faith, a feeling of importance for the family and education, courage, practical dress style, and determined spirit of a pioneer woman.
B. Try this! Visit a museum, such as the Ponca City Pioneer Woman Museum, and do a report on the household furniture, equipment, costumes, and other memorabilia of pioneer family life.

15

TERRITORIAL GOVERNMENT: ROAD TO STATEHOOD

The *Organic Act* provided a plan of government for the Territory of Oklahoma. An *executive branch* was headed by the governor. He was appointed by the president. A secretary, attorney, United States marshal, and postmasters were also appointed.

The territorial *judicial branch* was headed by a supreme court. The justices, three of them at first, were appointed by the president. The supreme court heard cases at Guthrie. Each of the judges also presided alone over a lower district court. The number of justices was increased to five in 1893 and seven in 1902.

The *legislative branch* consisted of two elected houses: the Council and the House of Representatives.

People in the territory were given no voice in national elections except to choose a *delegate to Congress* every two years. He represented the territory in Washington, D.C. The delegate could speak in the United States House of Representatives, but he had no vote. A Republican was elected at every election except 1896.

A large number of people in the Territory of Oklahoma tended to vote Republican. This party was popular in the West because it was responsible for passing the Homestead Act and the Free Homes Bill.

County elections were usually divided between the parties. Northern counties generally elected Republicans. The southern part of the territory was more Democratic. A small third party, the *Populists,* sometimes held the balance of power.

1. GEORGE WASHINGTON STEELE, THE FIRST TERRITORIAL GOVERNOR, DID A GOOD JOB BUT WAS CALLED A CARPETBAGGER.

George Washington Steele (1890–1891). The first governor was a lawyer and former congressman from Indiana. He was *appointed* by his friend, President Benjamin Harrison. Steele, like several other governors of the Territory of Oklahoma, had been an officer in the Union Army during the Civil War.

Governor Steele arrived at Guthrie, the capital, by train in May, 1890. He went to work at the governor's office above Moses Weinberger's saloon. One of his first jobs was to define the boundaries for the original seven counties. Only the county seats were named in the Organic Act. Steele also appointed the first county officers.

The governor then ordered that a census be taken. The population count was 60,417 in the seven counties. *Legislative districts* were then marked on the map. Steele set August 5 as the date for Oklahoma Territory's first election to choose legislators.

The housing of Oklahoma's convicted criminals was one of the first problems faced by Governor Steele. He signed a contract with Kansas officials to keep the prisoners at the penitentiary in Lansing, Kansas. Some of the convicts later worked in coal mines there to earn their keep.

First territorial legislature. Two elective houses made up the *Legislative Assembly.* The Council had thirteen members. The House of Representatives had twenty-six.

The first legislature met at Guthrie in late August, 1890. Most of the 120-day *session* was spent on the location of institutions and attempts to remove the *capital.* The work of putting together a code of laws was delayed until the last few days of the session.

George W. Steele, 1890-1891

Abram J. Seay, 1892-1893

William C. Renfrow, 1893-1897

Cassius M. Barnes, 1897-1901

William M. Jenkins, 1901

Thompson B. Ferguson, 1901-1906

Frank Frantz, 1906-1907

Every legislator was a booster for his district. He wanted to take home a college or some other institution to create jobs and business. When the smoke-filled rooms were cleared, Norman had the University of Oklahoma. Stillwater got an agricultural mechanical college that is now named Oklahoma State University. Edmond was given a teacher training college known today as Central Oklahoma State University.

The capital was considered the biggest prize. A representative from Oklahoma City got a bill passed to remove the capital there. He barely escaped a Guthrie lynch mob by hiding in the back of a butcher shop. Governor Steele refused to sign the capital removal bill. He also vetoed a second bill to make Kingfisher the capital. The territorial capital stayed at Guthrie.

The first legislature defeated a *civil rights* bill by just one vote. The bill was introduced by Green I. Currin of Kingfisher County. Elected in 1890, Currin was the first black to serve in an Oklahoma legislature.

Governor Steele resigned. Not all was smooth sailing for Steele. He was called a *carpetbagger* for vetoing the capital removal bills. Why? Steele was an appointed governor and only a temporary resident of the territory. The legislators, on the other hand, were elected by the people and a majority of them voted to remove the capital. They thought that the governor, an outsider, was keeping the people from doing what they wanted.

Steele's last official duty as governor was to supervise a land opening in 1891. Surplus lands of the Iowa, Sac and Fox, and Shawnee-Pottawatomie tribes were settled. These reservations were divided into two new counties: Lincoln and Pottawatomie.

First building at Oklahoma A and M (now Oklahoma State University)

2. WILLIAM C. RENFROW WAS THE ONLY DEMOCRATIC TERRITORIAL GOVERNOR (1893–1897).

President Grover Cleveland, a Democrat, appointed Renfrow governor for two reasons. Renfrow voted for Cleveland at the *Democratic National Convention*. He also suggested the name Cleveland for his home county. Renfrow was a well-to-do businessman in Norman.

A Confederate Army veteran, Renfrow would not sign a civil rights bill passed by the legislature. This bill would have ended separate schools for black children in 1895. Two years later, Governor Renfrow signed a law that created Langston University. Edward P. McCabe, a black leader and former state auditor of Kansas, donated forty acres of land for the school.

Renfrow also approved the bill that started a teacher's college at Alva. This school is now Northwestern Oklahoma State University.

In November, 1891, Governor Steele resigned and left office. He returned to Indiana and was again elected to Congress. His *tenure* as governor in Oklahoma was just one more event in Steele's active political career.

Robert Martin, the territorial secretary, became acting *governor*. He served until the next governor was appointed in 1892.

Abraham J. Seay was promoted to governor (1892–1893). Seay (SHAY), a lifelong bachelor from Missouri, had served as a colonel in the Union Army. President Harrison appointed him to the first territorial supreme court. Seay held district court in Kingfisher.

While Seay was governor, the Cheyenne-Arapaho surplus lands were opened to settlement. He picked the first ten officers for each of the six new counties that were created. Seay is also remembered for his "seeds to the seedless" program. The legislature voted money to buy seed for farmers who were too poor to do spring planting in 1893.

After leaving office, Seay prospered in banking and real estate in Kingfisher. His three-story mansion there is now open to the public.

3 WILLIAM McKINLEY, A REPUBLICAN, APPOINTED TWO TERRITORIAL GOVERNORS FOR OKLAHOMA.

Cassius M. Barnes (1897–1901). While Barnes was governor, the Spanish-American War broke out in 1898. He had two sons in the war in Cuba. Other Oklahomans, especially cowboys, joined the Rough Riders, a cavalry unit.

Edward P. McCabe. (OHS)

The statehood question split the Republican Party and caused Barnes's removal from office. He headed a faction that wanted the "twin territories" united as one state. On the other side, Delegate to Congress Dennis T. Flynn from Guthrie led a group that favored separate statehood for the *Territory of Oklahoma.* Flynn said that union with *Indian Territory* "would make Oklahoma a southern state." It would be controlled by the Democratic Party, he said.

For the sake of party unity, President McKinley did not reappoint Barnes as governor.

McCabe's Black State Plan. Like Flynn, Edward P. McCabe also favored separate statehood. But his goal was a state under the control of black Republicans. Black voters, if they outnumbered the whites, could elect a majority in the legislature and send two Republican black U.S. senators to Washington, D.C. With this plan in mind, McCabe encouraged black people to migrate to the Oklahoma territory.

In the early 1890s, McCabe founded the all-black town of Langston. Soon, farmers were growing cotton successfully there. As we have seen, the legislature created a black college at Langston. The next step was to increase black migration to all parts of the territory. For years, McCabe and other black leaders advertised this area in their newspapers which were sent to southern states. They wrote about the rich soil and favorable climate in "a new land where you will be free to vote as you please."

Many blacks came here from the South and from states bordering the twin territories. The percentage of blacks did not increase much, however. The 1910 census showed that the blacks were only 8.3 percent of Oklahoma's population.

Meanwhile, the territorial Republican Party remained split over the statehood issue. As in the past, statehood bills of all kinds were introduced in Congress to no avail.

William M. Jenkins (1901). President McKinley promoted Secretary Jenkins to governor. Jenkins took a neutral stand in his inaugural speech. "I shall make no promises or

Dalton gang robbing a train at Wharton, now Perry, in 1891.

say anything which you might remember or I might forget," he said.

The most important event of the Jenkins administration was the settlement of more surplus lands. As you may recall, the Comanche-Kiowa-Apache and Wichita-Caddo lands were opened by lottery. Jenkins appointed the first officers for the new counties of Caddo, Comanche, and Kiowa.

Governor Jenkins was criticized for pardoning convicts. He also asked the governor of Kansas to pardon Emmett Dalton. This outlaw was serving a life sentence for his part in a bank robbery at Coffeyville, Kansas. Emmett and several of his brothers in the notorious Dalton gang had been law officers in the Indian Territory before taking up a life of crime.

4. PRESIDENT THEODORE ROOSEVELT CHOSE THE LAST TWO REPUBLICAN GOVERNORS.

Thompson B. "Honest Tom" Ferguson (1901–1906). Ferguson was an "Eighty-Niner." His claim was near Edmond. Later, he published the *Watonga Republican,* a popular weekly newspaper. He also served as postmaster in Watonga and was chairman of the territorial Republican Party.

Ferguson disliked social affairs. His inaugural ceremony in Guthrie was simple. Called a "country editor" by reporters, he often appeared in public dressed in a blue workshirt.

While Ferguson was governor, the legislature passed a *quarantine law* to protect Oklahoma cattle from Texas imports. A reformatory was created for juvenile offenders. Buildings at Fort Supply were used to start a mental hospital (now Western State Hospital).

Frank Frantz (1906–1907). Frantz was a Rough Rider during the Spanish-American War. One of his commanders was Colonel Theodore Roosevelt. When Roosevelt became president, he appointed Frantz to several jobs. Frantz was the postmaster at Enid, an agent to the Osages, and finally governor.

Frantz tried to be governor for all the people. His staff filed lawsuits that forced railroads to lower freight rates. He helped the Kiowas, Comanches, and Apaches when their "Big Pasture" lands were opened to settlement. He insisted that the lands be sold to the highest bidders. This plan brought more money to the tribes than a land run or lottery.

Frantz also fought to protect mineral rights on school lands for the use of schools. He testified in Washington, D.C. when Congress was considering a bill to take these rights away. He persuaded a Senate committee to drop the bill.

Governor Frantz worked for the fair treatment of blacks and Native Americans. One of his biggest battles was with the "Con-Con." That was a short name for the Oklahoma Constitutional Convention. This body met at Guthrie in 1906–1907. Frantz warned the delegates not to treat minority groups unfairly. President Roosevelt would not approve a constitution that discriminated against blacks and Native Americans, the Governor argued.

The convention delegates, however, provided for "separate but equal" schools for blacks. But no *"Jim Crow"* provisions that discriminate against blacks were put in the constitution. The delegates decided to let the first state legislature debate that issue.

Frantz was the Republican nominee for governor of the new state in 1907. He was defeated by Charles N. Haskell, the Democratic nominee. After leaving office, Frantz went into the oil business. In 1932, he was elected to the Oklahoma Hall of Fame.

ROUNDUP

1. List the officers in the Territory of Oklahoma who were appointed by the president.
2. Which officers were elected by the people?
3. Make a chart about the territorial governors. Use these column headings: Governors, Term, Appointed by, Achievements or Main Events.
A. Try this! The U.S. marshal was an important officer. Find out about Marshal William C. Grimes (who later served as territorial secretary and acting governor) or one of his famous deputies—Bill Tilghman, Heck Thomas, and Chris Madsen who were called the "three guardsmen"—or Bass Reeves, the most famous black lawman. These men and others kept busy chasing horsethieves, train robbers, and outlaws who terrorized the settlers. Why do you think some of the bad hombres, unfortunately, are better known than the marshals?

16

INDIAN TERRITORY: PREPARATION FOR STATEHOOD

Before Oklahoma became a state, it was divided into two territories. The Territory of Oklahoma and Indian Territory were about equal in size and population. In 1907, each had about 700,000 people.

The *twin territories* were different in geography and in other ways. Take government, for example. As we have seen, western Oklahoma had territorial government. By contrast, each tribe in Indian Territory had its own chiefs, council, and courts.

Land ownership was another major difference. In the Territory of Oklahoma, any individual could own a farm or town lot. Property deeds were recorded at the county courthouse. The owners paid taxes to support government and schools. In Indian Territory, however, all land was owned by the tribes.

The federal government gradually took away tribal control of Indian Territory. Congress ignored treaties that gave this area to the Five Civilized Tribes forever. The tribes were forced to allot the land to individual Indians. After awhile, non-Indians gained the right to buy land from the natives.

1. NON-INDIAN INTRUDERS RAPIDLY FILLED UP INDIAN TERRITORY.

Many non-Indian newcomers came to Indian Territory after railroads were built. Railroaders, merchants, coal miners, lumbermen, and cowboys drifted in. White and black tenant farmers tilled the soil. They built houses and barns on land they could not own legally.

By 1890, the whites greatly outnumbered the Native Americans and *black freedmen* (former slaves of the Indians).

Towns in Indian Territory. The newcomers built towns. Some of these places became important shipping centers for cattle, coal, lumber, and farm products.

White merchants built stores on lots owned by the tribes. The white residents had no way to *incorporate* a town in Indian Territory. Thus they could not levy taxes to provide schools, roads, and other services.

Courts, crime, and civil law in Indian Territory. The Five Civilized Tribes had courts for their own people. Until 1889, the closest court for white pioneers in Indian Territory was at Fort Smith, Arkansas.

Crime was a problem in Indian Territory. Outlaws ran loose in the rural areas and in some towns. Most ordinary criminals went unpunished. U.S. marshals and their posses kept busy hunting the worst robbers and killers. Many of these renegades were sentenced to death by Judge Isaac Parker, the "hanging judge" at Fort Smith. The notorious horsethief Belle Starr got off easier. She and her Cherokee second husband, Sam Starr, were given a year behind bars.

Civil law for non-Indians hardly existed in Indian Territory. The cost of suing someone in Fort Smith was expensive. There was no cheap way to collect a debt or to settle a property dispute except "to shoot it out."

Finally, in 1889, a United States Court was established in Muskogee. The first courtroom was an upstairs room above the Muskogee *Phoenix* newspaper office. Later, Ardmore and McAlester also were given federal courts.

2. THE DAWES COMMISSION PREPARED THE INDIAN TERRITORY FOR STATEHOOD.

Dawes Commission. In 1893, Congress created the "Commission to the Five Civilized

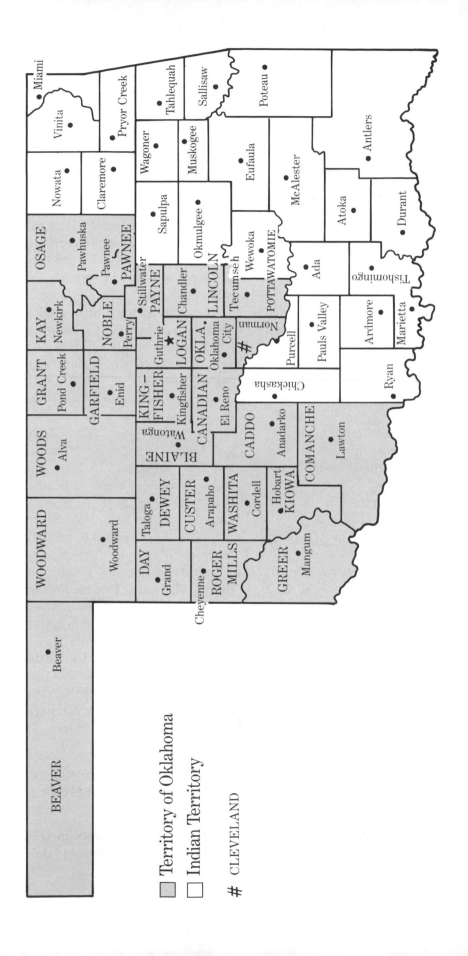

Territory of Oklahoma (Counties) and Indian Territory (Recording Districts), 1906

Territory of Oklahoma

Indian Territory

CLEVELAND

Judge Isaac Parker. (National Archives)

Tribes." This group was better known by the name of its chairman, Henry L. Dawes. He was a former U.S. senator from Massachusetts.

The purpose of the commission was to persuade each tribe to divide its land among tribal members. Each individual would receive his/her own allotment.

Congress ordered a survey of tribal lands. It also directed the Dawes Commission to compile a roll of citizens in each tribe. The survey and rolls would be used in making allotments.

Tribal rolls. More than 400,000 people claimed to be a member of the Five Civilized Tribes. Their claims were based on blood, marriage, or descent from former slaves of these tribes. About three-fourths of these applicants were rejected.

The commission enrolled 101,506 persons who could get allotments. By tribe there were 41,824 Cherokees; 25,168 Choctaws; 1,660 Mississippi Choctaws; 18,761 Creeks; 10,966 Chickasaws; and 3,127 Seminoles.

Curtis Act. At first, the Five Civilized Tribes refused to listen to the Dawes Commission. Only the Seminole people approved an allotment agreement.

In 1898, Congress passed the Curtis Act. This law gave the Dawes Commission power to force the division of *communal lands* held by the tribes. Also, the commission could abolish tribal government.

The Curtis Act did away with tribal courts. The law made everyone—Native Americans, blacks, and whites—subject to the laws of the United States.

Atoka Agreement. The Curtis Act gave the tribes no choice. They had to allot their lands to individual members.

The Choctaws and Chickasaw people voted to accept the Atoka Agreement which their chiefs had signed. Each man, woman, and child was allotted an average of 320 acres. The number of acres depended on the kind of land—rich bottom land or rough mountain country. Black freedmen got only 40 acres each.

The Atoka Agreement also set aside three million acres of coal, asphalt, and timber. These lands were for the benefit of all tribal members.

Creek allotment agreement and the Crazy Snake Rebellion. "If we had our way we would be living on lands in common," Chief Pleasant Porter said. "But this (white) civilization came up against us and we have no place to go."

Chief Pleasant Porter. (OHS)

Chitto Harjo. (OHS)

The Creek people reluctantly approved an agreement signed by Porter and other leaders in 1900. Every Creek man, woman, and child was given 160 acres. Black freedmen got the same acreage.

Chitto Harjo, known as Crazy Snake, opposed the allotment agreement. He and his full blood Creek followers set up their own tribal government. They arrested Creeks who took allotments and whipped them in public.

Chief Porter and the Dawes Commission called on the federal government for help. The United States cavalry from Fort Reno arrested nearly a hundred Creek rebels. Sixty-seven were put in jail at Muskogee and tried in federal court. The men were freed after they promised to take allotments and settle down.

Many of the Snakes, however, did not occupy their allotments. Some of them even sent back *oil royalty* checks after 1912. In that year, the great Cushing oil pool was discovered in Creek country. More than seventy Snakes had been forced to take land there.

Cherokee agreement opposed by the Nighthawk Keetoowah. In 1902, the Cherokee people voted to accept allotments. They were the last tribe to do so. Every person on the tribal roll got about 110 acres of average land. Descendants of Cherokee black slaves were given an equal amount.

A faction of full blood Cherokees refused to be enrolled for allotments. They were called the "Nighthawk Keetoowah." Their leader was Red Bird Smith. U.S. marshals rounded up some of the Nighthawks and put them in jail at Muskogee. Smith said they had to enrol for an allotment to get out.

Principal Chief William C. Rogers (grandfather of Will Rogers) signed deeds for the allotments until 1917. His office of chief was then abolished until 1970.

Towns incorporated. The Curtis Act provided for the incorporation of towns in the territory of the Five Civilized Tribes. All town residents of age were allowed to vote in elections for a local government. For the first time, white residents could buy lots.

Incorporated town governments began to levy taxes to start schools. They also built electric light plants, water systems, sewers, streets, and sidewalks.

The Indian Territory had nearly 150 incorporated towns by the turn of the century. The largest in 1900 were:

Ardmore (population 5681), Muskogee (4254), South McAlester (3479), Chickasha (3209), Durant (2969), Coalgate (2614), Wagoner (2372), Hartshorne (2352), Vinita (2339), Purcell (2277), Wynnewood (1907), Miami (1527), Lehigh (1500), Tahlequah (1482), Pauls Valley (1467), Tulsa (1390), Davis (1346), Sulphur Springs (1198), Poteau (1182), Duncan (1164), and Marlow (1016).

3. GRAFTERS CHEATED THE NATIVE AMERICANS OUT OF THEIR ALLOTMENTS.

More than fifteen million acres of tribal lands passed into the hands of individual Indians. The allotments in Indian Territory contained rich farmland and pastures, dense forests, and some of the best lead, zinc, coal, and oil deposits in the world.

Many of the allottees had no concept of private property or its value. They were easy victims for the crooks and shysters who were called *grafters.*

Grafters liked the system used by the Dawes Commission to allot land. An allottee was usually given two types of land. The *homestead* part could not be sold for a specified number of years. Full bloods, who were not experienced in the ways of white civilization, had to wait the longest. A second type of land, called *surplus,* could be sold sooner.

The Dawes Commission tried to give each tribal member a homestead in the hills where he had a cabin or home. The surplus part of an allotment might be choice prairie or valley land some distance away.

Full bloods seldom wanted more than the small holdings which they had been farming. They sold their surplus to the first person who approached them. Most of the natives were happy to pick up a few dollars from a grafter simply by making a mark on a piece of paper.

Grafters, many of whom were real estate dealers, used a clever scheme to get control over large tracts of land. They paid the transportation expenses of the poorer natives to a land office and helped them select allotments. The grafter tried to select surplus lands for a number of allottees in the same place. Then he would lease or buy the whole area for a fraction of its real value.

A similar plan was used by well-to-do tribal members whose large estates were reduced to average size by the Dawes Commission. Robert L. Owen, a future U.S. senator, was typical. Owen used the allotment system to save his ten thousand acre estate on Cherokee tribal lands. His agents persuaded Cherokee citizens to select their surplus allotments inside Owen's fences and rent the land to him. The allottees also agreed to deed the surplus to Owen as soon as the law allowed.

"Professional guardians" often worked with real estate dealers to cheat Indian children. Never were children so rich and yet so defenseless. Each child on the rolls of the Five Civilized Tribes got the same allotment as an adult.

U.S. Senator Robert L. Owen. (OHS)

But inexperienced parents often signed *waivers,* turning over control of their child's land to a guardian.

A *professional guardian* got waivers from the parents of a large number of children. He would lease their allotments to a *realtor* friend for practically nothing. The realtor then subleased the land to farmers for a huge profit. The children were thus cheated out of income from their allotments.

Town lots gave grafters another opportunity. The Curtis Act protected people who had built on town lots. They were allowed to buy the lots at a fraction of the market value. All town lots without improvements belonged to the tribe and were sold at auction.

Within a month after the Curtis Act was passed, speculators arrived in Indian Territory. To qualify for low prices on town lots, they made "temporary improvements," such as planting a tree or digging a well. Later, the speculators sold the lots at full market value.

4. THE SEQUOYAH CONVENTION FAILED TO GET SEPARATE STATEHOOD FOR INDIAN TERRITORY, BUT GREATLY INFLUENCED THE PRESENT OKLAHOMA CONSTITUTION.

The lands occupied by the Five Civilized Tribes "shall be...a State of the Union." In these

Chief Green McCurtain with wife Jane and daughters. (OHS)

"The chiefs agreed to support single statehood," Haskell said, "if they failed to get separate statehood for Indian Territory."

The chiefs called a constitutional convention to meet at Muskogee on August 21, 1905. Seven delegates were to be chosen from each of twenty-six *recording districts*. Both Native Americans and whites were elected. The Muskogee convention was the first major effort of the races to cooperate politically.

Sequoyah constitutional convention. The delegates assembled at the Hinton Theater. They elected Chief Porter president of the convention. "Sequoyah" was chosen as the name for the proposed new state.

A constitution committee worked day and night to complete its work. The chairman was W. W. Hastings, a part-Cherokee who later represented an Oklahoma district in the U.S. Con-

words the Atoka Agreement promised separate statehood for the Indian Territory. Congress, however, chose to make one state from the Oklahoma and Indian territories.

Chiefs call a convention. The tribal leaders made a gallant try to secure separate statehood for the Indian Territory. In July, 1905, the principal chiefs met at Muskogee. Present were Pleasant Porter of the Creeks, William C. Rogers of the Cherokees, Green McCurtain of the Choctaws, and John F. Brown of the Seminoles. Governor Douglas H. Johnston of the Chickasaws was represented by William H. Murray, the tribal attorney. Murray, a white man, was married to Johnston's niece.

Chief Porter sought the advice of his friend, Charles N. Haskell, a white railroad builder in Muskogee. Haskell told the chiefs that Congress was not likely to grant separate statehood even if they were entitled to it by treaty.

Chickasaw Governor Douglas H. Johnston. (OHS)

128

Mrs. William H. Murray.

gress. Haskell and Murray did much of the work on the constitution. Their special duty was to divide the State of Sequoyah into counties. To please nearly everyone who wanted a county, they ended up with forty-eight.

The Sequoyah Constitution. This document was long—about 35,000 words. Its clear, concise style was the work of Alexander Posey, a Creek poet and editor. He was secretary of the convention.

A *bill of rights* and sections on the three branches of government were not unusual. But the Sequoyah Constitution contained many new ideas. It provided for mine safety, regulation of child labor, pure food and drugs, and *prohibition* of alcoholic beverages. A corporation commission was created to regulate railroads and big business.

Voters in the Indian Territory went to the polls on November 7, 1905. They approved the Sequoyah Constitution by a vote of 56,279 to 9,073. One reason for the big yes vote was a special election rule. A person had to vote in favor of the constitution in order to take part in the selection of a county seat.

Four "congressmen" were elected to take the Sequoyah Constitution to Washington, D.C. Haskell and Murray accompanied this group. A bill was introduced in each house of Congress to ad-

mit the State of Sequoyah. But no action was taken on the bill.

Instead, Congress passed the *Oklahoma Enabling Act* to admit the twin territories as one state. President Theodore Roosevelt signed this law on June 16, 1906.

Significance of the Sequoyah Convention. The Sequoyah movement failed, but was highly important in the history of Oklahoma. Why? Leaders of the Five Civilized Tribes felt an honest effort had been made to organize Indian Territory as a separate state. Though disappointed, they were loyal to their promise to be satisfied with single statehood.

Also, far-sighted and ambitious white Democrats at the Muskogee convention gained experience in leadership and teamwork. They were able to dominate the Oklahoma contitutional convention at Guthrie in 1906. The Sequoyah Constitution gave Haskell, Murray, and other Democrats a *platform* of issues that a majority of people favored. Except for the Sequoyah convention, Murray said, the "railroad attorneys" would have controlled the Guthrie convention.

The *progressive* Sequoyah Constitution was a model for the Constitution of Oklahoma. Some provisions were adopted word for word.

ROUNDUP

1. How were the Oklahoma and Indian territories similar? How were they different?
2. Who was Judge Isaac Parker? Why was a U.S. Court established at Muskogee in Indian Territory?
3. Why did the Dawes Commission order a survey of tribal lands and compile a roll of Indian citizens? What were the main provisions of the Curtis Act of 1898?
4. Identify: Atoka Agreement, Pleasant Porter, Chitto Harjo, and the Nighthawk Keetoowah?
5. Why did towns in Indian Territory want the right to incorporate?
6. What two types of land were allotted to individual Indians? How did grafters take advantage of this system? How did other grafters cheat Indian children?

129

7. Who called for delegates to meet in the Sequoyah Convention? List some new ideas that were put into the Sequoyah Constitution.

8. For what reasons was the Sequoyah Convention important in Oklahoma history?

A. Think about it! "Within a generation," wrote historian Angie Debo, "these Indians, who owned and governed a region greater in area and potential wealth than many an American state, were almost stripped of their holdings, and were rescued from starvation only through public charity."

Do you think that ownership and control of Indian Territory by the Five Tribes could have been preserved? Did a choice have to be made between seventy thousand Indians and a million land hungry newcomers? Can you think of other policies or laws that would have been better for Indians than the Dawes and Curtis acts? Would the Indians be better off on reservations as in Arizona?

17

CONSTITUTION OF OKLAHOMA

In 1906, President Theodore Roosevelt signed the Oklahoma Enabling Act. This law, known as the Hamilton Statehood Bill, made it possible for the Oklahoma and Indian territories to enter the Union as one state.

A constitutional convention with 112 delegates was to meet at Guthrie. Each territory would elect fifty-five delegates. The Osage Nation would choose two delegates.

1. THE ENABLING ACT PUT RESTRICTIONS ON THE CONSTITUTIONAL CONVENTION.

Capital at Guthrie. The capital of the new state was supposed to be at Guthrie, at least until 1913. Henry Asp, a Republican leader, got Congress to include this provision in the act. Asp was the chief attorney for the Santa Fe railroad in Oklahoma.

Guthrie appeared to be a logical choice for the capital. In 1906, it was a prosperous city of 12,000 people. Nine railroads and forty-one daily passenger trains made Guthrie a railroad center. It was also the capital of the Territory of Oklahoma.

Prohibition in Indian Territory. Congress instructed the convention to prohibit the sale of intoxicants in Indian Territory. *Prohibition* also would apply to the Osage reservation.

The delegates, however, had a choice for the western part of the new state. This area could be *wet, dry,* or have *local option.*

State support for schools. The Enabling Act provided that school lands in the Territory of Oklahoma would be transferred to the new state. These lands amounted to two sections in each township.

No lands had been set aside for public schools in Indian Territory. As a substitute for school land in this area, Congress gave the new state $5 million for a *school trust fund.*

Congressional districts and senate seats. At its first election, Oklahoma was to elect five representatives to serve in the United States House. The Enabling Act defined the boundaries for each *congressional district.*

As in all the states, two United States senators were to be elected by the first state legislature.

Counties. The matter of county boundaries and county seats was left to the convention, with one exception. The delegates were directed to

Kate Barnard. (OHS)

William Jennings Bryan.

"constitute the Osage Indian reservation a separate county."

2. THE DEMOCRATIC PARTY ELECTED A BIG MAJORITY OF DELEGATES TO THE CONSTITUTIONAL CONVENTION.

In November, 1906, the Democrats elected ninety-nine of the 112 delegates. In the words of Charles N. Haskell, a convention leader from Muskogee, "the people sent ninety-nine Democrats to Guthrie and thirteen witnesses to watch them." The outnumbered Republicans were called the "Twelve Apostles." One delegate was an independent.

What were the reasons for the Democratic Party's success in 1906? A *coalition* of groups—a large southern white population, farmer ogranizations, labor unions, *social reformers* led by young Kate Barnard of Oklahoma City, and others—united to win a big majority of delegates.

The Democrats held a convention at Shawnee. They drew up the "Shawnee Demands" and promised to write a constitution with progressive *reforms*. They said that a bigger voice for the people in government was a major party goal.

Some famous speakers were imported to campaign for Democratic candidates. The best known was William Jennings Bryan, the "silver-tongued orator" from Nebraska. Huge crowds gathered in towns and at railroad whistle stops to hear Bryan speak.

Democratic committees at the precinct level worked hard to get out the voters on election day. The huge Democratic Party victory in 1906 was the beginning of half a century of almost solid Democratic rule in Oklahoma.

Who were the delegates to the constitutional convention? By occupation, 33 were farmers, 29 lawyers, 14 merchants, 7 teachers, 6 ministers, 5 stockmen, and 3 bankers. About a dozen had college degrees. Most had been educated in the "school of adversity."

By origin, seventy-five delegates came from former slave states in the Old South. Only thirty-five were from northern states. Two were foreign-born.

The oldest delegate was Clement V. Rogers of Claremore who was 68. The youngest was William C. Leidtke of Eufaula. He was 24. The president of the convention, William H. Murray, was 37.

The delegates were not impressed by lobbyists. The constitutional convention opened on November 20, 1906 at the Guthrie City Hall.

Guthrie City Hall.

When the delegates arrived in town they found most of the good hotel rooms reserved. Corporation *lobbyists* from northern cities had rented the rooms. But these people cancelled their reservations after Charles N. Haskell got the convention to pass an anti-lobbying resolution.

3. THE LEADERS OF THE CONSTITUTIONAL CONVENTION CAME MAINLY FROM INDIAN TERRITORY.

Charles N. Haskell was one of the leaders who emerged to guide the delegates toward their main goal of writing a constitution. Haskell chose not to run for president of the convention. He thought his past work as a railroad builder in Muskogee might be held against him.

As chairman of the important steering committee, Haskell was the "power behind the throne." He was able to work out compromises on *controversial issues* that divided the convention. Chief among these were prohibition and the location of county seats.

William H. Murray. Haskell supported Murray for president of the convention. Murray, after looking at the election returns, knew he could win the position. He was one of thirty-four dele-

Pete Hanraty. (OHS)

gates who had served in the Sequoyah Convention. Another thirty delegates from the Oklahoma Territory were, like Murray, members of the Farmers' Union.

Murray was called "Alfalfa Bill." He got the name when he farmed land in the Chickasaw Nation. A Tishomingo newspaper editor heard Murray speak to local farmers and wrote a story with the headline "Alfalfa Bill on Alfalfa." The name stuck.

Pete Hanraty of Coalgate was elected vice-president of the convention. Hanraty headed the Twin Territories Federation of Labor. He was responsible for the sections on labor in the constitution.

Robert L. Williams of Durant was the Democratic national committeeman from Indian Territory. In this position, he had the power to influence many delegates. Once a corporation lawyer, he gave up his free railroad pass and led the fight to regulate big business.

Like Haskell and Murray, Williams later became governor.

Walter A. Ledbetter of Ardmore was another convention leader. He resigned as attorney

Charles N. Haskell.

for several corporations and became part of the reform movement. Ledbetter served as legal advisor for the convention.

Leaders from Oklahoma Territory. Haskell, Murray, Hanraty, Williams, and Ledbetter—these influential delegates were all from Indian Territory.

The most prominent westsider was Henry S. Johnston of Perry. He presided over the convention when Murray took part in floor debate. Johnston also was destined to be governor of Oklahoma.

4. SEVERAL ISSUES DIVIDED THE DELEGATES UNTIL COMPROMISES WERE WORKED OUT.

The reform-minded Democratic delegates were ready to write the country's most modern constitution. Several issues, however, threatened to divide the convention. These included the location of county seats and county boundaries, *woman suffrage*, and the liquor question.

Compared to these disputes, naming the new state was a minor problem. The delegates wrangled for days, however, before deciding on "Oklahoma." This word is from the Choctaw *Okla-homma* meaning "red people." The name had been suggested earlier by Allen Wright, a Choctaw chief in the late 1860s, for an all-Indian territory.

County seats and county boundaries. "Delegates got to quarreling over county seats and county boundaries," said Haskell, "and I soon saw that it would be necessary to get that question out of the way before we could accomplish the really big things in the convention."

With Haskell's skilled guidance, the Committee on County Boundaries picked the seats for seventy-five counties. (Harmon and Cotton were added after Oklahoma became a state.) The shape of many counties was determined by political compromise, not by the logic of geography. Each county was allowed to change its county seat if it wished.

Prohibition of alcoholic beverages. The liquor question divided the delegates. The Enab-

ling Act required *prohibition* only in Indian Territory and on the Osage reservation for twenty-one years.

The convention was allowed to decide whether or not the Territory of Oklahoma had prohibition. As it was, nearly every town had a saloon. Liquor interests were strong politically in the territory.

Haskell said he was "opposed to any calico constitution that makes a thing a law in one part of the state and not in the other."

He feared, however, that a provision for state-wide prohibition might cause the constitution to be defeated. To avoid that possibility, Haskell and Murray persuaded the delegates to put a state-wide prohibition amendment on a separate ballot.

Woman suffrage. The privilege of female voting was a controversial issue at the convention. A majority of delegates were pledged to support *woman suffrage*. Many changed their minds, however, because of *racism*.

Haskell and Murray led the opponents of woman suffrage. They used a Guthrie school board election, at which women could vote, to make a point. More than seven hundred black women and only seven white women voted at this board election. Murray told the convention that adoption of the Hanraty amendment for woman suffrage would "mean giving the balance of power over to the Negro vote."

The anti-black convention voted to table the woman suffrage amendment 54 to 37. Twenty-one delegates didn't vote. A different result could have been expected from delegates who spoke loud and often about *social justice*.

Black suffrage. The Enabling Act required the delegates to include Amendment 15 of the federal constitution in the state constitution.

The fifteenth provides that: "The right of citizens of the United States to vote shall not be denied or abridged by the United States or any state on account of race, color, or previous condition of servitude."

Segregation of blacks. Most of the delegates were pledged to restrict the rights of blacks. As candidates, they promised separate schools,

75 Oklahoma Counties and County Seats, 1907

Counties which later changed the county seat.

Counties that were divided into two counties.

separate railway coaches, and separate waiting rooms for blacks. These *Jim Crow laws*, plus a provision to forbid whites to marry blacks, were in the first draft of the state constitution.

President Roosevelt said he would not approve the constitution with restrictions on blacks. With this advice, the delegates removed the *discriminatory clauses*, except for segregated schools. However, the convention passed resolutions urging the first state legislature to enact Jim Crow laws.

5. THE CONVENTION WROTE A PROGRESSIVE CONSTITUTION.

The convention delegates were almost unanimous in adopting progressive reforms. The negative votes on these issues could usually be counted on one hand.

Long constitution. The final draft of the constitution was one of the world's longest— about 50,000 words. Critics argued that it contained many sections that should be passed as laws by a legislature. A section in Article 20, for example, required that kerosene oil used for lighting have a flash point at 115 degrees Fahrenheit.

Murray admitted that many sections in the constitution didn't belong there. But the Democratic delegates included many reform provisions for a reason. Only the people can change the constitution. A law passed by a legislature, on the other hand, can be repealed by a later legislature.

Indeed, the Oklahoma constitution was outstanding—not for the length, but for its reforms. Murray said the constitution served the *"public interest"* (the people), not the *"special interests"* (corporations, in this case).

Regulation of corporations. The article on corporations was one of the longest parts of the constitution. An elective corporation commission of three members was created to enforce provisions in this article. Each commissioner had to take an oath that he had no financial interest in any railroad company or other corporation.

All corporations doing business in Oklahoma were required to have a state charter. Corporations were forbidden to form a monopoly.

Railroad companies were singled out for special control. They were not allowed to haul coal from their own mines. A two-cents-a-mile maximum passenger fare was set. Railroads had to pay a personal property tax on all rolling stock.

These and many other regulations were listed in the constitution.

The convention was guided by the slogan, "Let the People Rule." The delegates acted on the belief that the "cure for the evils of democracy is more democracy." The people were given more power through the initiative, referendum, and the long ballot.

The *initiative* is the process that begins with people writing a law or constitutional amendment. They have to get the required number of signatures on petitions to get the measure on the ballot. The voters pass or defeat the initiative at election time.

Two kinds of *referendum* are authorized in Oklahoma's constitution. The legislature can put a bill on the ballot voluntarily. Also, the voters can petition to get a bill, already passed by the legislature, placed on the ballot. The legislature can prevent a referendum by attaching the *emergency clause* to a bill.

The delegates showed their passion for *direct democracy* in another way. Nearly every state office was made elective. The result was a *long ballot*. Twelve elective officers were listed in Article VI: governor, lieutenant governor, secretary of state, state auditor, attorney general, state treasurer, superintendent of public instruction, state examiner and inspector, chief mine inspector, labor commissioner, insurance commissioner, and commissioner of charities and corrections.

The first eight officers on this list had to be "male citizens of the United States." The constitution writers used the phrase "his or her duty" only in connection with the office of commissioner of charities and corrections. The delegates expected Kate Barnard, the well-known social reformer from Oklahoma City, to be elected to that position. (She was.)

6. THE PEOPLE RATIFIED (APPROVED) THE CONSTITUTION BY A BIG MARGIN.

After the constitution was written, it had to be approved by the voters. Election day was set for September 17, 1907. The people were to vote on the constitution and prohibition separately. They also would elect five congressmen as well as state and county officers.

The merits of the constitution were debated before the election. Oklahoma was flooded with another wave of oratory.

Speakers in favor of adopting the constitution. Murray and other Democrats spoke for the constitution. Defeat the "corporations and carpetbaggers," Murray pleaded.

Bryan returned to defend the constitution. "I tell you that you have the best constitution of any state in the Union," he said. "This constitution was written from the standpoint of the people."

Speaking to large crowds, Bryan attacked the awkward position of the Republicans. He wondered how Republican candidates, if elected, could abide by the constitution that they opposed.

President Theodore Roosevelt was against the Oklahoma constitution. Roosevelt said his opinion of Oklahoma's radical constitution was "not fit for publication." His attorney general listed fifteen specific objections. Roosevelt especially disliked the way the black race was treated differently. People of African descent were defined as the "colored race" while everyone else was classified as "white."

Secretary of War William Howard Taft led the list of Republican "visiting statesmen" who came to speak against the constitution. Taft said the long document was not a constitution but a "code of by-laws." He argued that the provisions to regulate corporations would "scare away foreign capital."

Both the constitution and statewide prohibition were approved. The people went to the polls on September 17. Strongly in favor of statehood, they approved the constitution by a vote of 180,333 to 73,059. It got a favorable vote in every county.

President Theodore Roosevelt.

The people also voted for statewide prohibition. Only the approval of President Roosevelt was needed for Oklahoma to become the forty-sixth state. Oklahoma had to wait another two months for that.

7. THE DEMOCRATS WON MOST OF THE OFFICES IN OKLAHOMA'S FIRST STATE ELECTION IN 1907.

Democratic primary. In June, 1907, the Democratic Party held a *direct primary.* Democrats ran against Democrats.

Haskell defeated Lee Cruce, an Ardmore banker, to become the Democratic *nominee* for governor. Williams won a nomination for justice on the first Oklahoma Supreme Court. Hanraty was chosen the Democratic nominee for mine inspector. Murray easily won a seat in the state House of Representatives where he would be elected Speaker.

The Democrats countered a Republican charge that the "constitution convention clique" was trying to control the new government. Two Democrats who were not at the convention were selected for two United States Senate seats. The Senate race was only a *preferential primary.*

Statehood at last!

United States senators were chosen by state legislatures until Amendment 17 was added to the United States Constitution in 1913.

Robert L. Owen, Henry Furman, and Thomas Gore led a long list of candidates for the U.S. Senate in the preferential primary. Owen and Furman, who ran first and second, were both from Indian Territory. The Democrats had agreed that each territory should have a United States Senate seat. So Furman withdrew in favor of Gore who got the third highest number of votes. Gore was from Lawton in Oklahoma Territory.

No one was surprised that Kate Barnard was the Democratic nominee for commissioner of charities and corrections. This post had been created especially for her.

Republican convention. In 1907, the Republican nominees for state offices were chosen at a convention in Tulsa.

After a bitter factional fight, Frank Frantz was nominated for governor and became the party leader. The Bird S. McGuire wing of the party did not take defeat gracefully. This faction concentrated on getting McGuire elected to one of the five congressional seats. They gave no help to the rest of the Republican ticket.

Democratic nominees won big in the 1907 general election. The election on September 17, 1907, was almost a Democratic sweep. Haskell was elected Oklahoma's first state governor though he lost nineteen counties, including his home county of Muskogee.

Democratic nominees for Congress won four of five seats. McGuire was the sole Republican winner.

In the Oklahoma Senate, the Democrats outnumbered Republicans 39 to 5. The House of Representatives had 93 Democrats and only 16 Republicans.

At the county level, the Democrats won all or most of the offices in sixty-two of the seventy-five counties.

The overwhelming Democratic victory in 1907 was remarkable. A few years earlier, the party hardly existed in Indian Territory and it was usually defeated in Oklahoma Territory.

8. NOVEMBER 16 IS OKLAHOMA STATEHOOD DAY

President Roosevelt signed the *statehood proclamation* in Washington, D.C. on November 16, 1907.

Statehood celebrations. Oklahomans were ready to celebrate when the good news arrived by telegraph. Happy farm families went to town to share in the festivities. Brass bands and fireworks added to the holiday mood.

Thousands of people poured into Guthrie by train, wagon, or horseback. Statehood ceremonies were held on the steps of the Carnegie Library. A mock marriage symbolized the union of the twin territories. Miss Indian Territory, a beautiful Cherokee maiden dressed in beaded buckskin, was wed to Mr. Oklahoma Territory. He was a handsome, young man dressed in cowboy clothes and a Stetson hat.

Inauguration of elected officers. Governor Haskell, Lieutenant Governor George Bellamy, and other elected people took the oath of office. After the Governor's inaugural address, the crowd enjoyed a barbecue in the park. By sundown, most of the celebrants were on the way home. They experienced the greatest day in Oklahoma history.

Not everyone was happy with statehood. Many full blood Native Americans mourned the passing of the old way of life. The story is told

"The Wedding" statue at Guthrie. (Fred Marvel)

about one Cherokee woman who refused to attend a statehood celebration with her white husband.

Late in the evening he returned home and said, "Well, Mary, we no longer live in the Cherokee Nation. All of us are now citizens of the State of Oklahoma."

"It broke my heart," the woman recalled many years later, "I went to bed and cried all night long. It seemed more than I could bear that the Cherokee Nation—my country and my people's country—was no more."

ROUNDUP

1. List the restrictions that the Enabling Act put on the constitutional convention.
2. Give four reasons why the Democratic Party did so well in electing delegates to the convention.
3. What leadership jobs did Haskell, Murray, and Hanraty have at the convention?
4. On what basis were many county lines drawn? How did the delegates prevent the prohibition question from defeating the constitution?
5. Why did the delegates decide against including Jim Crow provisions in the constitution? What was the exception?
6. Define initiative, referendum, and long ballot.
7. For what reason did Bryan say Oklahoma had a good constitution? What did Taft mean when he said it really wasn't a constitution?
8. How were U.S. senators picked and how were they officially chosen in 1907?
9. Why was the Democratic sweep of state officials in 1907 so remarkable?
A. Think about it! Explain how the convention delegates succeeded in starting "a government of the people, by the people, and for the people." How did they fail to do this?

18

EARLY STATEHOOD YEARS, 1907–1919

Oklahoma started as a *one-party state.* A *two-party system,* where either party can win and be responsible for governing, was a long time coming.

Every governor, until 1963, was a Democrat. The legislature had a large Democratic majority. Victory in the Democratic primary was *tantamount* to election. The Republican Party had little chance to win in the general election. Why? For one reason, the legislature denied the vote to most blacks who were mainly Republican then. Also, many Oklahomans came from the Old South which was solidly Democratic after the Civil War.

The goals of the Democratic Party began to change after statehood. The coalition of labor unions, farmers, and social reformers, which wrote the nation's most "radical" constitution in 1907, fell apart. Middle class professional and business people gained a bigger voice in the party. The first three governors—Haskell, Cruce, and Williams—were lawyers and businessmen. They encouraged corporations to invest in Oklahoma.

Many debt-ridden farmers and some miners and city laborers began to flirt with *socialism.* "Socialism grows when every other crop fails," said Oscar Ameringer. He was a Socialist Party organizer who used the style of an evangelistic preacher. His week-long camp meetings in the farm country attracted large crowds. Ameringer entertained them with music and sometimes a hypnotist-mind reader. Socialist speakers appealed to *tenant farmers* and *sharecroppers* who wanted their own land.

The Socialist appeal was short-lived, however. Party membership fell as farm prices rose during World War I. Some Socialist leaders were put in jail for criticizing the government and encouraging young men to evade the draft.

World War I was a patriotic war. Americans dreamed of saving the world for democracy. More than ninety thousand Oklahomans were in the armed services. On the home front, people bought Liberty bonds to finance the war. They produced more food so that America's allies in Europe could be fed.

Oklahoma celebrated with the rest of the nation when Germany surrendered on November 11, 1918.

1. CHARLES N. HASKELL WAS THE FIRST STATE GOVERNOR.

Haskell's early life was a "rags to riches" story. Oklahoma's first governor was born in a log cabin in Ohio. His career began with a teaching job at age seventeen. Three years later he passed the Ohio bar exam. Haskell practiced law and promoted railroads. He was a wealthy widower with three children when he settled in Muskogee in 1901.

His first project in Indian Territory was a railroad between Muskogee and Fayettesville, Arkansas. Haskell also built a hotel, an office building, and an opera house in Muskogee. He published a weekly newspaper and was active in civic affairs. As we have seen, Haskell played an important role in the statehood movement. He was elected governor in 1907.

Haskell's first action as governor. Oklahoma is now a state! This good news arrived by telegraph from Washington, D.C., shortly after 9:16 a.m., Oklahoma time, November 16. Governor-elect Haskell was waiting in his hotel room in Guthrie and immediately took the oath of office.

Before the public inaugural ceremony at noon, Governor Haskell sent a telegram to Frank Canton at Bartlesville. Canton, the first head of

U.S. Senator Thomas P. Gore. (OHS)

the Oklahoma National Guard, followed the governor's orders. He stopped construction on a gas pipeline into Kansas.

Why did Haskell take this action? At that time, he thought Oklahoma's supply of cheap gas should be used to attract new industries and jobs to Oklahoma. He soon came to realize, however, that the state's oil and gas industry would benefit by piping these products to other states.

First state legislature organized. On December 2, 1907, the legislature met in Guthrie. Governor Haskell spoke to a joint session, outlining Oklahoma's needs.

William H. Murray was elected the first Speaker of the House. Henry S. Johnston was chosen President of the Senate.

The Democratic legislature chose Thomas P. Gore and Robert L. Owen as Oklahoma's first two United States senators.

Billup's Booze Bill. Haskell advised the legislature that prohibition had to be enforced. Senator Richard Billups introduced a bill for that purpose. This measure coupled enforcement with a state dispensary system. Each dispensary could sell liquor only by a doctor's prescription.

Enforcement of prohibition proved to be no easy job. *Moonshiners* made illegal whiskey in copper stills. They often paid local officers to leave them alone. Faced with this problem, Governor Haskell ordered State Attorney Charles West "to dry up" Oklahoma. West brought charges against corrupt sheriffs, judges, and county commissioners. *Bootleggers* continued to peddle booze, however. (The voters finally repealed prohibition in 1959).

State banking system. Haskell considered the *bank guaranty law* the greatest accomplishment of his administration. This law protected depositors from bank failures. A number of banks had gone under during the national *Panic of 1907.*

The Oklahoma Banking Board was given power to assess member banks one percent of their deposits. This money was kept in the *Oklahoma Depositors Guaranty Fund.* All state-chartered banks were forced to take part. The Noble State Bank sued Haskell. The bank's lawyers argued that the new law violated its 14th Amendment rights. The bank guaranty law was upheld, however, by the United States Supreme Court.

Six banks failed while Haskell was governor. Not one depositor lost a dime, thanks to the bank guaranty law. The Oklahoma law served as a model for other states. In 1933, Congress created a similar system known as the Federal Deposit Insurance Corporation (F.D.I.C.)

New institutions. The Democratic legislature argued over the location of institutions. Every legislator wanted an income-producing college, prison, asylum, or state home for his district. Most of the new prizes went to the old Indian Territory.

McAlester got the state prison. Oklahoma convicts were brought back from the Kansas penitentiary. They were put to work on "Big Mac." The prisoners made bricks and did construction inside an electrified barbed wire fence.

Seven new colleges were established. A school of mines was located at Wilburton and a college for girls at Chickasha. Teachers's colleges were established at Ada, Durant, and Tahlequah. Lawton and Goodwell in western Oklahoma got agricultural and mechanical schools.

Nearly every part of the state that didn't have an institution got something.

Labor gains. The First Legislature passed a labor code that pleased the Oklahoma Federation of Labor. The nation's first public employment agencies were established. *Blacklists* and *yellow dog contracts* were outlawed in Oklahoma. Labor Day was made a state holiday. Other laws provided for safety regulations in mines and factories. The work day was limited to eight hours on state projects.

The Democratic coalition fell apart over a child labor bill. House Speaker Murray and farmers opposed the bill. It restricted child labor on farms. The legislature barely passed the bill and Governor Haskell vetoed it.

Segregation law. The first bill passed by the legislature was a *"separate but equal" segregation law.* Known as the "Jim Crow Code," this law swished through the Senate by a vote of 37 to 2 and the House 95 to 10. It required railroad companies to provide separate waiting rooms, train seating, and other public facilities for blacks and whites. Schools were also segregated.

Blacks were understandably angered by this discrimination. Riots broke out in black towns. People in Taft burned down the railroad station.

A grandfather clause disenfranchised black voters. The Republican Party elected more congressmen and state legislators in 1908. A. C. Hamlin of Guthrie, the first black to serve in the state legislature, was elected to the House. The Republican Party's success was partly due to the solid support of black voters.

Alarmed at Republican gains, the Democratic legislature decided on the *literacy test* as a way to keep blacks from voting. A constitutional amendment was referred to the voters. It was approved in 1910.

A *grandfather clause* exempted from the literacy test all persons who could vote on January 1, 1866 (whites) and their descendants. Foreign immigrants were also excused. In effect, only blacks had to take the literacy test. Election officials could make the test difficult enough to deny blacks the suffrage.

Capital moved to Oklahoma City. Haskell's most famous action as governor was to move the state capital. He and other Democrats were anxious to take it away from Guthrie, a "Republican nest."

The location of the capital was a topic for endless debate in the legislature. The members agreed only that it should be near the center of the state. A few members wanted to build a new community west of Oklahoma City for the capital. It would be called New Jerusalem.

Finally, the legislature allowed towns to petition for the capital. Among the bids was one from Granite. This town offered the state a forty-acre tract on a granite mountain. In the end, three cities met all the requirements. Governor Haskell called a special election for Saturday, June 11, 1910, to decide the location of a permanent capital. The voters chose Oklahoma City by a three-to-one margin over Guthrie. Shawnee came in third.

Haskell ignored the Enabling Act restriction that the capital remain in Guthrie until 1913. He cleverly set Saturday as election day. Hoping Oklahoma City would win, Haskell planned to move there over the weekend. The courts would be closed and could not issue an *injunction* to stop removal of the capital from Guthrie.

On election day, Haskell voted in Muskogee and attended a banquet in Tulsa. He rode a night train to Oklahoma City. Meanwhile, his secretary brought the state seal from Guthrie by automobile. On Sunday morning Haskell was in his temporary governor's office at the Lee-Huckins Hotel.

"Under the law, Oklahoma City is the state capital," he told reporters, "and I have simply done my duty."

In 1911, the United States Supreme Court upheld the capital removal. The court said that a senate could locate its capital wherever the people wanted it.

Evaluation of Haskell. Haskell was one of the most capable leaders to serve in the governor's office. He got the machinery of government running. The first two legislatures passed some

Governor Haskell at his desk in the Lee-Huckins Hotel.

constructive laws. In general, Haskell's administration was progressive except for the segregation and *disenfranchisement* of black citizens.

Later life. Haskell finished his term in January, 1911, and returned to private business. In 1917, he moved to New York City and became wealthy by organizing oil companies.

Haskell was invited to Mexico to write oil laws for that country. He then returned to Oklahoma City to practice law and died there in 1933. A tall marble shaft marks his grave in Muskogee.

2. GOVERNOR LEE CRUCE PROMOTED OKLAHOMA'S ECONOMIC GROWTH AND TRIED TO ENFORCE THE LAWS.

Lee Cruce, an Ardmore banker and lawyer, was elected governor in 1910. Cruce defeated "Al-falfa Bill" Murray in the Democratic primary. He won the general election with a *plurality* of 49 percent. Four parties had *nominees* who split the votes.

Governor Cruce was a *business progressive*. He wanted to promote economic growth by encouraging corporations to invest here. Another goal was efficient, businesslike government.

Department of Highways. Oklahoma's growth depended on good highways. In 1911, the legislature created a highway department. Cruce appointed Sidney Suggs, an Ardmore newspaperman, as director.

Suggs traveled over the state in a horse and buggy. He often spoke to students and urged them to work on roads near their homes. He told them to use this slogan: "A good road for tire and hoof."

Capital punishment controversy. Governor Cruce was against the death penalty. He *commuted* to life in prison the sentences of all men condemned to die at the McAlester prison.

Judge Henry Furman of the Criminal Court of Appeals expressed the view of many Oklahomans who favored the death penalty. "No Governor has the right to substitute his own views for the law on capital punishment," the judge said.

Most of the state's newspapers objected to Cruce's commutation of death sentences. Nothing

Governor Lee Cruce (front car, back seat, right side) on his way to the State Capitol. (OHS)

143

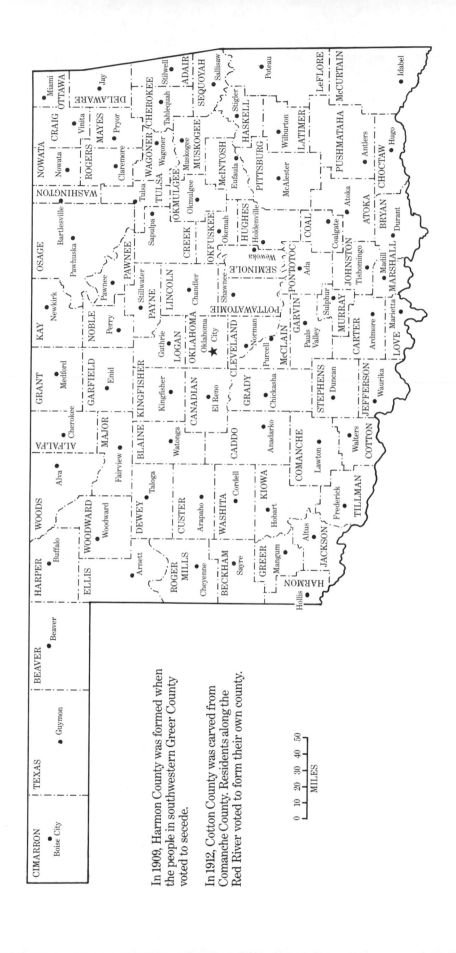

In 1909, Harmon County was formed when the people in southwestern Greer County voted to secede.

In 1912, Cotton County was carved from Comanche County. Residents along the Red River voted to form their own county.

77 Oklahoma Counties and County Seats Today

Governor Robert L. Williams. (OHS)

he did during his administration brought out more criticism.

Moral decency laws. Governor Cruce tried hard to enforce prohibition. He even accompanied several raids on Oklahoma City's bootlegging joints.

"You raid joints and pour out the liquor into the sewers," the buttermilk-drinking governor told a church audience. "Before you get home the bootlegger is back in the joint with twice as much booze."

After the people passed an anti-gambling referendum, Governor Cruce sent the National Guard to the Tulsa racetrack. Illegal betting on the horses was a problem there. Guardsmen had to fire over the heads of nervous jockeys before the races were stopped.

The Governor also used the National Guard to prevent prizefights in several towns. He was embarassed when a group of legislators were found in the fight crowd at an Oklahoma City auditorium. (In 1959, the legislature repealed the law against prizefighting.)

Later life. At the end of his four-year term, Cruce returned to Ardmore. Oil was discovered on his land, making him a wealthy man.

3. GOVERNOR ROBERT LEE WILLIAMS CUT STATE EXPENSES AND LED OKLAHOMA DURING WORLD WAR I.

Robert L. Williams was elected to Oklahoma's first supreme court. Williams was a railroad lawyer, banker, and farm owner from Durant. He was a lifelong bachelor though a sympathetic biographer called him a bigamist— "married to Oklahoma" and "wedded to history."

Unusual elections in 1914. Judge Williams ran for governor. Two other men named R. L. Williams filed for the office to confuse voters but were denied a place on the ballot.

The judge ran a model "We Will Win With Williams" campaign. He began a typical day with a Democrats for Williams Club meeting. Then came a church dinner. Finally, the candidate gave a speech in the public square. This pattern was repeated in another town the next day. Williams won the Democratic primary with a plurality of only 27 percent.

Al Jennings, an ex-convict, ran third in the Democratic primary. A lawyer, Jennings began robbing trains after his brother Ed was killed in a Woodward gunfight. Al was sentenced to five years in prison for his part in a Rock Island train holdup near Chickasha. He then returned to the

Al Jennings posing for a political campaign photo, 1914. (OHS)

practice of law. Jennings was a colorful candidate. Large, curious crowds turned out to hear the "convict who made good." Jennings carried three counties: Oklahoma, Logan, and Stephens.

Williams won the general election with a plurality of only 40 percent. A large vote for the third place Socialist Party nominee kept Williams from getting a majority. In 1914, the Socialist Party in Oklahoma had more than 11,000 members—more than any other state.

State spending reduced. A strong governor, Williams ran the state like a business. He set an example for economy by firing unneeded employees in the governor's office.

Williams decided that a planned capitol dome was an ornament Oklahoma could not afford. He also cut prison costs. Convicts were taught to make bricks, brooms, and shoes to help pay the expense of keeping them. The Governor closed five junior colleges to save more money. Some of the colleges were reopened later, however.

Oil and gas conservation. Williams was proud of laws that gave the corporation commission power to cut production. Rich oil discoveries at Cushing and Healdton had resulted in an oil glut and low prices. Oil companies were pumping more crude than the pipelines could handle. Much of it was run on the ground and wasted.

Other states copied the Oklahoma conservation laws.

The grandfather clause was declared unconstitutional. The "grandfather clause" in Oklahoma's constitution was like the one used in Southern states. Its purpose was to deny the vote to black citizens. The blacks, mainly Republican at that time, were a threat to the Democratic majority.

In 1915, the United States Supreme Court decided, in the case of *Guinn versus United States,* that Oklahoma's grandfather clause was unconstitutional. It violated the Fifteenth Amendment in the federal constitution. The right to vote cannot be denied "on account of race, color, or previous condition of servitude."

Highway construction. After the United States got into World War I in 1917, highways became a war priority. Good roads were needed to

World War I soldier. Note the gas mask and flat helmet. Wool leggings were rolled around between the shoe tops and knees like a bandage.

move troops, food, and was materials to railroad centers. Oklahoma got more federal funds to build roads.

Governor Williams inspected construction of new roads. He encouraged local people to grade the dirt roads and repair culverts. Williams Highway was named for the governor. It ran from Hot Springs, Arkansas to Durant and on to Fort Sill.

4. WORLD WAR I WAS THE FIRST WAR IN WHICH OKLAHOMA, AS A STATE, WAS INVOLVED.

World War I was in its third year when the United States declared war on April 6, 1917. German submarines were trying to sink everything

146

Joseph Oklahombi and wife after World War I. (OHS)

that floated, including American ships. Soldiers in two lines of trenches faced each other over a no man's land in France. Fresh American troops turned the tide of war. Germany surrendered on November 11, 1918.

Oklahoma men in uniform. More than ninety thousand Oklahomans—National Guard, draftees, and volunteers—served in the army or navy.

Most of the Oklahoma and Texas National Guard units were combined to form the 36th Infantry Division. The insignia of this division was a "T" on a blue arrowhead. Other Oklahoma Guard soldiers were in the famous Rainbow Division (42nd Infantry). These divisions were in combat in France.

Many young men were drafted through the Selective Service System. A draft board in each county registered eligible men. They were classi-

fied on the basis of physical exams, marital status, and occupation. Class 1A, healthy single men, were called to duty first. They went in the order that their numbers were drawn from a fishbowl in Washington, D.C. Farmers who produced crops needed in the war effort usually were exempted.

Private Joseph Oklahombi was the state's greatest hero. He was a Choctaw from McCurtain County. On one occasion, Oklahombi rushed a German outpost defended by more than fifty machine guns. He captured 171 prisoners singlehandedly.

Oklahoma's casualties in World War I totaled 1,064 killed and more than four thousand wounded.

Anti-draft violence—the "Green Corn Rebellion." Oklahomans were patriotic. They were enthusiastic about President Woodrow Wilson's "war to save democracy." But Oklahoma was the only state to experience violent resistance to the war.

The "Green Corn Rebellion" was staged in the blackjack country along the South Canadian River east of Oklahoma City. Poor whites, blacks, and some Native Americans in this area barely eked out a living. They were sharecroppers and tenant farmers. Debt-ridden and discontented, they joined the radical Working Class Unions. They were stirred into rebellion by radical leaders of another union, the I.W.W. (Industrial Workers of the World).

"We can beat the army draft by using matches," one rebel leader said. Night riders wore masks. They burned farmhouses, barns, and railroad bridges. They used wet ropes to flog farmers who opposed them. Posters had this message: "Now is the time to rebel against the war with Germany, boys. Don't go. Rich man's war. Poor man's fight."

The rebels planned to join a war protest march to Washington, D.C. They intended to live on green roasting ears foraged from fields. About four hundred rebels camped at "Roastin Ear Hill" near Sasakwa. But the men fled when a Pottawatomie County sheriff's posse surprised them. About a hundred rebels were captured and jailed.

A gun battle was fought near Calvin when several draft resisters refused to surrender.

A few of the anti-war rebels were imprisoned at McAlester. But most of the men got no punishment. They returned to their homes. Some of them moved out of state because their landlords would no longer rent land to them.

Oklahoma Council of Defense. A few days after Congress declared war, Governor Williams created a state Council of Defense. One of the first jobs of this council was to get people behind the war effort. Speakers, called "Four Minute Men," took the message of patriotism to every crossroads. They handed out red, white, and blue pamphlets. The council also released a weekly news summary. Every newspaper was requested to run it in a fixed place. The heading was "We Must Win the War." Remember there was no radio or television in those days.

The Council of Defense sponsored Liberty Day parades to promote the sale of war bonds. The purchase of Liberty Bonds was made a test of loyalty to the United States. The Cleveland County Defense council, for example, built a "slacker pen" for residents who didn't buy war bonds.

The state and local defense councils cooperated with Food Administrator Herbert Hoover's efforts to save food. "Food Will Win the War" signs were everywhere. Oklahoma housewives signed pledge cards to observe "meatless" and "wheatless" days. Produce more, consume less—that was the objective.

Discrimination against German-Americans. The German-Americans were Oklahoma's largest foreign-born ethnic group at the time of World War I. Many had opposed American entrance into the war against their fatherland. They were suspected of disloyalty and became victims of a hate campaign.

The German language was banned in schools, churches, telephone conversations, and newspapers. This sign was posted on some German churches: "God Almighty understands the American language. Address him only in that tongue." A local defense council in Enid shut down a German newspaper even though the editor, Ernst

Denner, had two sons fighting in Europe for American democracy. The publication of another German newspaper, the *Oklahoma Vorwarts* at Bessie (south of Clinton), was halted after a mob threatened to destroy the printing equipment.

German Mennonite families were afraid for their safety. Some moved to Canada until the war was over. Most German-Americans continued to till farms in north-central and western Oklahoma. They bought war bonds and showed their loyalty in other ways.

Three Oklahoma towns changed their German names. Kiel in Kingfisher County became Loyal. Bismark (Bismarck) became Wright in honor of the first McCurtain County soldier to die in World War I. A patriotic change in spelling from Korn to Corn did not take away the rich German heritage of this Washita County town.

Germany defeated. The German government surrendered on November 11, 1918. An armistice was signed before noon. The time was much earlier in Oklahoma, but people were out of bed in a hurry when the news arrived. Church bells rang. Guns and revolvers were fired. Steam whistles blasted away. The great war was over. The boys were coming home.

Some of the Oklahoma troops arrived in May, 1919. With them was General John J. Pershing who commanded the American army in Europe. He rode in a parade car with Mayor Jack Walton down Broadway and Main streets in Oklahoma City.

The returning soldiers were discharged and went home to civilian life.

Spanish influenza epidemic. During the winter of 1918–1919, an estimated 22 million people in the world died of the Spanish flu. The disease spread like wildfire across the United States. It killed more than a half million Americans.

By October, 1918, the flu reached Oklahoma. The Oklahoma Health Commission forbade public gatherings. Schools, churches, and movie theaters were closed. Even handshaking was discouraged. Despite these precautions, an estimated seven thousand Oklahomans died from flu during the epidemic.

Governor Williams. Two months after the armistice, Williams completed his term as governor. He was appointed federal judge in the Eastern District of Oklahoma. In 1936, Williams was promoted to the United States Court of Appeals where he served for two years.

The Williams administration is remembered for two things: "cruel economy" in cutting government spending and strong leadership on the home front during World War I.

ROUNDUP

1. How did the Democractic Party change after statehood?
2. Identify: Billup's Booze Bill, bank guaranty law.
3. List three labor reforms passed by the first legislature.
4. What were the main provisions of the Jim Crow laws? How did the grandfather clause deny the vote to blacks? Why was it declared unconstitutional?
5. What argument did the U.S. Supreme Court use to uphold Haskell's removal of the capital from Guthrie?
6. Why was Governor Cruce criticized? Which moral decency laws did Cruce have trouble enforcing?
7. Give examples of Governor Williams's economy. How did Oklahoma take the lead in oil conservation?
8. For what action is Joseph Oklahombi called Oklahoma's greatest World War I hero?
9. List the causes of the Green Corn Rebellion.
10. How did the Oklahoma Council of Defense help win the war?
11. Why did three Oklahoma towns change their names during World War I?
A. Think about it! Governor Haskell, speaking on the subject of prohibition, said, "I assure you that no one within our borders will violate this law. It will be enforced!" Contrast this statement with an often heard quote in later years: "The wets have their liquor and the drys have their law."
B. Governor Cruce tried hard to enforce laws against the sale of liquor, betting on horse races, and prizefights. Explain how Cruce's job would be easier today. What present-day social evil, however, might Cruce be fighting?

19

GOLDEN TWENTIES

The 1920s was a time of rapid and exciting change. More than anything else, the low-priced automobile replaced the horse. Electric lights took the place of kerosene lamps, especially in the cities. Washing machines, refrigerators, radios, and many other inventions made home life more pleasant for many people.

Oklahoma's towns and cities had all the signs of prosperity. Merchants did a good business selling new products. Streets were crowded with automobiles. *Picture shows* were a popular entertainment. New mansions symbolized wealth made in the oil industry. The state's population continued to grow. It increased from 2,028,283 in 1920 to 2,396,040 in 1930.

Most Oklahoma farmers, however, did not share in the prosperity of the "Golden Twenties." During the World War I years they had planted more acres because crop prices were high. Then came the bust. A big surplus of farm produce glutted the market. Prices fell. Agriculture, then the main source of employment in Oklahoma, was in trouble. The farm depression was to last about twenty years—until World War II.

1. PROSPERITY IN THE 1920s WAS DUE MAINLY TO TECHNOLOGY.

Assembly line production reduced the cost of factory goods. In the 1920s, workers could afford things once available only to the rich. They could buy hundreds of new products ranging from linoleum and rayon stockings to automobiles. Many people, of course, followed the advice of advertisers to "buy now and pay later." Buying on the *installment plan* became common in the "Prosperity Decade."

Impact of the automobile. The first "horseless carriages" were not much more than playthings. Many a stalled motorist had to suffer the jeer "Get a horse" from people riding in a passing buggy. The early cars were sold as a sideline by bicycle stores and wagon makers. Livery stables were turned into garages and blacksmiths learned how to repair broken parts.

By the 1920s, auto makers were producing cheaper, more powerful, and usually reliable cars. A large number were Model T Fords. Henry Ford's factory made these hand-cranked "Tin Lizzies" quickly and sold them for less than $300. Ford said the buyer could have any color he wanted—as long as it was black. The number of registered motor vehicles in Oklahoma increased from about 200,000 in 1920 to 600,000 ten years later.

The impact of the automobile on Oklahoma life was tremendous. Thousands of new jobs were created. The oil business, in particular, boomed as hundreds of derricks mushroomed over the countryside. *Filling stations*, garages, tourist cabins (motels), hamburger drive-ins, and other car-related businesses were built along the roadside.

Auto and bus travel ended the isolation of many Oklahomans. The economic center of rural life shifted from the crossroads store to larger

A 1917 Model T Ford. (OHS)

This automobile had to be pulled out of the sand. Few roads were first-class in the 1920's. (Rena Matthews collection)

towns where families went to shop. People began to take vacations or make a trip to the state fair in Oklahoma City. The "auto bus" also made the consolidation of rural schools possible.

Not all social changes brought by the zooming motor car were good. Some drivers and passengers were injured or killed in car accidents. Home life broke down as joyriders took to the wide open spaces. The morals of *flaming youth* declined—at least in the judgment of their elders. Bank robberies and other crimes increased in the 1920s because gangsters could make a quick getaway.

Despite these problems, few people wanted to return to the old horse and buggy life. The car, at first a luxury, became a necessity. It provided both needed transportation and a means to spend leisure hours more pleasurably.

Roads and highways in the 1920s. A former traveling salesman was asked what has changed the most in Oklahoma since the 1920s. "The roads," he said without hesitation. The salesman sold sheetrock (drywall) in nineteen counties of western Oklahoma. He covered this territory from his headquarters at Woodward in a 1923 Dodge. The whole area had only forty miles of paved road, including the main streets in towns.

Most of the roads were labelled "principal

trails" on the map. They were dirt or mud, depending on the weather. Few roads had bridges over the streams.

Driving under these conditions was not always a pleasure. Even when the road ran smoothly, the car often did not. Tires with inner-tubes were easily punctured. A motorist going very far was advised to carry spare tires, a tire repair kit, a tool box, a tow rope, chains, mud hooks to get the car out of ruts, wheel cup grease, and extra oil and water.

Until the mid-1920s, county commissioners were in charge of most road building. The main job of the Oklahoma Highway Department was to distribute federal money to counties. This system led to a patchwork of roads. The only paved highways were near the thickly settled cities.

Governor Martin Trapp (1923-1927) succeeded in giving the state a major role in highway construction. At his urging, the legislature created a highway commission. Revenue for state highways came from a gasoline tax, an auto license tax, and federal funds.

By 1929, the highway department controlled more than 6,000 miles of Oklahoma's roads. Three-fourths of the roads, however, were unpaved. State roads were maintained by local patrolmen who used their own horses and graders. A few big bridges were built, including one across the Red River near Hugo.

On December 7, 1930, people gathered at Ardmore to celebrate completion of the first paved road across the state. This route was begun

Construction work on old Highway 66.

An early WKY Radio sound effects booth.

in 1919. It was called the Suggs Highway and then the T-K-O. A north-south road, it is now U.S. Highway 77.

The first paved road between Oklahoma City and Tulsa was also finished in 1930. It passed through Guthrie, Cushing, and Sand Springs.

The era of mud had a few years to go before the state constructed the fine network of hard-surfaced highways that Oklahomans enjoy today.

Radio. The radio was an exciting invention of the 1920s. The first radios were *crystal sets*. Ham operators listened with earphones.

One of the first radios in the town of Apache (north of Lawton) was bought by the local druggist. At World Series time a crowd gathered at his store. A person with earphones told the others what was happening. An assistant drew a miniature baseball diamond on a piece of wood. He used little cards with the names of players to follow the progress of the game. Spectators were as excited as they would have been in the grandstand.

The nation's first commercial broadcasting station, WWJ in Detroit, went on the air August 20, 1920. A few months later, KDKA in Pittsburgh broadcast the news of Harding's election as president. The audience was small because the radio was a novelty then.

The new invention quickly became popular across the United States. By the end of the 1920s, one American home in three had a radio. In 1927, Congress created the Federal Radio Commission.

This commission assigned wavelengths to stations to bring order to the air waves. Many stations joined one of the networks. NBC was founded in 1926 and CBS the following year.

WKY in Oklahoma City was the first broadcast station west of the Mississippi River. WKY got a federal license in April, 1921. It had been operating for more than a year as an amateur station. WKY's first studio was a small garage behind H.S. Richards's house. He and Earl C. Hull were co-owners of the 20-watt station. Eventually, WKY increased its transmitting power and moved to a larger downtown studio.

WKY had two daily programs in the early years. People with radio sets could listen at noon to hear news, weather, sports scores, and music played on the studio's *phonograph*. A "special program" was aired at 8:15 p.m. This evening program usually consisted of local talent from glee clubs, church choirs, and music schools. The violin, ukelele, and other stringed instruments sounded best on the first radios. Base notes on a piano came through like the roar of a lion.

KFJF (later KOMA) was a WKY rival in Oklahoma City. It began broadcasting in 1922. KFJF operated night and day—a rarity in the early days of radio. Its programs were soon among the best in the country.

KFRU began operating at Bristow in 1925. W.G. Skelly, an oilman, bought this station and moved it to Tulsa. By that time the call letters were KVOO. This station became famous for country-western music. Bob Wills, the "King of Western Swing," got his start at KVOO.

Gene Autry also launched his career at KVOO. Known as "Oklahoma's Singing Cowboy," Autry composed many hit songs. The first was "That Silver-Haired Daddy of Mine" in 1930.

Radio greatly changed people's way of life. Families enjoyed sitting around the radio after supper to listen to their favorite programs. They tuned in to hear *Amos 'n Andy* and other comedy series. They got the news and heard both classical music and "hit" tunes. Sports events like the famous Dempsey-Tunney heavyweight boxing championship in 1927, had many listeners.

Radio reduced the isolation of Oklahoma

Tom Mix in *The Untamed*.

Guthrie saloon. He became a national rodeo champion and performed in Miller's Wild West Show. Today, the Tom Mix Museum in Dewey displays many of his saddles, trophies, and clothes.

The first *talkie* film was *The Jazz Singer* starring Al Jolson. It was shown in Oklahoma in the late 1920s. By that time, nearly every major town had at least one moving picture theater. The fancy ones were called "movie palaces."

The silver screen had a great social impact on people. The picture show was an escape from the drab reality of everyday life. The movies set standards for dress, songs, and morals. Like the motor car and the radio, motion pictures made life in Oklahoma more uniform with the rest of the nation. People living in small towns saw how the rest of the world lived, dressed, talked, and traveled. They idolized the same stars: Charley Chaplin, Douglas Fairbanks, Greta Garbo, Mary Pickford, Rudolph Valentino, and the Barrymores.

One of Oklahoma's first movie stars was Lucille LeSueur. As a child, she learned dances from performers at her stepfather's open-air theater in

farmers. It brought them storm warnings and market news. Radio unified the nation as never before. It set standards for music, humor, and language. Radio advertising commercials were pefected to an art.

Motion pictures. The first silent picture shows came to Oklahoma before statehood. The early movie houses were set up in empty store buildings. They were called *nickelodeons* because the admission was five cents.

The Great Train Robbery, made in 1903, was the first movie to tell a connected story. This breathtaking *melodrama* was followed by other *flickers*. A piano player usually accompanied the silent movies. Sometimes, live stage entertainment was part of the program. Will Rogers got his start by performing rope tricks on the stage of the Yale Theatre in Claremore.

Westerns became popular by the 1920s. Tom Mix was the most famous star of silent westerns. Before going into the movies, Mix worked in a

Joan Crawford.

Lawton. After the family moved to Kansas City, Lucille worked her way through high school and then entered show business as a chorus girl. An active teenager, she loved the Charleston—an arm-flinging, leg-pitching dance craze in the 1920s. Lucille's dancing and personality got her a movie contract in Hollywood. She took the name Joan Crawford and acted in more than eighty movies.

2. THE REBORN KU KLUX KLAN WAS STRONG IN OKLAHOMA DURING THE 1920s.

The "roaring 20s" was a time of great social change. The automobile, movie theater, and dance hall began to rival the church and schoolhouse. Bootleg whiskey was carried in hip flasks. *Flappers* wore short dresses, bobbed hair, and kiss-proof lipstick. Some women even dared to smoke in public. The crime rate grew. Law officers could not enforce prohibition.

Many Oklahomans looked to the reborn Ku Klux Klan to enforce laws and morals. About 100,000 people in this state joined the KKK. They came from every walk of life—businessmen, lawyers, college professors, mechanics, farmers, politicians of both major parties, and many Protestant ministers.

Like the old Klan, the new KKK was secret, wore sheets and pillowcases, and used violence to terrorize blacks. The new Klan was different in that it also preached morality and Americanism. They were anti-Catholic, anti-Jewish, anti-immigrants, and anti-radicals.

Faced with the power of the Klan, some ethnic minorities tried hard to prove their patriotism. In 1921, for example, the Jewish owners of several clothing stores in Oklahoma changed their name from "Madansky Brothers" to "May Brothers." They wanted to prove they were "American in every sense of the word."

Klan activities. Klansmen sometimes appeared at a church service to make a donation and speak about law and order. They marched in parades with signs like "We Stand for Purity" or "Bootleggers Get Out." The Klan enforced its own ideas of private morals with warnings, burning crosses, and the whip. Some victims were branded with a KKK. Violence of this sort reached a peak in 1923.

Opposition to the Klan. The Klan was politically powerful. Some candidates for office in 1922 openly asked for Klan endorsement. The Klan's violence, however, caused many people to leave the organization.

An anti-Ku Klux Klan convention met in Oklahoma City in 1923. The next year, the legislature passed an anti-mask law, making it illegal to parade in hooded sheets. After that, the Klan gradually lost influence and membership.

3. THE YEAR 1920 WAS A BANNER YEAR FOR REPUBLICAN CANDIDATES AND FOR WOMEN.

Harding landslide. In 1920, Oklahoma gave its *electoral votes* to a Republican presidential candidate for the first time. Warren G. Harding of Ohio led his party to a sweeping nationwide victory. Many Republican candidates at the state and local levels rode his coattails into office. People were tired of the emotion-packed World War I years. They liked Harding's idea of returning the country to pre-war *normalcy*.

Republicans won a majority in the Oklahoma House of Representatives for the first time. They also elected five of the eight congressmen. John W. Harreld, a Republican congressman from Oklahoma City, was elected to the United States Senate seat held by Thomas P. Gore. Gore had been defeated earlier in the Democratic primary. Harreld was Oklahoma's first Republican United States senator.

Congressman Manuel Herrick. The election victory of Manuel Herrick in the northern eighth congressional district was both accidental and unexpected. Popular Republican Congressman Dick Morgan died a short time before the primary. It was too late for another Republican of any standing to file.

Herrick, a preacher without a church, won the primary without opposition. A big loser in previous elections, he had spent time in the in-

Alice M. Robertson. (OHS)

sane asylum. The Harding landslide, however, swept Herrick into office. After one term in Congress, he was committed to a mental hospital in California.

Alice Robertson. Another new Republican member of Congress was Alice Robertson. Born at an Indian mission near Muskogee, "Miss Alice" was well-known for her public service. She and her mother established a school and orphanage for Creek Indian girls at Muskogee. This school eventually grew into a Presbyterian college. It was moved and became the University of Tulsa.

During World War I Miss Robertson met the trains at Muskogee. She gave free refreshments from her cafeteria and farm to the soldiers.

She ran for Congress in 1920 on a simple platform: "I am a Christian. I am an American. I am a Republican." This slogan was good enough to win.

Woman suffrage. Some people were surprised that Miss Robertson agreed to run for Congress. She was a leading foe of woman suffrage.

In February, 1920, however, Governor James B. Robertson, no relation to Alice, had called a special session of the legislature. Purpose? To ratify the Nineteenth Amendment giving women the vote. This amendment became part of the United States Constitution when three-fourths of the states, including Oklahoma, approved it.

Women voted for the first time in an Oklahoma general election in 1920.

4. THE TULSA RACE RIOT IN 1921 ATTRACTED NATIONAL ATTENTION.

Causes. On May 31, 1921, the worst violence in Oklahoma history broke out in Tulsa. It began with the arrest of a nineteen-year-old black shoeshiner named Dick Rowland. He was accused of assaulting a white female elevator operator.

A white mob gathered to take Rowland from the courthouse jail. They intended to lynch him. Armed blacks were already there, however, to prevent Rowland's removal. A full scale riot broke out when a white man tried to disarm a black war veteran who resisted.

"The race war was on and I was powerless to stop it," said Sheriff Willard McCullough. The outnumbered blacks retreated to Greenwood Avenue, the black district which had about 11,000 people in 1921.

Black section looted and burned. On June 1, a white mob began looting and burning in the Greenwood district. More than a thousand homes, businesses, schools, churches, and other property soon lay in ruin.

Governor Robertson declared martial law and sent National Guard units to restore order in Tulsa. By that time, several hundred people had been killed or injured. Estimates of the dead range from 27 to more than 250.

Aftermath. Many blacks lived in tents until they could rebuild the Greenwood Community. Prosperity returned and Tulsa's black-owned business district became known nationally.

The elevator girl refused to prosecute. Dick Rowland was freed on all charges.

155

Governor Jack Walton. (OHS)

5. THE RED RIVER BOUNDARY DISPUTE WAS SETTLED BY THE UNITED STATES SUPREME COURT.

In 1918, oil was discovered on the south side of the Red River near Burkburnett, Texas. Immediately, the river bed became a "black gold" mine. Both Oklahoma and Texas claimed the river and began issuing overlapping oil leases. Civil war nearly broke out between the Oklahoma National Guard and the Texas Rangers.

Oklahoma filed a suit with the United States Supreme Court. In 1923, the court made a decision. The political boundary between the two states is the south cut-bank where vegetation stops.

Who owns the river? Oklahoma owns only the north half of the river bed. The United States was given the south half as trustee for the Native Americans.

6. FIVE GOVERNORS SERVED OKLAHOMA DURING THE 1920s.

The 1920s was the *impeachment* decade. Two governors, Walton and Johnston, were impeached, convicted, and removed from office. A third, Robertson, escaped impeachment by only one vote. A fourth, Trapp, was impeached but not convicted when he was lieutenant governor.

James Brookes Ayers Robertson (1919–1923). Robertson was a Democrat and a lawyer from Chandler. He is called the "father of good roads in Oklahoma." While he was governor, about 1300 miles of road were paved by the counties.

Other accomplishments include a teacher retirement system. Also, Oklahoma became one of the first states to test water and milk samples for signs of typhoid. This program reduced the number of typhoid cases.

A strong governor, Robertson used his military power to maintain law and order. When coal miners went on strike in 1919, Robertson sent the National Guard to McAlester, Henryetta, and Coalgate to protect mine property. He also used the Guard during several other strikes and at the Tulsa race riot.

While governor, Robertson was indicted by a grand jury. He was charged with accepting a bribe for helping to keep a bank at Okmulgee open. He was cleared of this charge, but not until after the end of his term. Meanwhile, the House of Representatives tried to use the bank scandal to impeach him. They failed by a dramatic 42 to 42 vote.

The deciding "No" vote was cast by a representative who was confined to a sickbed at home. John T. Jerkins, an Oklahoma City policeman on leave, was loaded on an ambulance. On the way to the capitol, the driver swerved to miss a boy on a bicycle. The ambulance turned over. A passerby took Jerkins to the capitol in time for him to vote against the impeachment of Robertson. Close call!

John C. "Jack" Walton (1923). Mayor Walton of Oklahoma City was elected governor in 1922. He was called "the hero of the common people." The whole state was invited to his two-day inaugural barbecue and parade.

Governor Henry S. Johnston receiving a gift of apples. (OHS)

Once in office, Walton quickly antagonized many groups. Conservative Democrats in the legislature opposed his demands for spending increases. Newspapers criticized him for pardoning convicts whose families gave money to his political machine. Many people objected to his stand against the death penalty. "No one is going to the electric chair while I am governor," he said.

Patronage was the root of another Walton problem. When he replaced the president of Oklahoma A and M (now Oklahoma State University), many people at Stillwater protested. The new A and M president did not have a college degree. Walton threatened to send the National Guard to tell the protesters "when to go to bed and when to get up."

Walton also had trouble with the Ku Klux Klan. While governor, he joined the KKK, but he never liked the "Kluckers." For one reason, the Klan was anti-Catholic. Walton's wife was Catholic.

In November, 1923, the House voted to impeach Walton. The Senate, sitting as a jury, removed him from office by a vote of 42 to 0. Legally, Walton deserved to be impeached for corrupt and unconstitutional actions. But the Senate trial was too hasty and disorderly to be fair. Many of the senators were members of the KKK.

Martin E. Trapp (1923–1927). *Lieutenant Governor Trapp* had been impeached but not convicted. He replaced Walton as governor. With the help of the legislature, Trapp reduced Walton's "wild spree" budget by a third. But aid to education was reduced and the free textbook law was repealed. Trapp's greatest achievement was the state highway system connecting every part of the state.

Trapp added two important state agencies. They were then called the Fish and Game Commission and the State Crime Bureau. Crimes, including train and bank robberies, were a major problem in the 1920s. The oil boom town of Cromwell, for example, had a dozen unsolved murders. Bill Tilghman, then the aging town marshal, was killed there. The job of the State Crime Bureau was to help local peace officers.

Henry S. Johnston (1927–1929). Johnston, a Democrat from Perry, was not a strong executive. He would not listen to advice from party leaders and legislators. The lawmakers disliked his personal secretary, Mrs. Mayme Hammond. Some people called her the "acting governor." She screened visitors who wanted to see Johnston. Legislators often were kept waiting and unannounced.

Johnston seemed strange because he was interested in astrology. He sometimes waited to sign a bill until the Zodiac signs were right.

The 1928 election sealed Johnston's doom. Johnston was a Protestant, a dry, and a favorite of the Klan. But he supported his party's nominee for president, Alfred E. Smith of New York,

Mrs. Mayme Hammonds.

Governor William J. Holloway. (OHS)

who was a Catholic and a wet. Smith was badly defeated, both in Oklahoma and in the nation, by Herbert Hoover, the Republican nominee. State Democratic leaders blamed Johnston, unfairly, for the party's losses in 1928.

The House impeached Johnston. The Senate convicted and removed him from office for *general incompetency* by a vote of 35 to 9.

William J. Holloway (1929–1931). Lieutenant Governor Holloway completed Johnston's term as governor. A good diplomat, Holloway restored dignity to the office. He tried to appoint good people, regardless of party, to key jobs. Holloway was a Democrat but he chose Lou Wentz, a Republican, to head the highway commission. Wentz was a respected oilman from Ponca City.

Some important laws were passed while Holloway was governor. These included a new mining code, child labor laws, and a forty-five mile-an-hour speed limit. The Governor's biggest disappointment was the legislature's refusal to approve a $150 million bond election to pave all state highways.

The *Great Depression* hit Oklahoma after the 1929 stock market crash on Wall Street in New York City. Jobless workers began lining up at public soup kitchens. Some unemployed people ran for office in 1930. More than a hundred candidates filed for fifteen state offices.

ROUNDUP

1. Tell how the automobile changed life in Oklahoma.
2. What terms do we use today instead of filling station, picture show, flaming youth, and installment buying?
3. Describe the roads of the 1920s and how they were constructed.
4. Identify: WKY, KFRU, Bob Wills, and Gene Autry. Explain why the radio was so important to Oklahomans.
5. Who were the following: Tom Mix and Lucille LeSueur? Where is the Tom Mix Museum located?
6. What did the KKK stand for in the 1920s? How did the Klan appeal to many law abiding people?
7. Who was the first woman to represent Oklahoma in Congress? When did women vote in a general election for the first time in Oklahoma? Why then?
8. What were the outcomes of the Tulsa race riot?
9. Who owns the Red River, according to the U.S. Supreme Court?
10. For what purposes did Governor Robertson call out the National Guard?
11. List reasons for the impeachment of Governor Walton. Explain why impeachment and conviction are not the same.
12. What two agencies did Governor Trapp start? Why?
13. Politically speaking, why was Governor Johnston's support for the Democractic nominee for president in 1928 unusual?
14. List the achievements and disappointments of the Holloway administration.
A. Think about it! Explain this statement: "In the 1920s, prosperity resulted from mass production and consumer spending." Why weren't all Americans prosperous? Find out what similar problems we have today.
B. Why do you think people are prejudiced? What are the best ways to overcome discrimination?
C. Try it! Look at the list of Motivating Projects and Activities for project ideas that can be related to the 1920s.

20

GREAT DEPRESSION OF THE 1930s

The Great Depression of the 1930s was the worst ever. Millions of Americans were unemployed. Many banks failed and people lost their savings. Farm and oil prices were down. In Oklahoma, the depression struck hard.

Overproduction was one cause for the depression. The farms, factories, and mines produced more than customers could buy. *Too much credit* was another cause. People had been buying on the installment plan. They were deeply in debt and had to stop spending.

Too much speculation also helped bring on the depression. So many people were borrowing money to buy corporation stocks, the prices went sky high. Stocks were selling for much more than they were worth. On October 29, 1929, the *Wall Street stock market* crashed. Everyone with stocks tried to sell at the same time. Prices plunged down. Many investors lost all they had.

At first, each family did its best to get by. The pioneer practices of "make it over," "wear it out," and "eat it up" were repeated. Churches and private charities helped out. In Shawnee, for example, the Baptist Rescue Mission served nearly 37,000 free meals during the first three months of 1933. By that time, many Oklahomans eagerly sought federal aid.

1. ALFALFA BILL MURRAY, OKLAHOMA'S MOST COLORFUL AND CONTROVERSIAL GOVERNOR, FOUGHT THE DEPRESSION.

In the 1920s, William H. Murray led a group of colonists to Bolivia. The colony failed and the penniless Oklahomans returned home. In 1930, Murray borrowed forty dollars from a Tishomingo bank and ran for governor again.

Murray campaigned as the champion of downtrodden rural people. Murray traveled from town to town in an old Ford. He wore an old brown sweater held together in front with a safety pin. He let his long underwear show beneath his trouser legs. Murray's seedy appearance, including a walrus moustache and untrimmed hair, became his trademark.

Sometimes Murray sat on a curb to eat cheese and crackers. His favorite meal was "pot likker and corn pone." Pot likker is the liquid left after greens have been boiled, usually with salt pork or bacon. Corn pone is a bread made in a skillet with cornmeal, salt, and water. One big city newspaper said the unbathed Murray ate pancakes and syrup with his bare hands. None of these descriptions hurt Murray's standing with the common folk.

To get his viewpoints to the public, Murray bought the *Blue Valley Farmer*, a weekly newspaper at Roff. Copies of the newspaper were hand-delivered wherever Murray was scheduled to speak.

Murray and most other Democratic nominees won in 1930. Voters were blaming President Hoover and Republicans for the worldwide depression. Unemployment, bank failures, and mortgage foreclosures were becoming problems in Oklahoma.

Murray's tax reform program. As governor, Murray demanded tax relief for low income farmers and homeowners. He wanted the tax burden shifted to corporations and wealthy people. He also favored a *sales tax* on luxuries.

In 1931, the legislature passed a state *income tax* bill. The rates were lower, however, than Murray requested. Two years later, the legislature fulfilled a Murray dream. It abolished the state

Governor Murray with the National Guard at the Red River.

property tax. To make up for the lost revenue, the legislature approved a state sales tax of one percent.

State and federal emergency relief. Before the 1930s, counties were expected to take care of needy people. But during the Great Depression, state and federal governments had to help.

Oklahoma was one of the first states to start a state *relief fund*. This fund provided some food, clothing, and fuel to poor people. Free seed was given to needy farmers. Also, revenue from a state gasoline tax was used to hire some unemployed men. They worked on farm-to-market roads. A small dent was made on the depression in other ways too. Murray, for example, ordered land near the governor's mansion plowed up so poor families could grow vegetables.

Murray got federal money from the Hoover administration for some projects. Workers built roads, bridges, dams and shelters for the homeless. Murray spent part of the federal grants money on free textbooks for needy families.

Governor Murray used the National Guard to enforce his decisions. In 1931, Murray was in the national limelight. Oklahoma had an oil crisis when the price dropped to eighteen cents a barrel and Murray took decisive action to solve the problem. He ordered more than 3100 wells closed down temporarily. He sent the National Guard to enforce this order. Production limits were set after the oil fields were allowed to reopen. The result of this action was spectacular. Oil prices rose to a dollar a barrel.

Governor Murray used the National Guard twenty-seven times to enforce his decisons. His most famous use of troops was in the 1931 Red River "bridge war." Murray won the thanks of both Oklahoma and Texas residents. He kept three new state bridges open. These bridges spanned the Red River south of Durant, Marietta, and Ryan.

The "war" started when owners of nearby toll bridges got a federal judge to close new free bridges. Murray defied the court. He sent National Guard troops to open the new free bridge between Durant and Denison, Texas. He personally took charge. National magazines and newspapers ran pictures of "Horatio at the Bridge" (Murray) directing traffic. Finally, a federal court upheld Murray's action because Oklahoma owned both banks of the Red River.

Candidate for president. Murray's decisive actions made him one of the nation's best-known governors. Reporters loved to quote his witty comments. In 1932, Murray ran for president and made the front cover of *Time* magazine.

This cartoon was used by eastern newspapers to ridicule Murray's candidacy for president.

Murray took his "Bread, Butter, Bacon, and Beans" campaign to southern and midwest states. He spoke out for federal relief to help the jobless. He also wanted federal old age pensions. And the farmers needed more credit, he said.

Murray didn't do well at the Democratic National Convention. The delegates nominated Governor Franklin Delano Roosevelt of New York for president.

Murray became anti-New Deal. Murray's plea for federal relief was answered by President Roosevelt's *New Deal*. But the Governor had mixed emotions about the New Deal programs.

Murray sincerely wanted help for Oklahoma's poor people. On the other hand, he personally hated the new president. He knew that the rich, Harvard-educated Roosevelt thought of him as a *hayseed* and a *demagogue*. Also, Murray believed in *states' rights* without federal interference. He had conflicts with New Deal officials over control of federal funds for relief jobs.

After leaving office in 1935, Murray became very anti-New Deal. In 1940, he campaigned against Roosevelt, supporting the Republican nominee for president.

2. THE NEW DEAL WAS A NATIONAL EFFORT TO OVERCOME THE DEPRESSION.

President Roosevelt, known as FDR, took the trial-and-error approach to the depression. "Try something," he said. "If it fails, try another."

At first, the New Deal gave money to the states. This money was handed out as *direct relief*. Unemployed people, however, wanted jobs, not charity.

The next New Deal programs were *make work projects*. Men on relief picked up litter in parks. They smoothed out roads with shovels and mule-pulled scrapers. Women sewed clothes for the needy.

Finally, programs were designed to provide useful work. Most of these programs were best-known by the initials of their three-word titles.

PWA. The Public Works Administration gave contracts to private companies to build public

WPA workers building a sidewalk. (National Archives)

projects. Much of the PWA money went for materials. But the companies also hired workers.

Oklahoma's first PWA project was the rebuilding of Jefferson School in Shawnee. This school had been damaged by a tornado. Franklin School, in the same town, was built by another agency, the WPA.

WPA. The Works Progress Administration soon became the nation's chief relief agency. It was based on the belief that every employable person has the right to useful work. "The WPA was a big blessing," one former WPA worker said. "It gave men honor."

WPA workers improved highways. They built school buildings, post offices, libraries, water systems, sidewalks, and bridges. Nearly every community in the state benefitted by WPA projects. A new high school, built of native stone in Boise City, was a typical project. In 1939, students proudly moved across the street from old wood frame buildings to the new school.

The WPA employed people in all walks of life. The Oklahoma Writers' Program, for example, provided work for writers and researchers. They traveled across the state to interview thousands of pioneers and Indians. Typed copies of these interviews were bound into 112 precious volumes which now reside at the Oklahoma Historical So-

CCC crew sloping sides of eroded gully and planting Bermuda grass. (USDA, Soil Conservation Service)

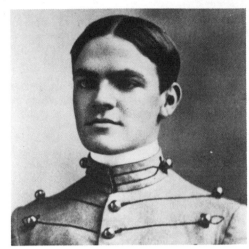

West Point Cadet Hugh S. Johnson from Alva later became a general and the NRA administrator.

ciety and the Western History Collection at the University of Oklahoma. The writers also did a book, *Oklahoma: A Guide to the Sooner State.* It gives us a good picture of what the state was like in the 1930s.

Another interesting WPA project was the excavation of a dinosaur quarry in Cimarron County. The largest animal found was a sixty-five feet long brontosaurus.

NYA. The National Youth Administration was a division of the WPA. Many students in Oklahoma colleges and high schools were given part-time work.

CCC. The Civilian Conservation Corps was one of the most popular of the federal relief programs. It provided useful work and vocational training for young men, ages 18 to 25. They were paid $30 a month. Of this amount, $25 was sent home to needy parents or dependents. The men received food, shelter, and education.

More than forty CCC camps were located in Oklahoma. The men built their own barracks. They were supervised by Army officers and by LEMS, short for "local experienced men." The "tree army," as the CCC was called, did a variety of work.

More than half the Oklahoma CCC camps did soil conservation projects. The camp near Blackwell, for example, surveyed fields for contour farming. They built check dams in eroded gullies and constructed ponds. They planted trees and grass to stop wind erosion. Control of soil erosion was the most outstanding CCC accomplishment.

The CCC also made improvements in parks and forests. At Platt National Park, CCC crews built mineral spring shelters with native stone. In Oklahoma City, the CCC began work on Lincoln and Will Rogers parks. The men built the amphitheater in Lincoln Park. Another CCC city project was Tulsa's Mohawk Park.

Many of the CCC's young men later went into the armed services during World War II.

NRA. The National Recovery Administration was headed by General Hugh Johnson. He was a crusty, outspoken Oklahoman. As a boy, Johnson came to Alva on a Cherokee Outlet land run train in 1893. His father was Alva's first postmaster.

One purpose of the NRA was to spread the work around. More jobs can be created by cutting down the hours worked by each employee. Merchants all over Oklahoma signed up with NRA. They displayed the "blue eagle" with the slogan "We do our part" in store windows.

Oklahoma City led the nation in NRA pledges. The grocery stores alone were able to hire 500 new employees with a six-hour day. Oil companies and other businesses added many workers with a shorter work week.

162

Governor Ernest W. Marland. (OHS)

AAA. The Agricultural Adjustment Act tried to raise farm prices by paying farmers to cut down their acreage.

Oklahoma cotton farmers eagerly signed up with the AAA. They were paid to plow under part of their 1933 crop. With less cotton on the market, the price rose from five to nine cents a pound. The AAA used similar plans to cut production of wheat and other crops as well as livestock.

Big farmers benefitted the most from the AAA. They received large payments for unused land. Landlords could profit more by taking land out of cultivation than by renting it. Sharecroppers were pushed off the land. A familiar picture of the 1930s was the poor farmer and his family headed down the road in an overloaded jalopy.

3. THE NEW DEAL WAS THE MOST HOTLY CONTESTED ISSUE IN STATE POLITICS IN THE 1930s.

Many farmers and jobless Oklahomans took help from New Deal agencies. Oklahoma voters gave Franklin Roosevelt a big majority every time he ran for president. Nevertheless, there was much opposition to the New Deal in this state. Opponents didn't like federal *regulation* and *bu-reaucracy*. They believed the New Deal was a threat to states' rights.

Two of Oklahoma's three Democratic governors in the 1930s were anti-New Deal. Only Marland favored it.

Governor Ernest W. Marland. Many people have visited Marland's beautiful fifty-five room mansion in Ponca City. It is now a national historic site. The Pioneer Woman Statue, in the same city, is Marland's best-known civic project.

In the late 1920s, Marland lost his oil empire to New York bankers. The Marland Oil Company became Conoco. Marland then went into politics. After one term in Congress, he was elected governor in 1934.

Marland worked hard to bring more New Deal programs and jobs to Oklahoma. That was perhaps his greatest achievement as governor. He failed, however, to fulfill his dream of a "Little New Deal" in Oklahoma. He wanted a huge state public works program. It would be financed by both federal funds and increased state taxes. The legislature, led by House Speaker Leon C. "Red" Phillips, refused to go along with most of Marland's plans.

Some important boards and agencies were created, however, while Marland was governor. The highway patrol was started in 1937. The Interstate Oil Compact Commission was created to promote oil conservation and keep oil prices steady. Marland also got the legislature to establish the Oklahoma Planning and Resources Board. He thought the state needed to plan in order to grow and attract new industries.

Governor Leon C. "Red" Phillips. Phillips, a lawyer and state representative from Okemah, was elected governor in 1938. He fulfilled an election promise to balance the state budget. Spending was slashed. Taxes on gasoline and other items were raised.

Phillips then persuaded the voters to approve a "balanced budget amendment" to the constitution in 1941. This amendment put Oklahoma on a "pay-as-you-go" basis. It has been called "the single most notable achievement of any governor in the 1930s and 1940s."

Phillips was a conservative Democrat. He

A black blizzard rolls into Goodwell, Oklahoma on June 4, 1937. (No Man's Land Museum, Goodwell)

didn't believe a government should spend more than it can afford. This belief is one reason he was against the New Deal. Phillips refused to support Roosevelt for a third term in 1940. After leaving office, he switched to the Republican Party.

New Dealers were shocked when Governor Phillips opposed the construction of a huge federal flood control and hydroelectric project on the Red River. He argued that Denison Dam would take 100,000 acres of rich farmland off the Oklahoma tax rolls. The dam was completed, however, in 1944. It backs up Lake Texoma, Oklahoma's second largest lake.

4. THE DUST BOWL INCLUDED NORTHWEST OKLAHOMA AND PARTS OF ADJACENT STATES.

In pioneer days, settlers rushed into the Great Plains. They "busted" the sod and planted wheat. In the spring, restless winds bent vast fields of ripening grain into golden waves as far as the eye could see. Year after year, the rains came and crops were harvested.

Prosperous farmers gradually replaced rude dugouts with comfortable frame houses. They bought tractors, combines, trucks, and automobiles which changed farm life. Little towns sprang up. Old trails became roads. Railroads were built to haul grain and other freight.

Dust Bowl. A severe drought in the 1930s turned the high plains into a *Dust Bowl*. Farmers suddenly realized they had given too little attention to conserving moisture and humus in the soil.

"There are fields which, because of the soil characteristics, should have been left in grass," said one big farmer-rancher in the Panhandle. "In the main, however, our blunder was not in breaking the sod but in farming methods we used afterwards."

The heart of the Dust Bowl was in a five-state

164

A Dust Bowl scene near Felt in Cimarron County. (National Archives)

area. It included northwestern Oklahoma and parts of Kansas, Colorado, New Mexico, and Texas. Most of this plains region had been stripped of its natural grass cover. The land had no defense against the winds and drought.

Dust storms. Two types of dust storms swept over the plains in the "dirty thirties." They were the *black blizzard* and the *sand storm.*

An approaching black blizzard looked like a rolling wall, often more than a mile high. The dirt was lifted higher and higher by atmospheric electricity.

One of the worst blizzards struck on Black Sunday, April 14, 1935. No one who experienced it will ever forget. In mid-afternoon, a warm, clear day with fresh, blue skies suddenly turned cold. Birds fluttered nervously. There was no sound, no wind—just a huge cloud of dust rolling in from the north. When it arrived, the world turned to darkness. Chickens went to roost early.

The day after Black Sunday the Dust Bowl got its name. A Denver reporter traveling in the Panhandle wrote an article which began: "Three little words, achingly familiar on a Western farmer's tongue, rule life in the dust bowl . . . if it rains."

The sand storm was a more frequent occurrence in the Dust Bowl. It was stirred up by the low winds, usually from the southwest. Beginning in March, sandy soil in plowed fields drifted into dunes along the fence rows and ditches. Aban-

doned farmhouses and farm machinery were partially buried. The sand storms eroded fields, leaving them as bare and hard as a table. Native American campgrounds were exposed and arrowhead collecting became a hobby.

During bad dust storms, travelers pulled off the road. Trains slowed to a crawl or stopped when sand drifted across the rails. People were uncomfortable as dust filled the nose, eyes, and throat. Goggles and a big handkerchief or dust mask helped a little. Housewives could not keep the powdery dust from sifting in. They tried to seal cracks in windows with gummed-paper used in wrapping packages. Metal weather stripping was tacked around openings. But nothing was fully effective.

The Soil Conservation Service counted the dust storms. A storm was counted if it cut visibility to less than a mile. The worst years were 1935 with forty, 1936 with sixty-eight, 1937 with seventy-two, and 1938 with sixty-one. The number of hours of dust storm weather was also recorded. In 1937, for example, Guymon in Texas County had 550 hours of countable dusty weather.

Woodrow Wilson "Woody" Guthrie (1912–1967). Guthrie recorded two albums of "Dust Bowl" ballads. He was able to put into music the agony of Dust Bowl people who struggled to survive in the midst of a dream gone suddenly wrong.

An Oklahoma folk hero, Guthrie was born in Okemah. He left home at age 16 "to see the land

"Drouth Survivors" (Alexander Hogue painting, 1936)

Woody Guthrie.

A Dust Bowl farm in 1936.

and the people." Woody survived by playing the harmonica and guitar and singing in pool rooms, migrant camps in California, and labor union halls. Eventually he sang folk songs on radio shows in Los Angeles and New York City. Guthrie composed more than a thousand ballads, including "This Land Is Your Land." He has been called the father of modern folk music.

One of Guthrie's popular ballads about the dust that darkened the sun went like this:

"The telephone rang, it rang off the wall
It was the preacher a-makin' his call.
He said, 'Kind friends, this may be the
   end;
May be your last chance at salvation
   from sin.'

"The church it was crowded, the church
   it was packed,
But the dusty old dust storm blowed up
   so black,
That the preacher could not read a word
   of his text,
So he folded his specs,
Took up a collection and said,

"So long, it's been good to know you,
So long, it's been good to know you . . ."

Changes in Dust Bowl farming methods.

The U.S. Soil Conservation Service and other federal agencies worked with farmers to save the Dust Bowl. A program of improved farming methods stressed three points: conservation of moisture, use of cover crops, and stopping the practice of planting wheat in a dry seedbed.

Moisture was saved by *contour farming*. Each furrow was plowed on the level—around the slopes instead of up and down the hill. Water would then stay in the furrows and sink into the soil. To save even more water, some farmers also built broad, low *terraces* along the contour lines.

Many farmers had better luck with the damming or basin *lister*. This tillage implement made a small earthen dam about every ten feet in the furrow. Bill Baker, the Cimarron County farm agent, said the basins held the rain as well as contour furrows.

A new *cover crop*, dwarf milo maize, helped save the Dust Bowl. It was developed by a plant breeder at the Woodward experiment station. The dwarf milo, no more than two or three feet high, could survive winds and hot summer sun that bent down taller milo and kaffir. Combine milo, as plains farmers called the dwarf milo, matured before frost. It was harvested with a wheat combine. Strip farming—the planting of cover crops in alternate strips with wheat—helped to check wind erosion.

The same farm in 1937 after the planting of combine (dwarf) milo.

Circular irrigation—fields watered by giant sprinklers.

Dry land researchers discovered a way to predict the chances of producing a wheat crop. If a farmer could not measure two feet of subsoil moisture at seeding time in the autumn, forget it. He was advised not to plant.

By the early 1940s the drought was broken. The Panhandle got more than 25 inches of rain in 1941. The dust was wet enough that the harshest winds could not disturb it. Today, some farmers in the old Dust Bowl irrigate crops with water pumped from deep wells.

5. OKLAHOMA'S POPULATION DECLINED AND ITS IMAGE CHANGED IN THE 1930s.

The Great Depression decreased the need for farm workers and tenants. Oklahoma suffered more than most states during the depression. Why? One reason is that the state depended heavily on farming. In the 1930s, the per capita income in Oklahoma was only half the national average. Low crop prices and drought forced many farmers to leave the soil. Foreclosures on farms and sheriff's sales were common in the 1930s.

Farmland was a drag on the market. The low point was reached when a quarter section in Cimarron County sold for only $25. Well-to-do farmers and businessmen bought up huge tracts of cheap land. The average size farm in Oklahoma nearly doubled between 1930 and 1950.

At the same time, many farms were mechanized. Tractors and modern equipment reduced the need for farm laborers and tenants. Also, as we have seen, the AAA programs caused many big farmers to stop renting out their land. They could make more profit by collecting federal subsidies for taking the land out of cultivation.

Many Oklahomans left the state. The Oklahoma economy could not support the population in the 1930s. Thousands of jobless people scattered in all directions. Many hit "that hot old dusty way to the California line."

Contrary to popular belief, not all the California-bound *migrants* were from Oklahoma. Many people left Arkansas, Kansas, Missouri, Texas, and other states. But in California, they were all called *"Okies."*

The typical "Okies," from whatever state, were young parents with one or two children. Most were farm workers or *tenants*. Some were unemployed town people. Very few were farm owners. Only six percent of the Oklahoma migrants came from the eleven northwest Dust Bowl counties—another myth shot down! Nearly two-thirds came from the southern tier of counties where cotton was the main crop.

Many migrants chugged along Highway 66 in a wheezy car. Called "tin can tourists," they had

167

Hard times drove many Oklahomans to California. (Library of Congress, a Lange photo)

only a few dollars for gas and a bit of food. Lacking education, most of them could not adapt to new occupations. Once in California, they eked out a poor living picking fruit and vegetables on huge farms.

Sooner image tarnished. In 1939, Oklahomans celebrated the Golden Anniversary of the 1889 land run. In fifty years the word *Sooner* had come to mean a can-do, energetic, successful person. Oklahoma's boosters pictured the state as "The Land of the Fair God"—a land of prosperity and opportunity.

This positive image was captured by Rodgers and Hammerstein in the musical *Oklahoma*: "We know we belong to the land, and the land we belong to is grand." The ending of this song expressed the Sooner spirit exactly: OKLAHOMA-aaaH—OK!"

But the darker side of Oklahoma's heritage was hard to ignore in the 1930s. Hundreds of jobless country people camped in a shanty town along the Canadian River in Oklahoma City. The migration of poor farmers to California's "Okievilles" gave Oklahoma bad publicity. Then, in 1939, a WPA official estimated that half the state's population was on some kind of relief.

Grapes of Wrath. John Steinbeck, a California novelist, shocked Oklahomans with his *Grapes of Wrath* in 1939. Steinbeck could have chosen many other places as the setting for his book. But he picked Oklahoma to show how de-

pression, drought, and machinery forced tenant farmers off the land.

The *Grapes of Wrath* is the story of the fictitious Joad family. Like other "Okies," the Joads pack their belongings in a "tin lizzie" and hit the road for California. Unfortunately, the Joads became the *stereotype* for all the "real" migrants. The obscene language and dialect which Steinbeck had the Joads speak was a source of shame to all Oklahomans.

Furthermore, Steinbeck was hazy in his geography. Sallisaw, the Joad hometown on the Ozark Plateau, was located incorrectly in the Dust Bowl. The Sallisaw area had none of the huge mechanized farms that supposedly forced the Joads off the land. In fact, only forty tractors could be counted in all of Sequoyah County. And why would Grandpa Joad yearn for California grapes to squish all over his face? Sallisaw is one of the best grape-growing regions in the United States.

Much of what Steinbeck wrote, however, was true in a general way. His "Okie" tenant farmers never shared in Oklahoma's prosperous farms, oil wells, and cultural progress. Reality to them was poverty, disease, and ignorance. Despite all their problems, the "Okies" loved the land. They loved their families. They kept their human dignity and that was the moral lesson of the book.

Grapes of Wrath was a bestseller. The bottom line is that the novel burned "Okie" into the nation's vocabulary as a dirty word. Oklahoma was given an unfair image to live down.

6. WILL ROGERS AND WILEY POST WERE OKLAHOMA HEROES IN THE 1930s.

August 15, 1935 was a sad day! Oklahoma lost two favorite sons in an Alaskan airplane accident. Wiley Post, the pilot, was from Maysville. He hoped to find a mail and passenger route to Russia by way of Alaska. His famous passenger, Will Rogers, was a friend of aviation.

Post got lost in a dense fog while on a sidetrip from Fairbanks. Rogers wanted to interview "King Charlie" Brower, a whaler and trader, at Point Barrow. Less than twenty miles from this destination, Post landed on a frozen inlet. While he was getting directions from an Eskimo, the engine cooled. It stalled after takeoff and the nose-heavy plane plunged into the water. Both men were killed instantly. The nation mourned its double loss.

Will Rogers (1879–1935). William Penn Adair Rogers was America's best-loved "prince of wit and wisdom." His fame rested on his easy ability to make people laugh.

When asked where he was born, Rogers would say Claremore. He wasn't sure anyone could remember Oologah, the closest village to his birthplace. One-fourth Cherokee, Rogers would say, "My ancestors may not have come over on the Mayflower, but they met 'em at the boat."

The youngest of eight children, Rogers grew up on the family ranch at Oologah. He lacked discipline and did not do well in school. An expert rider and roper, he went to work as a cowboy in Texas.

In 1902, Will decided to see the world. After a short stay in Argentina, he worked on a cattle boat bound for South Africa. There he joined up with a wild west show as a trick roper. He later toured Australia and New Zealand with the Wirth Brothers Circus.

After two years roaming, Rogers returned to the United States and began a career in *vaudeville*. Not content with performing his rope act silently, Will began chatting with his audiences. "Swingin' a rope is all right," he would drawl, "when your neck ain't in it." People loved his down-to-earth humor.

In 1908, Will married his long-time sweetheart, Betty Blake. She toured with him but took time out to bear four children: Will Jr., Mary, Jimmy, and Fred who died in infancy.

From 1915 to 1925, Rogers was in the famed *Ziegfeld Follies* in New York City. His lasso act and running commentary on all subjects drew praise. While performing in the Follies, he began acting in silent films for Sam Goldwyn. Before his untimely death, Rogers did fifty silents and twenty-one talking films. He also made a series of movie shorts that flashed on the movie screen like a news show.

The news shorts launched Rogers into an-

Will Rogers at age 25. His Cherokee ancestry shows in this picture.

other side career—writing weekly and daily newspaper columns. He wrote witty comments on timely events reported in the newspapers. "All I know is what I read in the papers," became his often-quoted byword. His short, crisp "Daily Telegrams" was probably the most popular and widely-read newspaper column of all time.

Rogers was also in demand as a lecturer. Between movies he was constantly on tour. "I don't make jokes," he would say to sympathetic audiences, "I just watch the government and report the facts and I have never found it necessary to exaggerate." He said he was born on election day and that gave him a natural right to "poke fun" at people in high places.

In 1927, Rogers extended his audience by venturing into radio. He imitated President Coolidge so well, most listeners thought the President was speaking. The Rogers's radio show became especially popular during the Great Depression. His humorous comments on current events lifted the spirits of people everywhere.

During his career, Rogers raised millions of

dollars for charity. He donated his time and talent for benefit shows. In 1931, Rogers borrowed a navy plane to make a twenty-day charity tour of Oklahoma, Texas, and Arkansas. His shows in Tulsa, Fort Worth, and other cities raised $250,000 to help needy people.

Rogers was the nation's number one booster of aviation. He often praised Charles Lindberg who made the first solo flight across the Atlantic Ocean. And Rogers reminded the public of speed records set by Wiley Post and other aviators. Unfortunately, it was Rogers's interest in aviation that brought about his death in 1935.

The public continues to honor Will Rogers. His statue is one of two that Oklahoma is allowed to have in the Capitol in Washington, D.C. Another statue at the Will Rogers Memorial in Claremore bears his best-known comment: "I never met a man I didn't like."

Wiley Post (1899–1935). Born in Texas, Wiley Post grew up on an Oklahoma farm. Like most farm boys, he was interested in machines. Wiley began dreaming of flying when he saw his first airplane at a county fair in Lawton at age fourteen. He read books on aviation and acquired a technical education. He attended an automobile repair school in Kansas City and studied radio in the Army.

Wiley broke into flying as a parachute jumper. He hired on with a barnstorming group after making his first jump at Wewoka. But public interest in this sport soon dropped off. Post then returned to the oil fields to work. An accident almost wiped out his dream to fly. A sliver from an iron bolt, which a fellow worker was pounding with a sledge hammer, hit Post in the left eye. The eye had to be removed.

Post, unwilling to give up, learned to judge distances with one eye. He bought an old airplane with $1,800 received as workmen's compensation. Before long, he was earning a living training student pilots and flying oilmen to their rigs.

In 1927, Post eloped with a Texas rancher's daughter. When the plane engine conked out, the couple landed in a harvested cornfield. They were married by a local parson.

Post had an opportunity to fly better planes when he took a job as personal pilot for F. C. Hall, a wealthy Oklahoma oilman. Hall bought a Lockheed Vega plane with all the latest improvements. It had a streamlined fuselage built around a laminated plywood frame. With a Pratt and Whitney 420 horsepower engine, the plane cruised at 150 miles per hour. It was named *Winnie Mae* after Hall's daughter.

Hall was an aviation enthusiast. He let Post enter the *Winnie Mae* in air races. In 1930, Post won the nonstop race between Los Angeles and Chicago. Hall let him keep the $7,500 prize money.

Twice Post flew the *Winnie Mae* around the world—with a navigator in 1931 and alone in 1933. Two new inventions helped Post set a record of 7 days 18 hours 49½ minutes in the solo flight. One was the *automatic pilot* that made use of gyrostat principles to keep the plane level. The other was an *automatic radio direction finder*. This radiocompass homed in on commercial radio broadcasts. Post could fly in the direction of a transmitting antenna simply by tuning in the station.

Post was given two New York City ticker-tape parades after his world flights. Presidents Hoover and Roosevelt invited him to the White House. Congress awarded him the Distinguished Flying Cross.

Post appreciated the honors for his world flights. But he thought his high altitude experiments at Bartlesville were his greatest contribution to aviation. He knew that a plane could fly faster in the thinner air of a high altitude jet stream. All he needed was a breathing apparatus. For this purpose, Post invented a pressure suit. Wearing this suit he climbed comfortably to 40,000 feet in the *Winnie Mae*. He predicted, correctly, that planes would be equipped someday with pressurized cabins.

In 1935, Will Rogers hired Post to fly him to Alaska so he could gather new material for his syndicated newspaper column. If all went well, the men would fly across Siberia and around the world. Post bought a second-hand plane for the trip. He attached pontoons to make it a seaplane for landing on Alaska's lakes. Unfortunately, the

A sad day for Oklahoma and the world!

pontoons were too big and made the plane nose-heavy. Rogers had to sit near the tail to counterbalance the nose.

The crash on August 15 shocked the nation.

The *Winnie Mae* and Wiley Post's pressure suit are now on display at the Smithsonian Institute in Washington, D.C. In principle, Post's suit had the same design as those worn by astronauts today.

ROUNDUP

1. List causes for the Great Depression.
2. Why did many poor people like William Murray? Give several examples of Murray's actions that made him a strong governor. Why did he dislike President Roosevelt?
3. Make a chart of the New Deal agencies using these headings: Agencies, Purpose, Examples of Projects in Oklahoma.
   Why did many Oklahomans oppose the New Deal? What was Governor Marland's plan for a "Little New Deal?"
5. For what law is Governor Phillips remembered?
6. What is the difference between a black blizzard and a sand storm? Describe discomforts of people in the Dust Bowl. Why is Woodie Guthrie famous?
7. List some new farming methods that improved the Dust Bowl.
8. Why did Oklahomans leave the state in the 1930s?
9. Explain how the musical *Oklahoma!* and the book *Grapes of Wrath* gave opposite impressions of Oklahoma.
10. Briefly summarize the career of Will Rogers. List the achievements of Wiley Post.
A. Think about it! Compare or contrast Oklahoma's economy today with that of the 1930s. Explain your answer with specific examples.
B. Try it! Interview someone who lived during the Great Depression. Write a report or present your findings to the class.

171

21

WORLD WAR II AND POSTWAR CHANGES: 1940S AND 1950S

While Americans were busy fighting the depression in the 1930s, Europe and Asia were moving toward war. In 1931, the military leaders of Japan invaded Chinese territory. Four years later, dictator Mussolini of Italy took over helpless Ethiopia in Africa.

Then Adolf Hitler ordered his Nazi army to gobble up Austria and Czechoslovakia. On September 1, 1939, Hitler smashed into Poland. World War II officially began two days later when Great Britain and France declared war on Germany.

The United States sympathized with Britain, France, and their allies. President Roosevelt gave these countries all the material aid possible short of going to war. The final step came after a Japanese sneak attack on Pearl Harbor, Hawaii on December 7, 1941. The United States Congress declared war on the *Axis powers:* Japan, Germany, and Italy.

World War II brought many changes to Oklahoma. Families were disrupted as young men were drafted or volunteered for the armed services. Prosperity returned with the demand for the products of Oklahoma's farms, mines, and oil fields. A favorable climate, central location, cheap fuel, and mechanically-skilled population made Oklahoma an ideal place for army camps, naval bases, airfields, and defense factories.

More Oklahoma men and women had jobs than ever before. They were paid the highest wages in history. Since there was a shortage of wartime consumer goods, people put their excess cash into savings. Oklahoma was one of the nation's top ten states in buying war bonds.

Volunteers in every town tried to dramatize the war bond drives. Bond-o-meter boards, which looked like giant thermometers, were displayed in downtown areas. People could easily see what percent of their town's bond quota had been met. Residents of Ponca City bought a B-17 bomber, the *Miss Ponca City*, that cost more than a million dollars. In Tulsa, bond buyers were given a dinner. They used Hitler's silverware to eat cake cut by Japanese Admiral Yamashita's sword.

Captured German canteens were given to volunteers who sold a certain amount of bonds during one drive. Auctions were another popular way to sell bonds. On one occasion, silver service pieces from the *U.S.S. Oklahoma*, sunk at Pearl Harbor, were sold to the biggest bond buyers. Governor Robert Kerr proclaimed the first day of one bond drive "Sooner Day." Anyone who bought a bond on that day got a lapel pin with the words "I got mine sooner."

Oklahomans had every reason to be proud of their war effort. The stage was set for many postwar changes in the state.

1. MANY OKLAHOMA MEN AND WOMEN WERE IN THE ARMED SERVICES DURING WORLD WAR II.

Almost a half million Oklahomans were in the armed forces during World War II. More than 192,000 enlisted. Another 300,000 men were drafted through the Selective Service system. Sooner men and women distinguished themselves all over the world. Seventeen Oklahomans won the *Congressional Medal of Honor.* Casualties included 6,463 dead and 10,120 wounded.

45th Infantry Division. The Oklahoma National Guard was called to active duty in 1940 before the United States entered the war. The Oklahomans were joined by other Guard units to form the 45th Division. The original insignia of

National Guard soldiers wave goodbye as they leave for active duty at Fort Sill. (Arizona Historial Society)

45th Infantry Division troops crossing the Moselle River in France, 1944.

this division was a gold *swastika*. It was changed to the *thunderbird* because Hitler made the swastika his Nazi Party symbol.

In 1943, the 45th fought its way across the island of Sicily. Landings were made on the bloody beaches at Salerno and Anzio in southern Italy. The next year, the division landed in southern France and pushed north toward Germany. Lieutenant Clarence Coggins of Poteau was a hero in this drive. He single-handedly took hundreds of German prisoners.

Two Native Americans in the 45th Division won the Congressional Medal of Honor. Lieutenant Jack C. Montgomery, a Cherokee from Sallisaw, captured three strong enemy positions in Italy. The other winner was Lieutenant Ernest Childers, a Creek from Broken Arrow. Both men won their officer commissions on the battlefield.

Some Comanche soldiers were trained for code talking. Their language is unwritten and has a number of dialects. The Germans could not "decipher" it.

General Raymond S. McLain went overseas as the artillery commander of the 45th Division. An Oklahoma City banker in civilian life, McLain rose fast in rank and responsibility. He was soon in charge of three other divisions. Known as "the fighting general," he would say, "If you get out there with them, they (the army) will move."

Twice McLain fought his way out of a German roadblock with his jeep-mounted machine gun.

The 45th took part in the final conquest of Germany. The Thunderbirds rescued some 32,000 living skeletons at the Daschau concentration camp. They captured Munich where Hitler started his Nazi movement. Germany surrendered on May 8, 1945 (VE Day). By that time the 45th had been in combat more than 500 days.

Cartoons by Bill Mauldin of Phoenix, Arizona, made the 45th Division famous. Mauldin

Bill Mauldin drawing a Willie and Joe cartoon. (Arizona Highways)

The Beaver family, including U.S. Navy WAVES Delores and Beulah, are welcomed by another Kiowa at the Anadarko Indian Exposition. (U.S. Navy photo)

created two humorous characters named Willie and Joe to show the war through the eyes of the common soldier. The cartoons appeared in both army and civilian newspapers. Today, the heroic Thunderbirds are honored by the 45th Infantry Division Museum in Oklahoma City.

2. MANY WORLD WAR II PILOTS, SOLDIERS, AND SAILORS WERE TRAINED IN OKLAHOMA.

Oklahomans were very involved in the war effort. New army posts, naval bases, and airfields dotted the map.

Army posts. During World War II, soldiers trained at twenty-eight camps in Oklahoma. Fort Sill, the best-known, was enlarged. It became the largest artillery training center in the world. Here, men from all over the country learned to fire the big guns. Also, thousands of young Oklahomans were inducted into the army at Fort Sill—including the author of this book.

Camp Gruber, one of the new camps, was built in the Cookson Hills east of Muskogee. The quiet hilly country became a beehive of activity.

Naval bases. Whoever heard of an inland naval base? Many World War II sailors were surprised to be stationed at bases on the prairie near Norman, Clinton, Purcell, and other Oklahoma cities. They received needed technical training in naval aviation, mechanics, and other fields.

The Women's Naval Reserve (WAVES) had a training "ship" on the university campus at Stillwater. They did basic and advanced training there.

Air bases. Year round flying weather made Oklahoma an ideal location for Army and Navy flight training. The Army Air Force operated Will Rogers Air Base, using Oklahoma City's municipal airport. Training centers were established at Cimarron Field near Yukon and Vance Field at Enid. Pilots flew from these and other bases to auxiliary landing fields all over the state.

Navy flyers trained at North Base near Norman, at a base near Clinton, and other places.

Tinker Field at Oklahoma City was the largest Army Air Force installation in the state. It was named for General Clarence Tinker, an Osage native from Pawhuska. Tinker was killed in a 1942 bombing raid on the Japanese in the Battle of Midway. During the war, army bombers were brought to Tinker Field for repair. The B-29s that dropped atomic bombs on Hiroshima and Nagasaki in August, 1945, were modified at Tinker.

The Spartan School of Aeronautics at Tulsa trained Royal Air Force cadets at Miami for the British government. By the war's end, fifteen air-

General Clarence Tinker. (OHS)

174

Men and women working on B-24s at Tinker Air Force Base during World War II. (OHS)

men had died in plane crashes. A Miami resident, Mrs. Claude A. Hill, began looking after their graves. She was awarded the King's Medal of Service by the British ambassador in Washington, D.C.

POW camps. FIRST BATCH OF HUN CAPTIVES—that was the headline in the *El Reno American* on July 8, 1943. Fort Reno had one of the eight prisoner of war compounds in Oklahoma.

Many of the German prisoners in Oklahoma had surrendered in North Africa. They were part of Hitler's *Afrika Korps*. Indoctrinated with Nazi ideas, most of the captives still believed that someday Hitler would conquer the world. The POWs sometimes tossed pro-Hitler propaganda leaflets out of passing trains or from trucks taking them to work areas.

Very seldom did prisoners try to escape. One military policeman was assigned to every eight prisoners. Besides, where would an escapee go? Two young Germans who walked away from a work project in October, 1944, discovered they could not return to Germany. Hans Kaiser and Karl Haas hid the "P" painted on their clothing

by reversing their raincoats. They hid in barns and deserted farmhouses for two weeks. Then they surrendered at the El Reno train depot.

The prisoners actually helped the American war effort. To relieve their boredom, they worked willingly on farms and at military posts. Noncooperative, diehard-Nazi prisoners from POW camps all over the country were gathered together at a stockade near Alva. These POWs were guarded very closely and had very few privileges.

3. OKLAHOMA'S ECONOMY BOOMED DURING WORLD WAR II.

Oklahoma was prosperous during the war. The military bases brought millions of dollars into the state. Wheat combines rolled again across a wetter Dust Bowl. The state's farm crops, oil, and minerals brought high wartime prices.

New factories. Oklahoma's manufacturing industry grew dramatically during World War II. New defense factories were built in Oklahoma City, Tulsa, and other places.

English language classes were a popular activity in prisoner of war camps.

The most spectacular of the plants with government contracts was the great Douglas Aircraft bomber assembly plant at Tulsa. Dupont's smokeless powder plant at Chouteau was another important factory. Tulsa workers made the forty-mile trip daily to the plant in "share-the-ride" cars. A Tulsa mill made prefabricated houses for many workers at Chouteau and other towns.

Oklahoma City became a national aviation center during the war. Douglas Aircraft Company located a plant next to Tinker Field. The Douglas factory turned out C-47 cargo and troop transport planes.

4. ROBERT S. KERR USED HIS POLITICAL SKILLS TO PROMOTE THE ECONOMIC GROWTH OF OKLAHOMA.

Background. Robert S. Kerr had the perfect background for political success. He was born in a log cabin near Ada in the Chickasaw Nation in 1896. His father was a self-educated tenant farmer who knew his Bible well. The elder Kerr taught his children to work hard, get an education, and take part in civic affairs.

As a young boy, Robert told his father he wanted three things in life: a family, a million dollars, and the governorship. By 1942 he had all these things. During his campaign for governor that year, Kerr told crowds that turned out to hear him, "I'm just like you, only I struck oil."

Rich man with the common man's touch. Kerr was a great speaker. He had a sense of humor and a knack for getting people to like him. A good example was his reaction to a rumor spread by his Democratic primary opponent in 1942. Supposedly, Kerr was traveling with "two blonds." After finishing a speech in Seminole, he said, "And now I want you to meet those two blonds." Kerr introduced his wife and ten-year-old daughter.

Kerr was a self-made rich oil tycoon. But he had the common man's touch. On the campaign trail he rolled up his shirt sleeves and tugged at his red suspenders while speaking. For more than twenty years he taught a Sunday-school class at the First Baptist Church in Oklahoma City.

Governor Kerr (1943–1947). Kerr was elected the state's first native-born governor. He was lucky to be in office when Oklahoma was prosperous. During the war people had jobs. Incomes were rising. The taxes rolled in. The legislature had more money to spend for schools, highways, and public health. Surplus funds were used to wipe out the state debt.

Governor Kerr was willing to go almost anywhere to promote Oklahoma and the Democratic Party. His enemies called him "Travellin' Bob." The Tulsa newspapers gave him the name "Sorghum-Packin' Bob." While on a trip to New York City, he took a jug of sorghum molasses to a

Governor Robert S. Kerr shares some Oklahoma sorghum.

lady who had written to him. Surrounded by reporters and cameras, Kerr took advantage of the free publicity to brag about Oklahoma's agriculture.

In 1944, Kerr was invited to give the *keynote address* at the Democratic National Convention in Chicago. His rousing praise of Roosevelt's New Deal thrilled the delegates. Kerr's strong support for Roosevelt and Truman paid off for Oklahoma. The state did better than most in getting defense contracts and federal funds for roads, dams, and flood control projects.

U.S. Senator Kerr (1949–1963). In 1948, Kerr was elected to the U.S. Senate with the slogan "Land, Wood, and Water." He promised soil and water projects to "build Oklahoma." Kerr was called the "millionaire candidate" by opponents because of his huge spending for advertising on billboards, on the radio, and in newspapers.

Senator Kerr took great pride in the Arkansas River Navigation Project and other public works he got Congress to approve for Oklahoma.

Oklahomans were shocked when Senator Kerr died on New Year's Day, 1963. Then in his third six-year term, he had served his state well. A fellow senator called Kerr "the uncrowned king of the senate." President John F. Kennedy and other dignitaries attended the funeral in Oklahoma City. The state legislature made Kerr's birthplace near Ada a state memorial. He was buried not far from the restored log cabin where he was born.

Kerr bridged the gap between rustic frontier Oklahoma and the modern state. Before the 1940s, Oklahoma's economy rested on production of the 3 Fs: food, fiber, and fuel. Kerr was a leader in diversifying the economy. He promoted the state's potentials for manufacturing and recreation.

Kerr believed that all Oklahoma would benefit by development of the state's water resources. He studied plans of the Army Corps of Engineers to control floods, conserve soil, generate electricity, and provide recreation. Water control, Kerr said, would assure Oklahoma's future growth. Agriculture will prosper. Cities can attract new factories. *Tourism* will become a major

Congressman Carl Albert.

industry. Both rural and urban areas supported Kerr's efforts to change Oklahoma.

Visitors in the rotunda of the Oklahoma capitol have seen the paintings by artist Charles Banks Wilson of Miami. Only four great Oklahomans were honored: Sequoyah, Jim Thorpe, Will Rogers, and Robert S. Kerr.

5. OTHER GOVERNORS IN THE 1940s and 1950s PROMOTED INDUSTRIAL GROWTH AND STRUGGLED WITH OKLAHOMA'S NEED FOR CHANGES.

Robert S. Kerr set a pattern for the next three Democratic governors: Roy J. Turner (elected in 1946), Johnston Murray (1950), and Raymond Gary (1954). These governors promoted new industries. They kept taxes down and improved the highway system.

Turner was a self-made millionaire. His fortune came from oil-rich real estate and cattle ranching. For seven years he was a member of the Oklahoma City school board. His hobby was country music which he sang and composed.

In 1946, Turner became governor in the first postwar election. Four war veterans were elected to Congress that year. One of them was Carl Albert of Bugtussle. (Albert later was chosen

Governor Roy Turner visits with President Harry S. Truman at the White House, 1948.

ing office, Murray aired Oklahoma's unsolved problems in a *Saturday Evening Post* article.

He was correct in saying that Oklahoma needed new industries so young people would not go elsewhere to find better jobs. To help attract industries, Murray said Oklahoma needed "a gigantic state-wide water works" to trap water flowing through the state. Senator Kerr and others, of course, were hard at work on the water problem.

Murray suggested that much of Oklahoma's highway money was wasted by the county road system. "We have set up 231 (77x3) little kingdoms," he said. Each county commissioner had a free hand on road building in his district.

The ex-governor also said that the prohibition law was a joke. Only 3.2 beer was legal, but moonshiners did a thriving business. The State of Oklahoma collected no tax either on the illegal booze or the liquor that residents bought in other states. There was some truth to the expression, "The wets have their liquor and the drys have their law."

Why would a former governor say "Oklahoma is in a mess" in a national magazine? Murray ex-

Speaker of the U.S. House. This job was the highest political position ever held by an Oklahoman.)

Governor Turner, like Kerr, promoted new industries for Oklahoma. He sent a three-car railroad traveling exhibit to advertise "Made in Oklahoma" products in eastern cities. Turner's greatest achievement, of course, was in road building. The Turner Turnpike between Oklahoma City and Tulsa bears his name. Started in 1950, the turnpike was financed by revenue bonds sold to investors.

Johnston Murray was Oklahoma's first governor of Indian descent. He was an enrolled member of the Chickasaw Nation, his mother's tribe. The son of a former governor, he was proud to be called "Alfalfa Bill's boy."

Two toll roads were approved while he was governor. The Will Rogers Turnpike was completed in 1957 and the H. E. Bailey in 1964. They connected with the Turner Turnpike to become Interstate 44.

Murray wanted to streamline Oklahoma's government and cut out unneeded jobs. Little reform took place, however, partly because Murray did not get along with the legislature. He called the lawmakers "greedy" and "gutless." After leav-

Governor and Mrs. Johnston Murray at the Governor's Mansion. (OHS)

Governor Raymond Gary signing a bill. (OHS)

plained that he wanted to make Oklahomans angry enough to fight for change and reforms.

Raymond Gary. Governor Gary answered Murray's article with one of his own in the *Saturday Evening Post.* "I say Oklahoma's OK!" he said. "Oklahoma is a young and vigorous state—from tepees to towers in less than fifty years of statehood . . . We have not even approached our potential."

Gary, a son of tenant farmers near Madill, was the first governor born in Oklahoma after statehood. A former President of the State Senate, he understood the legislative process. He followed the four rules for getting along with the rural-controlled legislature.

First, nothing was to be said about the way the legislature was apportioned. By the 1950s, the legislative districts were very unequal. Why? The population had been shifting from rural to urban areas, but few changes had been made in district boundaries since 1907.

Second, the governor was not supposed to dispute the strong role of the legislature in filling state jobs. A legislator's local power depended on his ability to get jobs for friends.

Third, it was understood that a legislator was expected to bring home money for county roads. This system, of course, wasted much of the state's highway money. It also neglected urban areas like Oklahoma and Tulsa counties.

Despite this handicap, Governor Gary was able to improve the state's highway system. He got new funds from record gasoline tax revenue and from President Dwight Eisenhower's *interstate highway* program. Interstates 35, 40, and 44, centering on Oklahoma City, were part of the new national network.

Fourth, it was a "no-no" for a governor to ask for the repeal of prohibition. Most of the rural legislators, like the people they represented, were in favor of prohibition.

This rule was no problem for Gary. He was a strong Baptist and a dry. While he was governor, however, urban voters turned out in large numbers to defeat a *local option* initiative. This measure would have allowed any county to prohibit the sale of beer. Governor Gary worked hard for this amendment. He said he was "happy to stand on the side of 3,500 churches" against the beer industry.

Gary rated his handling of school desegregation as his top achievement.

6. GOVERNOR J. HOWARD EDMONDSON TRIED TO REFORM OKLAHOMA GOVERNMENT.

In 1958, J. Howard Edmondson was elected governor on a reform platform. He attacked Oklahoma's old style politics. At age 33, he was the state's youngest chief executive.

Getting elected was easier than being governor. Edmondson was county attorney in Tulsa County when he ran for governor. He was well-known for convicting a woman mass murderer. The woman met men at lonely hearts clubs, married them, fed them with arsenic, and collected their insurance.

Edmondson was the first candidate for governor to campaign statewide on television. His catchy jingle, "E-D-M-O-N-D-S-O-N spells

179

Governor J. Howard Edmondson. (OHS)

Repeal of prohibition. Governor Edmondson believed Oklahomans would repeal prohibition if it were enforced ruthlessly. He ordered law officers to arrest all bootleggers. Raids were made on private clubs that sold illegal liquor. The highway patrol set up roadblocks and searched cars.

As expected, angry citizens wrote to their representatives and senators. The legislators debated the question of repealing prohibition. By a slim margin, they put a repeal referendum on the ballot in 1959. The voters had a choice: enforced prohibition or legalized package liquor stores. A majority voted to repeal prohibition.

U.S. senator for awhile. Edmondson became a U.S. senator in a roundabout way. First, in January, 1963, Senator Kerr died. Edmondson resigned and Lieutenant Governor George Nigh took over as governor. Nigh then appointed Edmondson to fill Kerr's Senate seat until the next election.

Edmondson" caught on. Voters also liked his "Big Red E" symbol. Finally, he was a good speaker.

Promising to clean up Oklahoma politics, Edmondson ran first in a field of eight Democrats. He then piled up huge majorities in the runoff and general elections.

Once in office, however, Edmondson was soon squashed by the *Old Guard* Democratic legislature. The young governor was trying to rock the boat. He had to fight hard for the few reforms he got.

The legislature resisted change. Most of Edmondson's plans were designed to protect urban interests. He didn't follow the rules for getting along with rural politicians in the legislature. They naturally turned down the Governor's request for *reapportionment* of the legislature. Secondly, they didn't like his idea to transfer control of county road money to the State Highway Commission.

The legislature went along with a *merit system* for hiring state employees. People would have to be chosen on the basis of ability and qualifications. But part of the "good ol' boy" system was continued. Jobs for people who worked for elected officials were not included in the merit system.

7. THE WALL OF SEGREGATION BETWEEN BLACKS AND WHITES BEGAN TO TUMBLE AFTER WORLD WAR II.

Segregation before World War II. Beginning in territorial days, *Jim Crow laws* separated the black and white races in Oklahoma. Schools, housing, theaters, cafes, trains, buses, waiting rooms, and even mines were segregated.

Many black leaders fought for equality. One was Roscoe Dunjee, publisher of *The Black Dispatch* newspaper. He worked with black preachers and lawyers to bring an end to segregation. Their first ray of hope came after World War II. The first major victory over segregation came in the field of higher education.

The NAACP found a weak link in Oklahoma's segregation. Oklahoma provided separate schools for blacks and whites. But the state's black college, Langston University, offered only a bachelor's degree. Black graduate students had to go out-of-state to earn *advanced* or *professional degrees*. The State of Oklahoma paid them a small tuition grant. This grant did not cover their added expenses.

Black lawyers for the NAACP (National Asso-

Roscoe Dunjee. (OHS painting by J. Oxford)

Ada Lois Sipuel.

ciation for the Advancement of Colored People) decided to attack segregation at its weak point—graduate and professional education.

The Sipuel case. Ada Lois Sipuel was a bright young Langston graduate from Chickasha. In 1946, she tried to enroll at the University of Oklahoma Law School. Many faculty members favored her admission. She was turned down, however. A state law made it a *misdemeanor* for a school official to admit a black student into a white school.

Miss Sipuel went to court. The District Court in Cleveland County upheld the state segregation law. So did the Oklahoma Supreme Court. Sipuel's case was argued by Amos T. Hill, a Tulsa lawyer, and the NAACP's Thurgood Marshall. (Marshall was appointed later to be the first black justice on the U.S. Supreme Court.)

The nation's highest court said Oklahoma was violating the *Fourteenth Amendment.* The state was not providing "equal" legal education for Miss Sipuel.

State Officials then established the Langston Law School in rooms at the State Capitol. Local attorneys were hired as teachers. "A fake, fraud, and deception"—that is what a professor at the

University of Oklahoma called the new school. Miss Sipuel refused to attend.

McLaurin case. Several black graduate students were denied admission to the University of Oklahoma. One of them, 68-year-old George W. McLaurin, was picked by the NAACP for a test case. He was a married Langston teacher. In 1948, a federal district court ordered the university to admit McLaurin. The court, however, did not overturn Oklahoma's segregation laws.

McLaurin enrolled at the university but was segregated from white students. He was assigned a seat in a small room next to the main classroom. His lawyer, Thurgood Marshall, called the room a "broom closet." McLaurin also had a "separate but equal" table in the library and in the cafeteria.

"Stupid"—that was Marshall's description of these arrangements. He appealed the McLaurin case to the U.S. Supreme Court. In 1950, this court said the University of Oklahoma was depriving McLaurin of rights under the Fourteenth Amendment.

The Oklahoma legislature redefined "separate but equal." In 1949, the state legislature had changed the segregation law. Colleges

181

were authorized to admit black students to earn degrees not offered at Langston University. The blacks, however, were to be taught in separate classrooms or at different times.

At the University of Oklahoma, black students were assigned seats in a roped off section of classrooms. When Miss Sipuel entered law school in 1949, her seat was marked "For colored only." White students soon removed the sign and cut the ropes.

8. DESEGREGATION OF OKLAHOMA'S SCHOOLS AND PUBLIC PLACES.

In 1954, the U.S. Supreme Court decided that "separate but equal" schools for blacks and whites were not constitutional. This case was *Brown vs. Topeka Board of Education.* Oklahoma was one of seventeen states ordered to desegregate its schools. The court believed that the time had come for blacks to enter the mainstream of American life.

Governor Gary worked hard for a referendum called the "Better Schools Amendment." Oklahoma's first step toward school *integration* was to abolish the dual budget system. Money for white schools came from a school district property tax. Black schools were a county responsibility. The legislature gave the voters a chance to combine the two school budgets. The "Better Schools Amendment" was put on the ballot. Governor Gary led the drive to get it passed. It won by a three to one vote.

Schools integrated. Poteau was the first Oklahoma school district to integrate. By the fall of 1955, the state had 273 schools with black and white children in classes together.

Integration of schools in Oklahoma City seemed difficult. The main reason was segregated housing patterns. For seventeen years, U.S. District Judge Luther Bohanon forced changes in desegregation plans. Not until 1977 was he satisfied that the school board was complying with the Supreme Court's desegregation order.

Oklahoma City's lunch counter sit-ins, 1958–1964. On a hot day in August, 1958, thirteen black children began a *sit-in* at the Katz

Demonstration for civil rights in Oklahoma City, 1964. (OHS)

Drugstore food counter in downtown Oklahoma City. On the third day they were finally served. The Katz counter was desegregated. Other eating places held out much longer, however.

The blacks were members of the city's NAACP Youth Council. Their adult advisor was Clara Luper, then a history teacher at Dunjee High School. She was greatly influenced by the *civil rights* crusade of Dr. Martin Luther King Jr.

The Katz demonstration was the beginning of a six-year campaign of black sit-ins, *picketing*, and store *boycotts*. During that time, most of the stores and eating places in downtown Oklahoma City were desegregated.

Civil rights history was made in 1964. The Oklahoma City council passed a public accommodations ordinance. This law forbade operators of restaurants, theaters, and swimming pools to refuse service to anyone. The wording was similar to the federal Civil Rights Act of 1964 that applied to the whole nation.

ROUNDUP

1. Make a list of changes in Oklahoma resulting from World War II.
2. Identify: 45th Infantry Division, Clarence Coggins, Jack C. Montgomery, Ernest Childers, General McLain, and Bill Mauldin.
3. Make a chart of military posts and bases in Oklahoma during World War II. Use these headings: Type, Names of Specific Posts and Bases.
4. For what reasons did Oklahoma's economy boom during World War II?
5. Describe Robert S. Kerr as a person. Why was he governor at a good time? What was his greatest achievement as U.S. senator? In what way was the Kerr era a bridge in Oklahoma politics?
6. What did Governor Turner accomplish?
7. Why did a former governor, Johnston Murray, air Oklahoma's problems in a national magazine article? List three problems which he wanted to reform.
8. List the four rules that a governor had to follow to get along with the legislature.
9. Explain how Governor Edmondson violated the four rules. What were Edmondson's two main successes?
10. What weak spot did NAACP lawyers find in Oklahoma's school segregation system? For what will each of the following be remembered: Ada Sipuel, George W. McLaurin?
11. Identify: Brown versus Topeka Board of Education, Better Schools Amendment.
12. What technique did black students use to achieve lunch counter integration in Oklahoma City? Who was their adult advisor?
A. Think about it! The history of Oklahoma during the 1940s and 1950s teaches us that change is always going on. Make a list of changes that will likely take place in Oklahoma in the future.

Boise City is Bombed

In 1943, Boise City was bombed, not by the Japanese or Germans, but by our own air force. Residents of this town in the Panhandle had celebrated the 4th of July, but they heard more fireworks after midnight.

As people slept, a greenhorn navigator guided the pilot of a training bomber in the wrong direction from Dalhart Air Base. The plane flew due north to Boise City instead of northeast. From the air, street lights around the courthouse made the town look like the target range in Texas where the plane was supposed to be.

Circling the town, the crew began to drop practice bombs, six in all. One bomb exploded close to some loaded gasoline trucks that were parked near the courthouse. Another bomb grazed the wall of the nearby First Baptist Church.

The town awoke! The electrical power plant operator jumped out of bed, hurried to the plant, and switched off the lights. The county sheriff, whose family lived in the courthouse, and a Dalhart soldier on leave rushed frantically to the local telephone office to notify the air base.

Embarrassed by its goof, the bomber crew headed back to Dalhart with a few bombs still on board. Later, a large sign was erected at the base. It read, "Remember the Maine, Remember the Alamo, Remember Pearl Harbor, and, for God's sake, Remember Boise City."

The B-17 crew finished its training and became one of the most highly decorated outfits in World War II. The men were chosen to lead the first daylight bombing raid on Berlin in 1944.

Today, a bombshell-in-cement memorial in Boise City brings a smile to faces of people who recall the unusual bomb raid on their town.

22

OKLAHOMA GROWS AGAIN

The 1960 census showed that Oklahoma was growing again. The main reason is that manufacturing was becoming an important industry. Manufacturing gave the state a more *diversified economy* and provided jobs. During the 1960s alone, employment in manufacturing increased more than a third.

Workers for the new factories in Oklahoma's cities came from rural areas and from other states. Oklahoma became *urbanized*. By 1975, half of all Oklahomans lived in the metropolitan areas of Oklahoma City and Tulsa.

In the 1980s, the Oklahoma economy took a downturn when oil and farm crop prices fell. Oklahomans still depended greatly on the oil and agricultural industries. The drop in prices sent many oil drillers and farmers into bankruptcy. Some banks failed. Unemployment rose rapidly.

While experiencing these ups and downs in the economy, Oklahoma also underwent political changes. A major development was the beginning of a *two-party system*. Republicans began to challenge the Democrats for some offices.

Beginning in 1952, the Republican nominee for president usually carried Oklahoma. In 1972, Richard Nixon won all seventy-seven counties in defeating George McGovern.

In the 1960s, Republican candidates began winning races for governor and seats in the U.S. Senate. The Democrats, however, continued to hold most state offices, county offices, and congressional seats. The Democrats also had a big majority in the state legislature. That was true even after court-ordered *reapportionment* transferred control of the legislature from rural to urban voters.

How can the rise of the Republican Party in what was once a one-party Democratic state be explained? For one reason, most of the newcomers came from northern and border states where the Republican Party is stronger. By the 1970s, more than a third of Oklahoma voters were born outside the state.

The Republican Party also gained by urbanization—the movement of people to the cities. The rapidly growing white suburbs of Oklahoma City and Tulsa joined northern Oklahoma as Republican strongholds.

Oklahoma continues to change. Former Oklahomans who return to their native state are amazed. They see growing cities, a diversified economy, a two-party system, more social equality, recreation lakes, and modernized government.

1. OKLAHOMA GOVERNMENT IS BEING MODERNIZED.

Executive branch. Some streamlining of state government has made it more efficient and professional. The *merit system* for state employees, adopted in 1959, was a good beginning. Another improvement, the reduction of the number of executive offices to ten, was made in the 1970s. This change made the ballot shorter so people can vote more intelligently.

Reapportionment of the legislature. In the 1960s, the legislature was reapportioned so that each legislative district has about the same number of people. Many new lawmakers were elected from the bigger cities. The new legislature began to focus more on important statewide issues. It hired efficient staff members to help the committees. Less time was spent on politicking to get jobs for friends—thanks mainly to the merit system for hiring most people who work for the state.

Judicial reform. The judicial branch of government was also reformed in the 1960s. The Oklahoma Supreme Court and other appellate judges, who were once elected, are now appointed. When a vacancy occurs, the governor ap-

Tulsa skyline. (Don Sibley photo)

points a new judge from a list of lawyers recommended by a *bipartisan* nominating commission. Justice of the peace courts were abolished. All trials are now held in district courts.

2. HENRY BELLMON WAS OKLAHOMA'S FIRST REPUBLICAN GOVERNOR (1963–1967).

Republican political success in the 1960s and 1970s was due largely to two men: Henry Bellmon of Billings and Dewey Bartlett of Tulsa.

In 1962, Bellmon was elected governor. In 1968, he upset U.S. Senator Mike Monroney and served two six-year terms in the U.S. Senate. After a brief retirement, Bellmon won the governor's job again in 1986.

Bartlett replaced Bellmon as governor. In 1972, he joined Bellmon in the U.S. Senate. For the second time, Oklahoma had two Republican U.S. senators. (The single terms of J. W. Harreld, elected 1920, and W. B. Pine, elected 1924, overlapped for two years.)

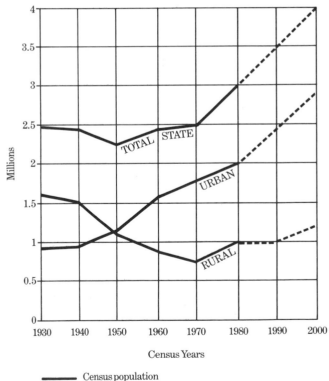

Oklahoma Population Trends

Census population
Future population trends

185

Governor Henry Bellmon, 1960s. (OHS)

Bellmon gave needed leadership to the Republican Party. The mastermind of the Republican victory for governor in 1962 was Henry Bellmon. He was a decorated World War II marine, a Noble County farmer, and a one-term legislator.

In 1961, Bellmon took over the thankless job of Republican state chairman. He had a plan to breathe life into the party. It was called "Operation Countdown."

Bellmon called a Republican state convention to create interest. He began a drive to register as Republicans the "300,000 Democrats who voted Republican in the last three presidential elections." The number of registered Republican voters was increased by 20 percent. Another project was to solicit small contributions. Why? The Republican Party wanted to break its past dependence on the oil interests for funds.

Improving party organization was given high priority. Bellmon replaced two-thirds of the Re-

publican state committee members with young energetic people. He established a Republican committee in every county that didn't have one. Finally, the party found good Republican candidates and trained them at "leadership seminars."

The party had come a long way since 1960. In that year, the Oklahoma County chairman ran ads in the *Daily Oklahoman* begging Republicans to run for office.

Having built up the party, Bellmon was a logical Republican candidate for governor in 1962. An honest, hardworking farmer, he was a "fresh breeze" in politics.

W. P. "Bill" Atkinson was the Democratic nominee for governor in 1962. Atkinson's background was a success story. While a journalism teacher at Oklahoma City University, he supplemented his income by selling real estate. During World War II, Atkinson shrewdly bought several farms near the future site of Tinker Field. He then developed Midwest City, the state's largest wartime suburb, and became a wealthy man.

Atkinson defeated former Governor Gary in the Democratic runoff by a narrow margin. Gary, who ran best in rural areas, refused to support Atkinson in the general election. With a divided Democratic Party, the Republicans had a chance to elect their first governor.

Bellmon was elected. As the Republican nominee, Bellmon had obstacles to overcome. How could he offset the heavy registration of Democrats and Atkinson's expensive advertising campaign?

The issue of taxes worked to Bellmon's advantage. He promised no new taxes. Atkinson, on the other hand, favored a one-cent increase in the sales tax. Also, many of Gary's rural Democratic followers voted for Bellmon.

Bellmon was elected with 55 percent of the vote. He got lopsided majorities in Oklahoma and Tulsa counties as well as in the Republican northwestern counties. Bellmon also did well in "Little Dixie" and other rural counties. He carried Gary's Marshall County with 61 percent of the vote.

Bellmon's victory was personal, however. No

other Republican won a state office. The Democrats still had a majority in the legislature.

While Bellmon was governor in the 1960s, the legislature created a state employees retirement system. The *oil depletion allowance* was increased. County attorneys were replaced by a district attorney system. The question of teacher salaries became a major issue.

Teacher salaries controversy. Oklahoma teacher salaries were too low. But the governor and legislature did not agree on the best way to provide money for the educators. The legislature preferred a sales tax increase. Bellmon suggested an indirect method. He wanted a bond issue to finance turnpikes. Money from the sale of bonds would free road money in the state budget to pay teacher salaries. Both of these plans were referred to the people and turned down in 1965.

The National Education Association (NEA) put the Oklahoma school system on its *blacklist.* The NEA censured any out-of-state teacher who took a job in Oklahoma. The association helped some Oklahoma teachers to find jobs in other states.

The legislature then passed a one-cent cigarette tax increase to help finance higher salaries for educators. Bellmon signed the bill, even though he had promised no tax increases, to raise needed money.

3. A COURT SCANDAL LED TO REFORMS OF THE JUDICIAL SYSTEM.

State Supreme Court Scandal. In 1965, N. S. Corn, a former justice of the State Supreme Court, was convicted on *bribery* and income tax evasion charges. Corn had been bribed $150,000 for a favorable decision in a case before his court in 1957. He paid $7,500 each to two other justices and later implicated them. Corn was paroled, after serving eighteen months in prison, because of old age.

Appellate court reforms. The Corn scandal led to a new way of selecting justices for the State Supreme Court and other *appellate* courts. These judges are no longer elected. Since 1967, they have been appointed by the governor.

This reform made it possible for the justices to concentrate on doing a good job. They don't have to worry about raising campaign funds and running for reelection.

How can an appellate court justice stay in office after the end of a term? First, the justice must agree to have his or her name put on the ballot. The voters decide to either retain the justice for another term or remove him or her from the bench. No other candidates can oppose the incumbent.

Lower courts. District judges are still elected. But they now run on a *nonpartisan* basis, not as Democrats or Republicans. The district courts are the only state trial courts. The justice of the peace system was abolished in 1967.

The legislature also replaced county attorneys with district attorneys elected every four years. Each county within a district has at least one assistant district attorney.

4. FEDERAL COURTS ENFORCED THE "ONE-MAN, ONE-VOTE RULE" IN OKLAHOMA.

Reapportionment of the legislature. The Constitution of Oklahoma requires the legislature to reapportion its districts after the census every ten years. The legislators, however, refused to fulfill this requirement. They ignored the shift of population from rural areas and small towns to the cities. In fact, the Oklahoma legislature was so malapportioned in 1962 that it ranked forty-seventh in the nation on this score. A fourth of the people could elect a majority of the legislators.

Reapportionment was forced on the legislature by a series of court decisions. In *Baker versus Carr*, a Tennessee case, the U.S. Supreme Court ruled that every legislator must represent about an equal number of people. This idea became known as the *one-man, one-vote rule.*

In the same year, a three-judge federal court panel in Oklahoma City ruled that the Oklahoma legislature's apportionment was unconstitutional, null and void. In 1964, the panel declared that

Governor Dewey Bartlett.

5. GOVERNOR DEWEY BARTLETT PROMOTED THE GROWTH OF MANUFACTURING AND PRIDE IN OKLAHOMA(1967—1971).

In 1966, Oklahomans went to the polls and elected another World War II veteran as the state's second Republican governor. Dewey Bartlett, a state senator and oilman from Tulsa, had promised economy and no new taxes. This simple platform and in-fighting among Democrats offset Bartlett's political liabilities. He was both Catholic and Republican in a Protestant Democratic state.

Oklahoma, Key to Indistrial Expansion. Though quiet in manner, Bartlett was enthusiastic about Oklahoma's future. He wore an *"OKIE"* button and worked hard to bring new factories and jobs to the state.

"Hello, I'm Dewey Bartlett, governor of Oklahoma."

Corporation executives all over the country heard this greeting. "Dynamic Dewey," as he was called, persuaded many business leaders to locate in Oklahoma. He gave most of his attention to outlying counties. "The only way I know how to help rural communities is to attract new industry," he said. "Oklahoma City and Tulsa can take care of themselves."

Dalton Foundries of Indiana built a new plant in Cushing. Uniroyal started making tires in Ardmore. The St. Joe Paper Company opened a factory in Sapulpa. Armco Steel expanded into Sand Springs. So the list went.

Bartlett knew that good transportation and a skilled work force were incentives for companies to locate in Oklahoma. He continued the construction of turnpikes and roads. He encouraged vocational training, especially programs to train workers for a particular industry. Lists of skilled workers, including former Oklahomans who wished to return, were provided to companies that were thinking about moving to Oklahoma.

Defeated for a second term. A change in the state constitution made it possible for a governor to run again. Bartlett tried for reelection in 1970. Overconfident, he was narrowly defeated by David Hall, the Democratic nominee.

the primary election for legislators that year was illegal.

The federal court then hired the Bureau of Government Research at the University of Oklahoma to redraw district boundaries. The new plan was close to perfect. No possible legislative majority could be elected with less than 49 percent of the people.

Governor Bellmon ordered a new primary election for September, 1964, to choose candidates in the new districts. The whole state, including the cities, were now fairly represented. The legislature had many new faces from the urban areas, but the Democrats still had a large majority.

Redistricting of congressional districts. Oklahoma was ordered to equalize the population in its six congressional districts. Governor Bellmon vetoed two redistricting plans of the legislature. He charged the Democratic lawmakers with *gerrymandering*—drawing boundary lines to benefit the majority party. The voters also turned down a legislative plan in 1966.

In 1967, a new Democratic legislature and a new Republican governor (Bartlett) agreed on a redistricting plan. The population in the districts was close to equal.

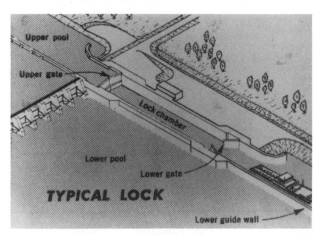

A typical lock on the Arkansas Waterway. (U.S. Army Engineer District, Tulsa)

In 1972, however, Bartlett won the U.S. Senate seat vacated by Fred Harris. Bartlett defeated the Democratic nominee, Congressman Ed Edmondson of Muskogee. Bartlett did not run for reelection in 1978. He had cancer and died the next year.

6. THE McCLELLAN-KERR ARKANSAS RIVER NAVIGATION PROJECT SERVES MANY PURPOSES.

Freight route. The U.S. Army Corps of Engineers completed a waterway on the Arkansas and Verdigris rivers in twelve years. Opened in 1971, the project was the most expensive waterway ever constructed. It cost $1.2 billion—four times as much as the Panama Canal.

The engineers tamed the wild Arkansas and Verdigris with a series of upstream lakes. These reservoirs provide a constant level of water nine feet deep in the navigation channel. The waterway stretches 450 miles from the Port of Catoosa, east of Tulsa, to the Mississippi River. Seventeen locks lift or lower barges along the route.

Seaports in the plains? Catoosa and Muskogee are Oklahoma's inland ports. Each of these ports has a concrete pier and steel *dolphins* where barges are loaded and unloaded. A typical barge load weighs about a thousand tons. Wheat is the major cargo that is shipped downstream. Steel for use in Oklahoma factories is the main

inbound load. The cost of transportation by barge is much cheaper than rail or truck freight.

The Catoosa and Muskogee ports have industrial parks with warehouses and factories. Many large corporations have built plants near the waterway. Armco Steel, Kerr-McGee, Phillips Petroleum, and many other companies employ thousands of workers.

Oklahoma shippers. Farmers in Oklahoma ship grain in barges to New Orleans for transfer to ocean-going ships. The coal industry got new life when the Arkansas waterway provided an outlet to coal markets all over the world. Oklahoma petroleum companies have shipped millions of barrels of crude oil down the Arkansas. Many other Oklahoma raw materials and manufactured goods are shipped over the waterway.

Other benefits of the McClellan-Kerr project. Flood control was a major goal of the project. The dams and lakes have prevented severe flood damage, especially during the high-water summer of 1973.

Water power is used at some of the lakes to generate electricity.

Recreation is another important benefit from the project. The U.S. Army Engineers built many recreational areas along the waterway. The largest is Sallisaw Park at Robert S. Kerr Lake. Thousands of tourists go to Sallisaw and other

Tulsa's Port of Catoosa and part of the McClellan-Kerr Waterway. (Don Sibley photo)

parks to camp, launch their boats, and fish. Lodges at some of the lakes attract tourists. By the 1980s, *tourism* was a major industry in Oklahoma.

7. STATE GOVERNMENT BECAME THE STORY OF BOTH REFORMS AND SCANDALS.

Governor David Hall (1971-1975). A Democrat and former Tulsa county attorney, Hall was elected governor on his second try. Not a wealthy man, he borrowed campaign money at the bank and passed the hat at bean suppers and watermelon feasts.

As governor, Hall saw the need for more revenue. Low taxes had attracted new industries and jobs to Oklahoma, but services had been neglected. More money was needed for schools, highways, and other state responsibilities. Hall proposed the first major tax increase since World War II. The legislature obliged with an increase in the state income tax. Taxes on oil, gas, and liquor were also raised.

Legislative accomplishments included the creation of a state-supported kindergarten system, ratification of the 26th Amendment to the U.S. Constitution that gave 18-year-olds the right to vote nationwide, and an increase in the term of county officials from two to four years. The legislature appropriated money for two new prisons to relieve overcrowding.

In 1973, a prison riot at McAlester got national attention. Fires were set. Four prisoners were killed. Guards were held hostages. The National Guard was called to restore order.

The high point of Hall's tenure as governor was the opening of the Arkansas River Navigation Project in 1971. President Richard Nixon took part in the ceremony at Catoosa.

Hall's administration ended in scandal. He was indicted by a grand jury and later convicted of accepting a bribe. Allowed to drive himself to a federal prison in Arizona, he served eighteen months of a three-year sentence.

Governor David Lyle Boren (1975-1979). A four-term Democratic state representative from Seminole, Boren was elected governor in 1974.

Governor David Hall (OHS)

Only 33 years of age, he was a graduate of Yale University as well as Oxford, where he was a Rhodes scholar, and the University of Oklahoma Law School.

Boren was scarcely known outside of Oklahoma Baptist University where he taught government. But his message caught on. He campaigned across the state with a broom sticking out the rear window of his green Ford. He promised a "clean sweep" of his party's corruption in state government. Sounding like Republican candidates, he said that lower taxes will attract new industries and jobs to Oklahoma.

Reforms in government highlighted the Boren administration. The people approved a referendum that helps make a *short ballot*. This measure gave the governor power to appoint three officers that had been elective—secretary of state, labor commissioner, and chief mine inspector. The first two had been involved in corruption prior to the changes.

The legislature passed a *sunset law*. This law provides that a certain number of state agencies must be studied each year to see if they should continue to exist. Another reform law changed the death penalty from electrocution to injection with a lethal drug.

Governor (later U.S. Senator) David Boren

Governor George Nigh

Thanks to an oil boom and increased state revenues, Boren was able to cut taxes as promised.

U.S. senators from Oklahoma. In 1978, Governor Boren won the U.S. Senate seat vacated by Senator Bartlett. Boren was re-elected in 1984 and 1990. He resigned in 1994 to become president of the University of Oklahoma at Norman. Congressman Jim Inhofe, a Tulsa Republican, was elected to complete the last two years of Boren's term.

Don Nickles, a Republican from Ponca City, was elected to Oklahoma's other U.S. Senate seat in 1980 when Senator Bellmon chose not to run again. Nickles was re-elected in 1986 and 1992.

Governor George Nigh (1979-1987). Nigh was in state government nearly a third of a century. He served four terms in the state legislature while a teacher of history and government at McAlester High School. At age 31, he was elected the state's youngest lieutenant governor and held that job nearly sixteen years. Twice he moved up to the governor's office to complete the terms of Edmondson and Boren when they went to the U.S. Senate.

While Nigh was governor, the Oklahoma economy had its ups and downs. In 1980, the population passed the 3 million mark and the state was booming. Oil drillers and farmers were borrowing money to buy more equipment. Manufacturing was growing. But in 1982, oil prices dropped and the economy went into a tailspin. Penn Square Bank in Oklahoma City failed as debtors defaulted on their loans. Unemployment rose.

Everyone could see that the state needed to diversify—to start more new industries so Oklahomans could share in the general prosperity of the country.

In 1981, a major scandal was uncovered. The FBI and IRS (Internal Revenue Service) finished an investigation of corrupt county commissioners in Oklahoma and several other states. Federal agents used audio and visual tapes to reveal a pattern of bribes, kickbacks, and phony purchase practices.

Operation Corcom (short for "corrupt commissioners") proved that graft in county government had been adding millions of dollars to Oklahoma's road maintenance costs. One building materials salesman, for example, admitted to making 8,400 payoffs to county officials. The FBI had tapes of payoffs in hotel rooms, pickup trucks, and county buildings.

Several hundred commissioners and businessmen were caught in the Corcom net and charged with crimes. Many pleaded *nolo contendere*—in effect, the same as an admission of guilt.

Governor Nigh expressed the reaction of most Oklahomans. "The shock is that a lot of these people didn't think they were being dishonest," he lamented. "They were told that this is the way you do business."

Nigh faced another problem in 1983. A prison riot broke out in the dining room at the new medium security prison in Hominy. Inmates, armed with makeshift weapons, went wild. They set fire to several buildings. To quell the riot, Nigh sent in the highway patrol and National Guard troops. Then the prisoners were transferred to other facilities until the Hominy prison could be rebuilt.

After leaving office, Nigh became president of Central State University at Edmond.

Governor Henry Bellmon returns (1987–1991). Bellmon, a Republican and a Noble County farmer, came out of political retirement to be elected governor again in 1986. The voters seemed to feel that his experience as a state legislator, governor, and U.S. senator would be helpful in solving Oklahoma's economic problems.

Bellmon set some high goals for the state: better education, an expanded economy, a decent job and suitable housing for everyone, equal opportunity and respect for human rights, and drug-free schools.

By the middle of Bellmon's term, spending for education was up. A roadbuilding project created some jobs. Unemployment dropped. A new tax program was enacted to keep revenues up.

The Main Street Program was a step in the right direction. Cities and towns began restoring downtown areas to attract new business. Horse racing and parimutuel betting at Remington Park in Oklahoma City gave a boost to the tourist industry and increased state revenues.

Progress was made in developing new industries to assure future economic growth in Oklahoma.

Governor David Walters (1991–1995). Walters was Oklahoma's first governor born after World War II. A farm boy from Canute, he earned college degrees at the University of Oklahoma and

Governor David Walters

Harvard. A Democrat, Walters narrowly lost in a race for governor in 1986. Four years later, at age 39, he won the office easily. He carried 75 counties after spending $2.7 million in his campaign.

As governor, Walters spoke for changes to prepare Oklahoma for the 21st century. He wanted increased spending for education with more emphasis on technology of the future. He called for improvements in health care and crime prevention.

At the same time, Walters stressed the need for fiscal responsibility—budget cuts for state agencies and a hiring freeze. His plan to create a state-run lottery to raise money was defeated by the voters.

While Walters was pushing for these changes, a grand jury indicted him for campaign violations. In 1993, he pleaded "guilty" to a misdemeanor charge of accepting more than the legal maximum donation from a supporter. Walters was given a deferred sentence and agreed to transfer his unspent campaign money to the Ethics Commission. When prosecutors dropped the grand jury's eight felony indictments against Walters, many angry Oklahomans called for him to resign or for

Congressman J. C. Watts Jr., 4th District

Governor Frank Keating

the legislature to impeach him.

"Enough is enough," Governor Walters responded. He tried to calm the political turmoil by announcing that he would not seek re-election.

8. IN 1994, VOTERS NATIONWIDE GAVE REPUBLICANS A CHANCE TO GOVERN.

"It may be our turn in the wilderness," sighed a prominent Democrat who was shocked by the Republican landslide victory in 1994.

Like people nationwide, nearly a million Oklahomans went to the polls and voted for change. A majority seemed to say "big federal government controls too much of our daily lives." Voters spoke out for lower taxes, cuts in spending, and more emphasis on family values.

Republicans won control of Congress. Since 1930, Democrats had controlled the U.S. Congress almost continuously. In 1994, however, Oklahomans helped the Republicans take over the U.S. Senate by electing Jim Inhofe. His victory gave Oklahoma two Republican senators for only the second time in history. Republican candidates also won five of Oklahoma's six seats in the U.S.

House of Representatives.

The state's southwest congressional district drew national attention with the election of J. C. Watts of Norman. A young member of the state corporation commission and a former star O U quarterback, Watts became the first black Republican elected to Congress from a southern state in 120 years. Representative Watts said he won by talking about the issues—lower taxes, welfare reform, strenghtening the family, and a strong military defense. "This win," he said, "also proved that the color of one's skin is not significant . . . I'm a Republican who just happens to be black."

Frank Keating was elected governor in 1994. A Tulsa lawyer and former state legislator, Keating became only the third Republican governor in Oklahoma history.

Keating said his priority was to promote growth and prosperity. He favored tax cuts and a right-to-work law to attract more business to this state. He called for stricter enforcement of criminal laws. "With a limited budget," he said, "we ought to focus on good roads and education. We should let the private system build prisons and we can lease the space."

193

Lt. Governor Mary Fallin

Governor Keating could count on support from the new lieutenant governor, Mary Fallin. A young legislator from Oklahoma City, she became the first woman and the first Republican to hold that job.

Keating was confident he could work with the Democratic majority in the legislature by using friendly persuasion. Only if that failed, the new governor said, would he use the veto or go directly to the voters with initiative petitions. See if you can find out how well he has done.

ROUNDUP

1. List six major changes in Oklahoma since 1960.
2. Explain how each of the three branches of state government has been modernized.
3. Why was Henry Bellmon a logical Republican candidate for governor in 1962?
4. Name three achievements of the first Bellmon administration. What was a major problem?
5. Why was a state supreme court judge sent to prison in 1965? What reforms in the court system resulted from this scandal?
6. Define "one-man, one-vote." How did this court ruling change the Oklahoma legislature?
7. Explain Governor Bartlett's "OKIE" program. Did it work?
8. Make a list of all the purposes served by the Arkansas waterway.
9. Which important amendment was added to the U.S. Constitution while David Hall was governor?
10. List three important reforms of Governor Boren's administration.
11. For what reasons did Oklahoma's economy slow down in the 1980s?
12. List Governor Bellmon's goals for a better Oklahoma.
A. Think about it! The true test of character when problems develop (in government, in society, or in one's personal life) is what we do about them. What do you consider the five most important current problems that Oklahomans should face up to and try to solve.
B. Try this! Fill in a chart with columns labeled Governors, Year(s) Elected, Political Party, and Important Events.

23

OKLAHOMA'S HERITAGE

Our study of Oklahoma's past gives us an appreciation for the lives and achievements of people who made the state what it is today. Contributions to Oklahoma's heritage have been made by people of *many different nationalities, races, and origins*. Men and women in *all walks of life* have played important roles on the stage of Oklahoma history.

Oklahoma's history has been shaped by *outside influences* too. Wars, the Great Depression, and many other national and world events have made a great impact on Oklahoma affairs. New inventions—the automobile, airplane, farm machines, radio, television, space satellites, and computers—have changed our lifestyles significantly. Since the 1940s, Oklahoma has become more and more like the rest of the nation.

Our study of Oklahoma's past makes us aware of *values* held by people who settled and built the state. The pioneers had dreams and visions for a better way of life. But they were practical, self-reliant, hard-working, and resourceful. While they greatly respected individual freedom, the pioneers also believed in cooperation and sacrificing for the common good. They put a high value on education and on service to the community.

We all share in the *material aspects* of Oklahoma's heritage. Highways, schools, and churches have been built for us. Parks, lakes, and recreation areas were located where we can enjoy outdoor fun. State and local governments strive to protect our property and perform other needed services.

In learning what Oklahoma's past generations have accomplished, we gain courage and inspiration to make the state an even better place in which to live.

Yes, we are a part of history too. A knowledge of the past makes it easier to understand our present problems. We gain a better *perspective* to make decisions for the future. We should all remember the native American who never got lost because he often looked back to see where he had been.

Oklahoma's *heritage* is remembered in many ways. Communities all over the state celebrate pioneer days with festivals that often last several days. The spirit of the Old West is rekindled with parades, rodeos, square dances, and many other special events that attract crowds. People also learn about their state's history by visiting museums and historic sites. And they read about past events in books and newspaper articles.

"Ride 'em, cowboy!"

Tom Mix Museum in Dewey. (Fred Marvel)

1. MUSEUMS AND HISTORIC SITES REMIND US OF OKLAHOMA'S HERITAGE.

Museums in Oklahoma. Ever go through a photograph album or see a movie about pioneer days? Museums give visitors the same kind of feeling.

Museums throughout the state help us remember the days of yesteryear. The spirit of early Oklahoma is kept alive in historic *murals* and *dioramas*. We are reminded of how things used to be by displays of cowboy regalia, gun collections, horse-drawn farm machines, firefighting equipment, mining or oil field tools, and rooms furnished as they were a century ago. Old buggies, wagons, stagecoaches, steam locomotives, and antique automobiles help us visualize changes in transportation.

The State Museum of Oklahoma is near the State Capitol in Oklahoma City. Exhibits there depict Oklahoma's colorful history since prehistoric times. A special gallery is devoted to Oklahoma's Native Americans.

Several Oklahoma museums specialize in Native American culture. Every year thousands of people visit Anadarko's Indian City U.S.A., the Southern Plains Museum and Crafts Center, and the National Hall of Fame for Famous American Indians. Tahlequah's ancient village of Tsa-la-gi and the Cherokee National Museum attract many visitors. Other museums with excellent displays of Indian artifacts are located in nearly every part of the state. The Woolaroc near Bartlesville and the Five Civilized Tribes Museum at Muskogee are two of the best-known.

Some museums bring back visions of cowboy heroes and life on the range. The National Cowboy Hall of Fame and Western Heritage Center in Oklahoma City is the most famous museum of this kind in the world. This museum honors working cowboys past and present. It is also a shrine for rodeo stars as well as for movie and television cowboy actors.

Cowboy and ranching life are also featured at the Will Rogers Memorial in Claremore. Other museums that honor the cowboy are the Tom Mix Museum in Dewey and the Chisholm Trail Museum in Kingfisher.

The Air Space Museum in Oklahoma City is concerned with the state's more recent heritage. This museum honors Oklahomans who have served as astronauts in the space program. The first Oklahoma astronaut was Gordon Cooper of Shawnee. He was in the spacecraft that orbited the earth in 1963. The museum has simulators that let visitors feel what it is like to fly.

The Oklahoma Historical Society has devel-

Overholser Mansion in Oklahoma City. (Fred Marvel)

89er celebration in Guthrie with Carnegie Library in background. (Fred Marvel)

oped a slide lecture to promote the use of state museums and to inform people about historic sites. The Society has also helped to organize Oklahoma Heritage Clubs for students. Some club members do volunteer work at museums in their area.

National historic sites. Once an old building or historic place is destroyed, it is gone forever. The Oklahoma Historical Society and other groups have worked hard to identify historic sites that should be preserved.

The Society's program for marking sites began in 1949. Representative John E. Wagner of Chandler got the legislature to vote enough money for the first 100 markers. Each marker was cast of aluminum. The letters were silver on a green enamel background. Most of the historic site markers were placed near a highway. They made Oklahomans more conscious of their state's history than they had ever been.

The U.S. Congress helped by passing the National Historic Preservation Act of 1966. By this law, the U.S. Department of Interior can pay 50 percent of the cost of preserving sites listed in the National Register of Historic Places. The National Park Service decides which sites are important enough to be listed.

Many Oklahoma houses are on the National Register. These include a "soddie" near Cleo Springs and Sequoyah's log cabin near Sallisaw. Others on the list are Governor Marland's mansion in Ponca City, the Overholser mansion in Oklahoma City, and Jim Thorpe's home at Yale. The house where Will Rogers was born had to be moved nearby when the Oologah Dam and Reservoir were constructed on the Verdigris River.

Other places classified as historic sites include old forts, battlefields, churches, school buildings, hotels, government buildings, bridges, business buildings, and statues. The Carnegie Library building in Guthrie is part of the city's historic district. This area has been restored to look like it did in pre-statehood days. The streets are paved with brick and lined with antique lampposts, creating an old-town atmosphere.

Oklahoma's historic sites and markers are listed and described in the book *Mark of Heritage* by Muriel Wright, George H. Shirk, and Kenny A. Franks. Wright led the effort to preserve historic sites as early as the 1920s. Her first site article was on the "Old Boggy Depot." She later helped to search out all twelve station sites in Oklahoma on the Butterfield Overland Mail route. Another good source is *Windows on the Past* by Kent Ruth and Jim Argo.

2. OKLAHOMA'S HERITAGE IS PRESERVED IN OLD DRAWINGS, PAINTINGS, AND HISTORICAL MURALS.

Early art has historical value. The art of Oklahoma's early inhabitants tells us much about cultures and lifestyles that no longer exist. We can learn about the advanced Spiro Mounds culture, for example, by studying their pottery and other artifacts.

People often draw pictures of what they value most. The Plains tribes painted warriors mounted on horses ready for battle. Sometimes it was a buffalo hunt. Drawings were made on buffalo robes and on the sides of tepees.

The Old West of the 19th century was put on canvas by professional painters who traveled in this area.

Visiting artists. George Catlin (1796–1872) was the first eastern artist to make a pictorial record of Native Americans on the western plains. In the 1830s he accompanied mounted dragoons from Fort Gibson into Pawnee and Comanche country. He painted Cherokees and other tribal members too.

Catlin's watercolor drawings give us a descriptive "look" at Native Americans—their clothing, headdress, moccasins, beads, jewelry, and many aspects of their lifestyles.

Charles Russell (1864–1926) was a working Montana cowboy, painter, and sculptor. He tried to record the glorious Old West in pictures and bronzes before it disappeared. His favorite subjects were cowboys and Indians in action.

Frederic Remington (1861–1909) was a New Yorker. He did many sketches while visiting frontier military posts. Remington traveled with cavalry troops on campaigns against warlike natives. His fame rests on hundreds of paintings and bronzes of soldiers, Native Americans, cowboys, and other frontier people.

The Gilcrease Institute of American History and Art in Tulsa has one of the world's best collections of works done by Catlin, Russell, Remington, and other painters of the Old West. Oil millionaire Thomas Gilcrease used part of his fortune to buy art works that document the cultural history of Oklahoma and the American West.

The Cowboy Hall of Fame in Oklahoma City and the Woolaroc Museum in Bartlesville also have valuable collections of western art.

Pioneer art. Most pioneers had little interest in paintings. They were busy trying to survive on a new frontier. Their art talents were expressed in making quilts, wagons, and other things they could use.

Most of the pioneers who painted were untrained. They simply drew or painted what came naturally. One of them, Augusta Metcalf, was

Woodrow Crumbo working on his mural "Wild Horses." (Bureau of Indian Affairs)

only fifteen when her family moved from Kansas to No Man's Land in 1886. Her paintings show farmers fighting a prairie fire, herding cattle, or scraping for water in a dry creek bed.

Metcalf's works and other pioneer paintings may not be perfect in technique. But they capture the spirit of hard work and frontier living. They are invaluable as a colorful record of Oklahoma's heritage.

One of the pioneer painters, John Noble, got an art education. After taking part in the Cherokee Outlet Run in 1893, he studied art in Europe. His painting *The Run* was one of his best works.

Native American Artists. Oklahoma Indian tribes have produced many excellent painters. A good example was Woodrow Crumbo, a half-Pottawatomie and half-white. He graduated as valedictorian from Shawnee High School and later attended the University of Oklahoma. Crumbo's murals of wild animals and Indian dancers show a creative, individualistic style. They can be seen in the Department of Interior building in Washington, D.C. and other places. He taught and painted at Bacone College in Muskogee.

Oscar Jacobsen, director of the School of Art at the University of Oklahoma for many years, recruited talented young Native American artists. Jacobsen was born in Sweden, reared in Kansas and educated in the east and in Europe. After coming to the university in 1915, he arranged special art classes for Indian students of the Kiowa and other tribes. They were encouraged to paint spontaneously. Today their watercolor paintings decorate the walls of many art galleries and public buildings.

The Philbrook Art Center in Tulsa has helped Native American artists. Housed in a mansion donated by oilman Waite Phillips, the Philbrook Center collects native art works. In the 1940s it began sponsoring exhibits of native paintings and awarding prizes for the best.

Artists can recreate history. Artists can recreate a past event or person. But they need factual information to make an accurate historical picture.

Charles Banks Wilson of Miami ranks as one of Oklahoma's most talented artists. His huge murals in the rotunda of the State Capitol portray a colorful summary of Oklahoma history. The murals cover 250 years of events from the Spanish explorers to the Land Runs that opened Oklahoma to settlers. In preparation for the murals, Wilson researched every historic aspect and made thousands of sketches.

Wilson also spent several years studying and painting murals of four heroic Oklahomans at the capitol: Sequoyah, Will Rogers, Jim Thorpe, and Robert S. Kerr. Wilson succeeded in painting the significance of each man's life.

Will Rogers is shown standing at an airstrip. He is slightly slouched like an old-time cowboy. His Stetson hat is tilted back, setting off his famous grin and cheerful face. A newspaper ("All I know is what I read in the papers.") is tucked in his coat pocket. Rogers was a likeable man and Wilson caught the essence of his warm personality.

Wilson painted Kerr as a farsighted man with great energy and ambition. Kerr is standing at his U.S. Senate desk. In the background are maps and charts of the inland waterway that bears his name.

When the portraits were finished, Wilson said the hardest part was doing Jim Thorpe's knee muscles. "It was like painting a bag of beans," he said, "they were so relaxed and so knit together." Thorpe was one of the world's all-time great athletes. Wilson captured the strength of both his body and character.

Oklahoma is fortunate to have so much of its history in pictures. Famous travelers, pioneer and Native American artists, and present-day historical painters have given us a colorful record of Oklahoma's heritage.

3. OKLAHOMA HAS A RICH HERITAGE IN MUSIC, DANCE, AND DRAMA.

The fine arts—including music, dance, and drama—have long been a part of Oklahoma's culture. Native Americans had dances and chants for every ceremonial occasion and need. Cowboys on the range sang to calm the cattle or to entertain themselves.

Pioneer settlers sang wherever they got together socially. Some families had a pump organ that they brought to Oklahoma by covered wagon. The early farmers and town dwellers danced away many an evening to fiddle music or the accompaniment of an harmonica. They also enjoyed plays and Christmas programs at the one-room school.

Traveling entertainment. A variety of professional entertainment was available in frontier towns. Companies of actors from the east sometimes performed on a candle-lit stage.

Wild West shows were started in Oklahoma by the Miller brothers, the Zack Mulhall family, and Gordon "Pawnee Bill" Lillie. Advance men would advertise the coming of these shows by pasting huge posters on the sides of store buildings or barns.

Live theatre and symphony orchestras. By the 1920s several Oklahoma towns had resident community theatres. Tulsa's Little Theatre has the longest continuous history. Started in 1922, it was the first theater to recognize the greatness of playwright Lynn Riggs. The Tulsa actors presented his *Big Lake*, a play about the Indian Territory. Riggs later went to France to

A scene from "Oklahoma" at Tulsa. (Don Sibley photo)

write *Green Grow the Lilacs* and on to fame in New York City and Hollywood.

Tulsa is still a cultural leader. The city has a variety of theatre and musical groups. One theatre company performs the musical "Oklahoma" during the summer at Discoveryland Outdoor Theatre. The Tulsa Opera, Tulsa Ballet Theatre, and the Philharmonic Orchestra are other cultural attractions in the state's second largest city.

The Oklahoma Symphony Orchestra is the state's best-known musical group. It was started in 1938 as a WPA project sponsored by the University of Oklahoma. The orchestra was established to help unemployed musicians but became a permanent group with headquarters in Oklahoma City. It plays both classical and Pops music at the Civic Center Municipal Hall. Performances are also given in other Oklahoma cities. The musicians earn a living at outside jobs.

Other well-known orchestras in Oklahoma include the Lawton Philharmonic, the Phillips-Enid Orchestra, and the Bartlesville Symphony.

Jazz musicians. Several Oklahoma black jazz musicians became famous. Charlie Christian (1919–1942) is considered one of the best jazz guitarists who ever lived. He played with Benny Goodman's orchestra.

Jimmy Rushing (1903–1972) was called the

Charlie Christian with drummer Gene Krupa.

"greatest living male blues singer." His voice was his instrument. A graduate of Douglas High School in Oklahoma City, he sang with Count Basie's orchestra for many years.

Several Oklahoma colleges and universities now sponsor jazz concerts. Some of the campus festivals focus on junior and senior high school competition.

Famous Oklahoma ballerinas. Ballet is quite different from Native American dances and pioneer square dancing. But ballet took root in Oklahoma. Five of the world's most outstanding ballerinas were Native Americans from this state.

Yvonne Chouteau, at age fourteen, was the youngest American ever chosen to dance with Ballet Russe de Monte Carlo. Yvonne grew up in Oklahoma City and returned to her native state after a brilliant career. In 1967, she performed in the "Four Moons" ballet in Tulsa.

This ballet was specially choreographed for Chouteau and three other famous Oklahoma ballerinas: Marjorie Tallchief, Moscelyne Larkin, and Rosella Hightower.

Maria Tallchief, Marjorie's older sister, was the best-known of Oklahoma's prima ballerinas. She gained international fame, proving that American ballet could equal European in quality. Maria was born in Fairfax, Oklahoma in 1925. Her father was Osage and her mother Scot-Irish. At age seventeen Maria began dancing with

Ballet Russe. Most of her career was with the New York City Ballet. She married the Ballet's director, George Balanchine.

Oklahoma has produced many stars of stage and screen. Will Rogers and Tom Mix got their starts in Wild West shows. They went on to stardom in the movies. Gene Autry, the "Singing Cowboy" from Achille, was a hero to many Americans who saw his western movies. Ben Johnson (Pawhuska) and Buck Jones (Red Rock) were also cowboy stars.

Other Oklahomans who have gained fame in movies or television include James Garner (Norman), Dennis Weaver (Norman), Dale Robertson (Harrah), Tony Randall (Tulsa), Jennifer Jones (Tulsa), Patti Page (Claremore), Ron Howard (Duncan), Joan Crawford (Lawton), Van Heflin (Walters), Dan Rowan (Beggs), Ginger Rogers (Blackwell), Vera Miles (Boise City), and Rue McClanahan (Healdton) who is one of the "Golden Girls."

Two Oklahoma ballerinas—Yvonne Chouteau (left) and Maria Tallchief (center)—dance with Pauline Goddard.

201

James Garner, a native of Norman, played the part of an Oklahoma railroad man in "The Long Summer of George Adams" in 1982.

4. OKLAHOMA'S SCHOOLS ARE A PART OF OUR HERITAGE

Indian, mission, and town schools in Indian Territory. The story of Oklahoma's schools begins with the Five Nations. Each of these tribes developed a public school system for its children. The tribes also welcomed missionaries who started private church-sponsored schools. In the 1880s, for example, the Presbyterians opened a day mission school in Tulsa. Two teachers taught all the grades in a room heated by pot-bellied stoves. The students sat at double desks with an ink well in the middle. A water pail, lunch baskets, and wraps were kept in an anteroom.

"I heard about sixteen classes a day," said Mrs. Lilah Lindsay. She taught at the day school for three years and then took a year off to rest. A member of the Creek Nation, Mrs. Lindsay's next job was as principal of the Coweta Indian Boarding School.

Later, Mrs. Lindsay started a private subscription school in a store building owned by her husband in Tulsa. Many white towns in Indian Territory had private schools. They could not levy taxes on Indian lands to provide public schools until 1898.

Federal control of schools in Indian Territory. The Curtis Act in that year allowed towns to incorporate and tax. The act also gave the federal government control over schools in the Indian Territory. The tribes had to cooperate to get federal funds. A federal superintendent brought more white and black children into the schools. He put more emphasis on vocational education. "Summer normal" classes for teachers helped to improve instruction.

Regardless of who was in control, the rural areas of eastern Oklahoma had few schools prior to statehood. Many rural children of all the races grew up with little or no formal education.

Local control of common schools in western Oklahoma. In 1890, the Territory of Oklahoma created a system of small district common schools. Most of them were one-room country schools. They were equipped with homemade furniture and had few books. The important point, of course, is that pioneer Oklahomans saw the need for education and provided what they could. As towns grew, graded schools and high schools were built.

Reservation Indians in western Oklahoma had mission schools run by Quakers, Presbyterians, Catholics, and missionaries of other denominations.

Higher education. The territorial legislature was optimistic about the future. It created colleges, giving western Oklahoma a headstart on public higher education. The Indian Territory did not have public colleges until after Oklahoma became a state.

Eventually, Oklahoma developed one of the nation's most extensive systems of state universities and junior colleges. Since 1941, these state schools have been governed by the State Regents for Higher Education.

There is an advantage in having a large number of colleges as well as vocational-technical centers. High school graduates can further their education close to home. The problem, however, is to provide enough funds to support all the schools.

Since territorial days, private church colleges have offered Oklahomans an alternative to public schools of higher learning.

Consolidation and centralization of the Oklahoma school system. At the beginning of statehood, Oklahoma was divided into 5,641 independent school districts. One-room country schools dotted the landscape. Each school was supported by taxes on the surrounding land. Lucky was the district that had a railroad or other valuable property to tax. At first, the teachers needed only an eighth grade education to apply for jobs. They attended county "institutes" during the summer to improve their knowledge of subjects taught.

During this century, the key words in Oklahoma's educational progress have been "consolidation" and "centralization." Small rural districts saw the advantages of combining. In 1903, before statehood, the first consolidated school district was organized around the little town of Quay. Students were picked up along county roads and transported in horsedrawn "kid wagons" to a central school. In later years, consolidation was speeded up by the school bus, better roads, and higher state curriculum requirements.

In 1947, the state legislature ordered smaller schools combined into larger ones. Thousands of country schoolhouses were boarded up. By the 1950s there were only about 600 districts. The largest district, in Cimarron County around Boise City, borders on three states. With consolidation came more graded schools, teachers, and course offerings. Bands, plays, sports, and other activities were added.

Another important trend in Oklahoma education has been an increase of state control over local schools—"centralization." The State Department of Education sets standards. Also, the state is now financing a larger portion of school costs. Why? The basic idea is to give every student, whether he/she lives in a poor or rich district, an equal educational opportunity. The state has broader means for raising revenue and can help equalize the tax burden statewide.

5. NATIVE AMERICANS AND OTHER MINORITY GROUPS HAVE BEEN MELTING SLOWLY INTO THE GENERAL POPULATION.

Oklahoma can boast of several ethnic minority groups. The Indians, blacks, Hispanic-Americans and others have contributed to our heritage. Since World War II, these groups have been moving up the economic and social ladder, getting closer to the "American dream." We have seen, for example, how the blacks struggled for integration and equal opportunity with the help of laws and court decisions.

Oklahoma's newest ethnic minority, the Vietnamese, arrived in the 1970s and 1980s. They had escaped to freedom when communist armies overran their South Vietnam homeland. Most of the Vietnamese-Americans who came to Oklahoma found homes in Oklahoma City and Tulsa. They have tried to hold on to their own culture (language, churches, and holidays) while learning English and adjusting to American life.

Native Americans. Oklahoma got its name from the "red people," the first residents in this area. Many tribes with different cultures have come here. The Indians, now constituting only about five percent of the state's population, still live mainly in rural areas. Adair County, which has the highest percent of native people, is one-third Indian. Thousands of Indians, however, have moved to the larger cities and mixed with the general population.

The federal government tries to help disadvantaged Indians. The Bureau of Indian Affairs (BIA) has guided Indians into businesses. The BIA sponsored the Chilocco Indian School to assist natives in both vocational and academic training. In 1946, Congress passed the Indian Claims Commission Act. This law allowed tribes to sue the federal government to get compensation for lands illegally taken from them. Among the first tribes to win settlements were the Cherokee Nation, Miamis, Pawnees, Sac and Fox, and Cheyenne-Arapaho.

The Indian Reorganization Act of 1934, encouraged the Indians to continue their tribal organization. They were allowed to adopt their own

Wilma Mankiller, Principal Chief, Cherokee Nation of Oklahoma.

Most Indians in Oklahoma, including mixed bloods, identify with a particular tribe. The old traditional way of life, however, is fading. For that reason, everything that represents the Indian has become precious. Ancient arts, crafts, tools, housing, clothes, and weapons are treasured.

Hispanic-Americans. After 1910, people of Mexican ancestry started coming to Oklahoma in large numbers. Poverty and a violent revolution caused them to leave Mexico. The Hispanics did hard work in cotton fields, on the railroads, and in coal mines. Eventually Mexican communities grew in Oklahoma City, Tulsa, Lawton, and other places.

A few Mexican-American ranchers ran spreads in the Panhandle. Like other Oklahoma ranchers and cowboys, they used equipment, methods, and language of Spanish-Mexican origin. From the Mexican cowboy (*vaquero*) came the lariat (*la reata*), horned saddle, and branding.

A Mexican vaquero roping a longhorn.

constitutions, hire lawyers, and start business corporations. Many tribes set up a tribal government with a council, chairman, and a tribal court with Indian judges. These courts handle only offenses against the tribal law and misdemeanors. More serious crimes are tried in state or federal courts.

A 1970 law allowed each tribe to elect a principal chief. The Choctaws elected J. W. Belvin, a prominent rancher from Durant. Cherokee tribal members chose W. W. Keeler, chairman of the board for Phillips Petroleum Company. In 1985, the Cherokees elected Wilma Mankiller, the first woman to serve as principal chief. She said her "long-term goal is to develop the economy of the tribe in fourteen counties of northeastern Oklahoma where many of our 67,000 members arc concentrated."

204

Dr. Angie Debo. (A Charles Banks Wilson portrait)

The Mexican expression *dale vuelta*, meaning to twist a rope around a saddle, became "dolly welter" or simply "dolly." The Spanish words corral, rodeo, and rancho also became a part of our ranching heritage.

6. THE PAST IS STUDIED FROM WRITTEN RECORDS AND THE THINGS LEFT BY PEOPLE WHO CAME BEFORE US.

No written records were kept in prehistoric times. But modern archaeologists use scientific detective methods to study Native American ruins that are unearthed. These scientists are slowly piecing together the story of Oklahoma's first people.

Fortunately, much of what has happened in Oklahoma since the 1500s was recorded. Early explorers and military men made reports and kept diaries. Many pioneer ranchers, farmers, businessmen, politicians, and other people have described their experiences to interviewers. Old newpapers provide *contemporary* accounts of important events. Government archives contain useful information. Historians have used these primary sources to write the story of Oklahoma's history.

Joseph B. Thoburn has been called Oklahoma's "pioneer historian and archaeologist." Beginning with his first book in 1908, Thoburn wrote a number of *comprehensive* histories of Oklahoma.

Thoburn was also the first person to become interested in Oklahoma's prehistoric sites. In the summer of 1916, he took a group of University of Oklahoma students on an archaeological dig at Big Mouth Cave near Gore in Delaware County. The young men frightened away a crowd of curious goldseekers by spreading a rumor about the "Hecome-hicome monster" that supposedly lived in the cave. The dig yielded some good artifacts—pieces of pottery, arrowheads, animal bones, and needles.

Angie Debo was known as "the first lady of Oklahoma history." Angie Debo came with her parents in a covered wagon to the Territory of Oklahoma in 1899. The family's hometown of Marshall became the subject of one of Debo's thirteen books about Oklahoma and western history. Named *Prairie City*, it was her only fictional book.

A scholarly historian who did extensive research, Dr. Debo wrote several books and articles about Native Americans. Her more general history, *Oklahoma: Foot-loose and Fancy-free*, was reprinted for the 80th anniversary of Oklahoma statehood.

Dr. Debo received many honors during her long life and after. She was the first woman and scholar to have her portrait placed permanently in the State Capitol rotunda. She was only the sixth person to receive the American Historical Association's "Award for Scholarly Distinction." Also, a one-hour documentary film on her life and works was shown on a national public television program shortly after her death in 1988 at the age of 98.

Oklahoma's heritage is preserved through historical publication. Oklahoma is fortunate to have a number of journals and magazines that publish historical articles. The *Chronicles of Oklahoma* is issued four times a year by the Oklahoma Historical Society. Each issue contains several well-researched papers on Oklahoma history. Scholarly articles can also be found in the *Great Plains Journal* (Lawton) and several other publications.

Oklahoma Today, a bimonthly, prints popular articles for the general reader. This magazine is ranked as one of the best state-published magazines in the nation.

Newspapers in the state also keep Oklahoma's heritage alive with frequent articles on historic events and places.

Research in Oklahoma history. Some valuable collections of historical materials are located in Oklahoma. They contain old photographs, family papers, letters, diaries, business records, and other items.

The Oklahoma Historical Society in Oklahoma City is a depository for materials ranging from records of state agencies and the Five Civilized Tribes to old newspaper files.

The University of Oklahoma Western History Collections are rich in *manuscripts*, photographs, and materials on Native Americans. The congressional papers of former Speaker of the House Carl Albert and U.S. Senator Robert S. Kerr as well as many other valuable records are deposited there.

Oklahoma State University, the University of Tulsa, and the Thomas Gilcrease Institute at Tulsa have important collections related to Oklahoma history. Many local museums and historical societies feature the photographs and possessions of early-day pioneers in their areas.

ROUNDUP

1. List four reasons why we should remember our state's history.
2. How do museums and historic markers help us preserve our heritage?
3. Name six artists who have put Oklahoma's past into paintings.
4. Describe the entertainment enjoyed by pioneer settlers.
5. Identify Lynn Riggs, Charlie Christian, and Jimmy Rushing.
6. Name five famous Oklahoma ballerinas.
7. How did the educational systems in the Indian Territory and Territory of Oklahoma differ?
8. What is the main advantage and the chief drawback to having a large number of colleges and vo-tech centers?
9. What are the key words in Oklahoma's educational progress?
10. Why has everything that represents Indian heritage become precious? What is Oklahoma's newest ethnic minority? Which ethnic group has contributed to our ranching heritage?
11. In what publications can you read popular articles about Oklahoma?
A. Try it! See the list of Motivating Projects and Activities for possible review contests.

GLOSSARY

acting governor: the officer who temporarily takes over the governor's office when the governor is out of the territory or state, resigns, or is dismissed (examples, the secretary in territorial days or lieutenant governor now).

advanced degree: a college degree higher than a bachelor's degree.

Afrika Korps: Hitler's army in the North African campaign against the British and Americans during World War II.

agribusiness: farming and all its related businesses, such as food processing and the manufacture of fertilizers

agricultural land use areas: the regions into which lands can be classified according to how they are used—grazing, cotton farming, vegetable growing, etc.

alliance: an agreement of people or nations to work together on some common interest.

allotment: a specific tract of tribal land that is assigned to each individual or family in a tribe when a reservation is broken up.

annuity: an allowance or income that is paid yearly.

antiquities law: an Oklahoma law that protects important prehistoric and historic sites from destruction.

appellate judge: a judge who has the right to hear appeals from a lower court.

appoint: to name or select a person for a job.

apportionment: the division of a state into legislative or congressional districts.

aquifer: the underground water-filled mass of rocks and sand from which water can be pumped.

archaeologist: a scientist who studies the remains of early human cultures.

artifact: anything made by human work or art.

assembly line production: the making of products step by step, each worker doing a specific job.

atlatl: a notched stick that was used by prehistoric Native Americans to hurl a spear with great force.

atrocity: an evil or cruel deed.

automatic pilot: a device that lets a plane fly level without a pilot.

automatic radio direction finder: a radiocompass that helps a pilot stay on course by tuning in on a radio broadcast.

Axis powers: the alliance of Germany (Hitler), Italy (Mussolini), and Japan (Tojo) during World War II.

bank guaranty law: an Oklahoma law that was passed by the legislature to protect deposits in state banks.

bill of rights: the part of a constitution that lists the rights of individuals, *e.g.* freedom of speech, religion, and assembly.

bipartisan: consisting of both Democrats and Republicans.

bison: another name for the North American buffalo that may have descendants in Canada today.

black blizzard: a high wind accompanied by rolling dust clouds.

black dog: a kerosene lamp that sometimes caused an explosion around oil wells.

black freedman: former black slave

blacklist: a list of persons, organizations, or states under censure; usually a list of workers who will be refused employment if they apply for jobs.

blizzard: a severe snowstorm accompanied by a high, cold wind.

bluff: a steep bank, as on the side of a hill.

Boomers: people who promoted white settlement in the Indian Territory.

booster: one who gives enthusiastic support, a boomer.

bootlegger: one who makes or sells liquor illegally.

boycott: an organized effort by any group that refuses to buy the products or services of a business which follows a policy (segregation, for example) that is objectionable.

bribery: the giving of money or a gift to influence, usually corruptly, some official action.

buffalo chips: dried buffalo manure that was used for fuel.

bureaucracy: the agencies and officials in a government who follow a strict routine (red tape) and have undue authority.

bushwhack: to ambush or attack from hiding.

business progressive: people who believe that corporations should be encouraged to invest their capital (money) so a state can grow and provide jobs.

butte: a hill with steep sides and a flat top.

capital: the city which is the seat of government.

capitol: the main building which houses a government, state or national.

carbon-14 process: a scientific method of dating ancient artifacts, which contain plant or animal tissue, by measuring the amount of radioactive carbon decay.

carpetbagger: a person appointed to govern in a place or territory that is not his/her home.

casinghead gas: natural gas that is found in association with petroleum; wet gas.

caucus: a private meeting of members of a political party to discuss candidates or decide which policies to follow.

Central Lowlands: (of the United States): a low plains area with rolling hills that stretches from central Oklahoma across Kansas and Iowa and eastward to the Appalachian Mountains.

Cherokee Neutral Lands: a district in southeast Kansas which was part of the lands given to the Cherokee tribe by the Treaty of New Echota in 1835.

Cherokee Outlet: a strip of land 60 miles wide on the Oklahoma side of the Kansas border that was given to the Cherokees in 1828 as an outlet to the Great Plains; also called the "Cherokee Strip."

Cherokee Strip: a ribbon of land 2½ miles wide along the north side of the Kansas line that the Cherokees had to give up after the Civil War.

chores: regular jobs and duties, as on a farm

churn: a vessel in which milk or cream is agitated (churned) to separate oily drops that form butter.

city: in Oklahoma, a place with more than 2,500 people.

civil law: the body of laws that spell out the rights and privileges of private citizens—contracts and property rights, for examples.

civil rights: the rights and privileges guaranteed to all United States citizens by the U.S. Constitution and the laws of Congress.

clan: a united group of relatives, or families, claiming a common ancestor.

climate: the general pattern of weather over a long period of time.

Clovis culture (phase): the lifestyle of the mammoth hunters who were the first people to live in what is now Oklahoma.

coalition: an alliance or agreement to act together by persons with a common interest.

Coastal Plains: the warm, wet area that extends from southeastern Oklahoma through east Texas to the Gulf of Mexico and to the Atlantic Coast.

collateral: property or belongings that a borrower must give up to a lender if a loan is not paid back.

commission: a group of persons, like a board, with authority to perform an assigned duty.

communal lands: lands owned in common by a community such as an Indian tribe.

commute: to reduce a fine or other punishment.

company town: a town owned by a mining, lumbering, or other company which rents houses to its employees and sells them goods at company-owned stores.

comprehensive: large in scope, including much.

compromise: to settle a difference by an agreement.

Confederate States of America (CSA): a league of southern states that seceded from the Union at the time of the Civil War (1861-1865).

congressional district: the area from which one person is elected to serve in the United States House of Representatives.

Congressional Medal of Honor: the highest U.S. military decoration awarded to one who risked his life for exceptional services beyond the call of duty.

conservation: the protection of natural resources such as forests or petroleum and natural gas deposits.

contour plowing (farming): plowing and planting along lines with the same elevation to conserve moisture and limit erosion.

controversial issue: a debatable matter on which people can honestly have different points of view.

council: name for a governing body that has legislative powers.

cover crop: a crop which farmers plant to protect the ground and keep it from eroding.

Cross Timbers: a belt of scrub trees and tangled brush in central Oklahoma.

crystal set: an early-day radio receiving set that operated with a crystal (Quartz) detector, not with electron tubes.

culture: the sum total of lifestyle and achievements of people in a certain area at a given time.

dasher: the plunger stick that is pushed up and down in a churn to make butter.

deficit spending: having more expenses than revenue needed to run a government.

delegate to Congress: the person elected to speak for a territory in the United States House of Representatives.

demagogue: one who leads the people by appealing to prejudices and emotions.

Democratic National Convention: a meeting of Democratic delegates from the states and territories to nominate candidates for president and vice president.

depression: a severe decline in business that brings unemployment and falling prices on goods that people can't afford to buy.

desegregation: the process of ending the separation of races in public schools and public facilities; see integration.

dinosaur: one of a group of extinct reptiles, including the largest known land animals, that lived on the earth during the Mesozoic Age.

diorama: an exhibit, as in a museum, that has small models set in a natural foreground which blends into a painted background.

direct democracy: government run by the people directly, not through representatives; examples: initiative and referendum.

direct primary: the election where each party chooses its nominees who will run in the general election; in the primary, Democrats run against Democrats and Republicans run against Republicans.

direct relief: a handout of money or food to the needy for which no work is expected.

discriminate: to show prejudice or bias.

discrimination: acting toward another person or race with prejudice.

discriminatory clause: a part of a law or constitution that shows prejudice against some group, race, or person.

disenfranchisement: condition of not being allowed to vote.

diversified economy: the producing of goods and income in a variety of ways, such as agriculture, mining, manufacturing, lumbering, tourism, business, and services.

dolphin: a device to which a boat can be moored.

Domebo site: a place near Anadarko where mammoth bones and Clovis points were dug up.

drought: a long dry spell with little or no rain.

drover: one who drives a herd of animals to market.

"dry": opposing or prohibiting the sale of alcoholic beverages.

dry gas: natural gas that is not found with petroleum.

dugout: an excavated shelter covered by a roof.

Dust Bowl: an area, including northwestern Oklahoma, where topsoil was blown away by winds during the 1930s drought.

earthquake: a vibration of the earth's crust caused by the faulting (splitting) of a mass of rock in the earth's interior.

Eastern Cherokees: the main group of Cherokees who remained in Georgia after some tribal members, the Western Cherokees, moved to Arkansas.

earmarking: the setting aside of money for a particular purpose.

economy, the: any system of producing goods and services, distributing income, and investing wealth.

electoral votes: the votes for president and vice president; the number of electoral votes for a state is equal to the number of U.S. senators (2) plus the number of United States representatives.

emergency clause: the clause that a legislature attachs to a bill to put it into effect immediately after the governor signs it.

emigrant: one who moves from one place within a country to another.

empire: all the land under the control of one ruler.

Enabling Act (1906): the law passed by Congress which "enabled" Oklahoma to become a state.

endangered species: any kind of animal, bird, fish, reptile, or plant that is in danger of dying off.

en masse: all together

Equal Rights Amendment: a proposed amendment to the U.S. Constitution that would provide women's rights.

erosion: wearing away of the earth's surface by wind, water, or glacier.

ethnic: of or belonging to a particular racial, cultural, or language division of the human race.

excursion: a trip taken by a group of people for relaxation or enjoyment.

executive branch: the branch of government that administers and enforces laws passed by the legislature.

expedition: a journey of a group of persons to explore, trade, or achieve some other objective.

faction: a subgroup that may disagree with the larger group (a political party, for example) of which it is a part.

fauna: wildlife.

filling station: gasoline station.

Five Civilized Tribes: southern tribes (Cherokees, Chickasaws, Choctaws, Creeks, and Seminoles) which adopted the white man's culture.

flaming youth: name given to young people in the 1920s whose moral standards dropped.

flannel: loosely woven warm cloth made of cotton and/ or wool.

flappers: girls in the 1920s who wore short skirts and bobbed hair and "flapped" their arms doing the Charleston dance.

flickers: a slang for motion pictures.

flora: plant life.

Folsom culture: the lifestyle of the bison hunters who lived in the plains area between the Clovis and Plainview cultures.

forest: trees covering a large tract of land.

Fourteenth Amendment: an amendment to the U.S. Constitution in 1868 that gave citizenship to former slaves as well as all privileges of citizenship.

freedman: an emancipated (freed) slave.

frontier: the part of a country that is just being settled.

general incompetency: not having the ability to perform the duties of an office.

geologist: a scientist who knows about the structure of the earth, including rocks, rock formations, and minerals.

gerrymander: to draw the boundaries of legislative or congressional districts so as to benefit the interests of the majority political party.

golden age: the time of greatest achievement, peace, and prosperity for a civilization.

graduated income tax: an income tax with rates that increase in percentage as the income increases—the higher the income, the higher the percentage rate of tax.

grafter: one who makes a profit or takes money and property by unfair or dishonest means.

grandfather clause: an Oklahoma constitutional amendment that excused most whites from taking a literacy test and forced most blacks to pass it before they could vote. Persons were excused from the test if they or their ancestors were eligible to vote on January 1, 1866. Very few blacks had been allowed to vote until the fifteenth amendment was ratified after that date.

grassland: land on which grass is the main vegetation.

Great Depression: the economic crisis of the 1930s when many people didn't have jobs, farm prices were low, some banks failed, and many factories closed.

Great Plains: a high plains region, east of the Rocky Mountains, that stretches from Canada to Texas and includes the Oklahoma Panhandle and northwest Oklahoma.

Greer County: land between forks of the Red River in present-day Oklahoma which the U.S. Supreme Court decided, in 1896, is part of Oklahoma, not Texas.

guerrillas: warriors or soldiers who fight in a small group using hit-and-run tactics, often inside the enemy's territory.

hayseed: another name for hick or yokel.

helium: an odorless, nonflammable, gaseous element that is found chiefly in natural gas deposits—used to inflate dirigibles.

ritage: the cultural tradition and knowledge that is handed down from past times.

High Plains: the high, dry land that slopes gently from the Panhandle and northwest Oklahoma to the Rocky Mountains.

high yield forestry: the practice of replanting trees in cut areas to assure a permanent supply of logs for sawmills.

homestead: a tract of free land, usually 160 acres, occupied under the Homestead Act of 1862; in Indian Territory, a homestead was the part of an allotment that the Native American owner could not sell for a specified number of years.

humidity: moisture or dampness in the air.

hybrid: a plant, animal, or fish that is a cross between two different varieties or breeds.

Ice Age: the age when the northern part of the world was covered four different times by a huge glacier.

impeachment: the trial of a public official—the House of Representatives makes the charges and prosecutes while the Senate sits as a jury.

inauguration: a ceremony at which an elected person takes office.

income tax: a tax on income (salaries, wages, business profits, etc.)

incorporate: to form a corporation with the right to act as an individual.

incorporated city or town: a place that has legal rights (to sue or be sued, for example) like an individual or a business.

incumbent: the person who holds an office.

independent: a voter or candidate who does not belong to any of the political parties.

Indian agent: a person who represents the U.S. government in relations with the Native Americans.

Indian Territory: (1) area covering all of Oklahoma, except the Panhandle, that was given to the Five Civilized Tribes before the Civil War, (2) eastern part of present Oklahoma that was occupied by the Five Civilized Tribes and smaller tribes after the Civil War.

initiative: the process by which the people can write a law or constitutional amendment and get it on the ballot for the voters to pass or defeat.

injunction: a judge's order requiring a person or company to do or not to do something.

integration: the process of making public schools, restaurants, parks, transportation, and other facilities available to persons of all races on an equal basis.

Interior Highlands: a tree-covered region that extends from the Ozarks and Ouachitas in eastern Oklahoma to the Atlantic Coast.

installment plan: a system of buying goods and paying a specific amount at regular times.

interstate highway: a road that passes through several states.

intruder: one who comes to a place or area without an invitation.

jerky: meat that has been preserved by drying in the sun.

Jim Crow laws: laws that segregated blacks and discriminated against them in other ways.

judicial: the branch of government, made up of courts, which interprets the law.

jury, grand: a group of people who are selected to consider evidence against a person and determine if he or she should be accused of a crime and sent to trial.

keelboat: a shallow freight boat that is moved with poles or by the current of a river.

keynote address: the main speech, especially at a political convention, that is supposed to inspire the delegates while presenting the main opinions or principles of the party.

"Kickapoos": members of the town company from Colony, Kansas who surveyed the second townsite in Oklahoma City; called "Kickers" by the "Seminoles."

kickback: money paid to an official who made it possible for a business to sell a product of some kind to the government.

labor union: an association of workers organized to improve working conditions and secure higher wages and/or other benefits.

landmark: a mountain or other land feature used as a guide by travelers or as a boundary.

legislative assembly: legislature of the Territory of Oklahoma.

legislative district: area from which a legislator is elected and which he or she represents in the legislature.

legislature: branch of government which makes laws.

lister: a plow with a double moldboard that produces a ridged furrow.

literacy test: a test of one's ability to read.

lobbyist: a person who tries to get legislators to vote for bills that favor the special interest (such as a union, business group, or organization) that he or she represents.

local option: the right of the people in a county or town to decide if the sale of alcoholic beverages will be permitted or prohibited.

long ballot: a ballot with many elective offices, candidates, and measures to be voted on.

Longhorn: a breed of domestic beef cattle with long horns.

lottery: a method of distributing prizes, such as homesteads, by drawing names or numbers from a container.

Lower Creeks: mixed blood Creeks who lived along the Alabama-Georgia line.

lumbering: the business of cutting trees and sawing the logs into boards, planks, and other kinds of lumber.

majority: more than half. An *absolute* majority is more than half of those eligible to vote. A *simple* majority is more than half of those who do vote.

make work project: relief work that is started just to create jobs.

mammoth: a giant, elephant-like animal that is now extinct.

manufacturing: the changing of raw materials into goods that have greater use and value.

manuscript: a typed or handwritten document, article, or book.

material aspects (of a culture): physical things.

melodrama: an emotional play or drama that has sensational incidents.

merit system: a system of hiring and promoting employees on the basis of their ability, qualifications, and job performance.

metal: any element that is usually hard, heavy, and lustrous; it also conducts electricity and can be hammered or rolled out without breaking.

metate: a stone on which seeds or grain are ground.

Mesozoic Age (roughly 200 to 70 million years ago): the age of the earth during which dinosaurs and other ugly beasts lived in swampy lands; sometimes called the "Age of Reptiles."

middleman: one who acts as a go-between, buying from producers and selling to others—a flour miller or cotton ginner, for examples.

migrant: a person who moves from place to place within the country.

migratory: roving or moving from place to place.

militia: a body of citizens subject to call for military duty.

mineral: any substance that can be extracted from the earth and used.

mineral fuel: a mineral that burns—examples are oil, natural gas, and coal.

minister (diplomatic): a person who represents his government to another government.

misdemeanor: a lesser crime

mission: a place where missionaries live and work, teach a religion, and/or do educational or charity work.

missionary: a person who is sent to another region or country to tell the people about a religion.

mixed economy: a variety of ways of making a living as opposed to dependence on just one.

moonshiner: one who makes liquor illegally.

municipal bond issue: the way a city borrows money by selling certificates of promise to repay later.

mural: a painting or decoration applied to a wall.

New Deal: name of President Franklin Roosevelt's programs for the economic recovery of the United States in the 1930s.

No Man's Land: the Oklahoma Panhandle area which was not a part of any territory or state between 1850 and 1890.

nickelodeon: a motion picture theater that charged an admission of five cents.

nolo contendere (plea): a plea by a defendant in a criminal action that has the same legal effect as an admission of guilt but does not prevent him/her from denying the charges in any other proceeding.

nomination: the act or condition of being chosen as a candidate; see nominee.

nominee: the candidate chosen by his or her political party to run against the nominees of other parties.

nonmetallic mineral: a rocklike substance that breaks up when hammered or ground.

nonpartisan: not identified with any political party.

normalcy: the usual, natural, or common condition.

norther: a cold storm from the north.

notary: a notary public—one who certifies contracts and other legal papers.

oil depletion allowance: the amount of reduction in the assessed value of oil property that is allowed by the government so that oil companies can reduce their taxes.

oil royalty: a share of the income from oil wells.

"Okie": the name that Californians called all migrants, regardless of the state they came from.

Oklahoma: named derived from two Choctaw (Muskogean) words: *okla* (red) and *homma* or *humma* (people).

Oklahoma Depositors Guaranty Fund: money collected from all state-chartered banks to insure depositors in any bank that might fail.

Oklahoma District: the "Unassigned Lands"—an area in central Oklahoma which the federal government forced the Creeks and Seminoles to set aside for other tribes but did not assign to anyone; the land that was opened to settlement in 1889.

Oklahoma Enabling Act: the law passed by Congress that made it possible for Oklahoma to become a state, combining the Territory of Oklahoma and the Indian Territory.

Oklahoma, Key to Industrial Expansion (OKIE): the slogan used by Governor Dewey Bartlett to promote the industrial growth of Oklahoma.

Old Guard: the people in a political party or government who are opposed to change and want to keep the existing way of doing things.

one-man, one vote rule: a decision of the U.S. Supreme Court that forced states to have about the same number of people in each legislative district and in each congressional district.

one-party state: a state where only one political party wins elections.

open range: a large area of unfenced grassland over which cattle or sheep roam and graze.

Operation Corcom: name given to the federal investigation of "corrupt commissioners" in Oklahoma counties that was completed in 1981.

Organic Act: the law passed by Congress in 1890 that created the Territory of Oklahoma in the area that is now western Oklahoma.

outside influences (on Oklahoma): the effects of events (such as wars, depressions, and inventions), ideas, and people outside the state on Oklahoma.

Paleozoic Age: geologic age of the earth lasting from 550 to 200 million years ago.

Panic of 1907: one of the times in American history when people were alarmed because of business and bank failures.

party: a group of persons associated together for some common purpose, such as a political party or an exploring party.

patronage: the power of deciding who will be appointed to jobs or offices; also, the jobs so distributed.

pemmican: a mixture of dried bison meat, berries, and animal fat.

perjury: the giving of false testimony under oath.

personal property tax: a tax on moveable property such as furniture or railroad cars.

perspective: the judging of facts or a situation with the advantage of experience and knowledge.

petroglyph: a prehistoric carving, usually pictorial, on a rock surface.

phonograph: a record player.

physiographic region: an area with the same kind of relief.

picketing: a demonstration of people who usually carry signs to call public attention to their grievances against a business, company, or public official.

picture show: movie or film.

pioneer: one of the first explorers or settlers in a new region or country.

plain: a fairly level, unforested land.

Plainview (Plains) culture: lifestyle of the bison hunters who also gathered food; the bridge between the hunting and the hunting-gathering cultures.

plateau: elevated, nearly-level land.

platform: a list of the principles, policies, and views on issues put forth by a political party.

plurality: more votes than any other candidate for an office.

pocket veto: an indirect veto—method used by a chief executive to stop a bill passed by a legislative body from becoming a law by holding it, without signing or vetoing it outright, at the time the legislature adjourns.

polar continental air: cold air from the North polar region.

poll (polling place): the place where voters in a precinct vote on election day.

Populists (People's Party): a political party, formed in 1891, that favored cheap money, free coinage of silver, income tax, public control of railroads, and limitation on the amount of land a person could own.

prairie: a plain that usually has tall grass.

prairie coal: buffalo or cow chips used for fuel.

precipitation: the falling of moisture (rain or snow) on the earth.

preferential primary: an election at which voters recommend candidates to be chosen later by a convention of delegates.

prehistoric: the time before written history.

prizefight: a boxing bout between professional fighters for a prize or sum of money.

professional degree: an advanced college degree in a field such as law or medicine; also a bachelor's degree in a field such as engineering or teaching.

professional guardian: in Indian Territory, a person who made a living by caring for the property of Indian children and adults who were not competent to act for themselves.

progressive: favoring reforms; a progressive constitution is one that gives the people a big voice in government.

prohibition: the forbidding of the making or sale of alcoholic beverages.

projectile points the sharp, pointed flint or metal pieces attached to a spear or arrow.

property tax: a tax based on the value of the land, buildings, and improvements.

proration umpire: a state official appointed by Governor Murray to hold oil production down and prices up by limiting the amount of oil pumped at each well.

public domain: land that belongs to all the people in a nation.

public interest: that which helps most people rather than a few persons or groups.

quarantine law (for livestock): a law to stop infected livestock from entering a certain state or area.

quarter section: 160 acres.

racism: the belief that people of another race should be discriminated against and/or treated as inferior.

raft: debris that packs up in a stream and blocks boat traffic.

railhead: a railroad terminus; the farthest point to which rails have been laid.

range cattle industry: the business of raising cattle on large tracts of grazing land.

ration: an allowance of food and supplies, especially as given to Native Americans confined to a reservation.

realtor: a person in the real estate business.

reapportionment: the changing of the shape or the number of legislative or congressional districts.

rearguard: a body of troops assigned to protect the rear of an army.

recall: the process by which voters may remove an elected official from office before the end of his or her term.

recording district: one of the twenty-six areas into which the Indian Territory was divided, each district having a town where Indians recorded their allotments.

recruit: a newly enlisted person in the army, navy, or air force.

referendum: a bill that is referred by the legislature to the voters to pass or defeat.

refinery: a plant where crude oil is purified into gasoline and other oil products.

reform: a change to make something better by correcting abuses or evils.

reformatory: an institution where juvenile offenders are kept.

regulation: control, as by a government bureau or agency.

relief (charity): charity or aid, such as food or money, that is given to the needy.

relief (land): the unevenness or flatness of the land surface.

relief fund: money set aside to help poor people.

removal treaty: a treaty signed by Indian leaders, voluntarily or by force, agreeing to give up lands and move west.

remuda: a herd of extra mounts used by cowboys in a roundup or trail drive.

Republican National Committee: the top committee of the Republican Party, consisting of one man and one woman from each state. The Democratic Party also has a national committee.

Republican National Convention: a meeting of Republican delegates from the states and territories to nominate candidates for president and vice president.

reservation: a tract of government land set aside for a special purpose—for the use of Indians, to preserve forests and wildlife, or for some other purpose.

reservoir: a basin, either natural or manmade, where a supply of water is collected.

rider: an addition or amendment, not likely to pass on its own merit, that is attached to an important bill certain to pass.

rural (Bureau of Census definition): any area away from cities in the country or in towns with fewer than 2,500 people.

Sabbath law (blue law): a law that prohibits stores to open and public entertainment on Sunday.

sales tax: a tax on money paid for goods.

saltworks: a place where large amounts of salt are made for sale.

sand storm: a dust storm stirred up by low winds.

savanna-woodland: a grassland partly covered by trees or shrubs.

school lands: lands that were set aside in each township for the benefit of schools.

school trust fund: money set aside by the state government to help support public schools.

scrip: a piece of paper that certifies the holder is to receive something else later, such as money or goods at the company store.

secede: to withdraw from a political association—as the southern states withdrew from the United States in 1861.

section: a square mile of surveyed land containing 640 acres.

sedition: language or conduct that incites disorder or revolt against the government.

seditious: pertaining to or taking part in the incitement of disorder or dissension against the government.

segregation: separation of people because of race.

seismograph: an instrument for recording automatically the size, direction, and duration of an earthquake—used in oil exploration.

selenite: a clear, sparkling gypsum found in the Glass Mountains.

self-binder: a farm machine that cut and tied grain stalks or stems into sheaves (bundles) for later threshing.

"Seminoles": members of the Seminole Land and Improvement Company who came, as Sooners, to lay out the first town lots in Oklahoma City.

separate but equal segregation law: a law that required a duplication of schools, waiting rooms, train seats, etc. for the black and white races.

session: the term or time during which a legislature meets to conduct business.

severalty: the holding of land in one's own right.

sharecropper: a farmer who pays a share of his crop to a landlord as rent on the land.

short ballot: a ballot which has only a few offices listed so that people can vote intelligently on the candidates.

sit-in: a peaceful demonstration in which people excluded from a public place, such as a lunch counter, enter and remain seated until served or forced to leave.

skirmish: a small battle between two sides at war.

sloth: a slow-moving, tree-dwelling mammal.

smelter: a plant where metal is separated from ore.

social justice: equal treatment of everyone under fair laws.

social reformer: a person who works to make society better for the disadvantaged.

socialism: a belief in the public ownership of the basic means of production, distribution, and trade; an economy where everyone is supposed to get a share of the goods and services produced.

society: the system of people existing together for the benefit and protection of all.

sod house: a house having sod or turf walls and a wooden roof used by early settlers on the plains.

Sooner (original definition): a person who slipped into an area to get land before the official starting time of a land run.

Sooner (new definition): a can-do, energetic, successful person in Oklahoma.

special interests: groups or individuals that seek special favors from the legislature or other government officials.

species: a grouping of animals or plants.

squatter: one who settles on land without permission.

staples: basic foods such as flour or sugar.

state park: land set aside by the state for public use.

statehood proclamation: the president's public announcement that a territory has become a state.

states' rights: the rights that states have in running their own governments free of federal control or direction.

stereotype: a fixed pattern that doesn't vary; a person who has the characteristics or qualities that typify, at least in the popular mind, a particular group.

stockade: a line of stout posts set upright in the earth to form a fence around an enclosed fort.

stockyard: a place where cattle or other livestock are kept in pens for shipment or slaughter.

strip mining: the mining of coal or other mineral by first taking off the surface soil and rock to expose the mineral vein.

stripper well: a low-producing oil well, often operating in a nearly-pumped out field.

subsistence farming: the raising of food for survival, not to sell.

suffrage: the right or privilege of voting.

sunset law: a law that requires government agencies to be evaluated to determine if they should continue to exist.

surplus allotment: the part of a tribal member's land allotment that could be sold sooner than the homestead part.

surplus lands: the part of a reservation that was opened for homesteading after tribal members selected their allotments.

swastika: a symbol of a cross with each of the four arms bent in the middle at a right angle; an ancient Indian symbol of good luck and later the emblem of Hitler's Nazi Party.

syllabary: a list of symbols or characters that stand for syllables in a language—Sequoyah's syllabary for the Cherokee language, for example.

talkie: a film with sound.

tantamount: equal to; the same same as.

tapir: a large, nocturnal mammal having short, stout legs and a big, flexible nose.

temperance: self-control in not using alcoholic drinks.

tenant: renter, as on a farm.

tenure: the time during which an office or a job is held.

terminus: the farthest station or town on a railroad; railhead.

terraces: in farming, the level spaces on which water is retained by ridges running along the contour lines.

territory: a political region of the United States having a certain degree of self-government but not the powers of a state—for example, the Territory of Oklahoma, 1890–1907.

Territory of Oklahoma: the western part of present-day Oklahoma that was created as a territory in 1890.

tornado: strong winds whirling in a circle at high speed.

tourism: tourist travel, especially when regarded as a source of income for businesses (such as motels, restaurants, and gasoline stations) that profit from the sale of goods and services to travelers.

towns: in Oklahoma, a place with fewer than 2,500 persons.

township: a unit of surveyed land containing 36 square miles or sections.

townsite: place where a town is built.

trading post a building or small settlement in an isolated place where a trader barters.

"trail of tears": the forced journeys westward of the Five Civilized Tribes when many Indians died of disease, cold, and hunger.

tramway: a railway for transporting goods or passengers.

treaty: an agreement between two or more nations.

trespassing: to enter wrongfully or illegally upon another's land or property.

tributary: a stream that flows into a larger stream.

tropical air: warm, moist air from the region that is along both sides of the equator.

turn state's evidence: to admit guilt to a crime and agree to become a witness for the state in testifying against accomplices.

turquoise: a blue or green gemstone consisting of aluminum phosphate colored by copper.

twin territories: Indian Territory (eastern Oklahoma) and the *Territory of Oklahoma* (western Oklahoma).

two-party system: a system where either of two major political parties is strong enough to win offices in a general election.

Unassigned Lands: see Oklahoma District.

underground shaft mining: a method of using tunnels to get to coal or other minerals to be mined.

unit plan: a plan whereby the corporation commission can choose one company to develop an oil field in order to conserve oil and natural gas.

Upper Creeks: full blood Creeks who lived in northern Alabama.

urban (Bureau of Census definition): any city or town area having more than 2,500 people.

urbanization: the movement of people to the cities.

value: the worth, importance, or desireability of something

vaudeville: a variety show, popular in the early part of the 20th century.

vertebrates: any creature (animal, bird, fish, or reptile) with a backbone.

volcano: an opening in the crust of the earth from which steam, hot gases, and ashes are expelled, forming a conical hill with a central crater.

waiver: in law, the voluntary giving up of a right or privilege.

walks of life: occupations, professions, or ways of making a living.

Wall Street stock market: the stock exchange in New York City where stocks and bonds are bought and sold.

weather: a combination of various atmospheric elements—sunshine, rain, snow, wind, temperature, and humidity.

Western Cherokees: the first-arriving Cherokees in Arkansas and northeast Oklahoma.

wet: favoring or permitting the sale of alcoholic beverages.

wet gas: see casinghead gas.

wildcat driller: one who drills oil wells in unproven territory.

wobblies: members of the radical Industrial Workers of the World.

woman suffrage: the privilege or right of women to vote.

wrangler: a herdsman, usually of saddle horses used by cowboys in a roundup or trail drive.

yellow dog contract: an agreement with an employer in which a worker agrees not to join a labor union.

SUGGESTED READINGS

Chapter 1

Gould, Charles N., *Travels Through Oklahoma*. Oklahoma City: Harlow Publishing Company, 1928.

Jordan, Robert Paul and Robert W. Madden, "Oklahoma, the Adventurous One," *National Geographic*, Vol. 140, No. 2 (August, 1971), pp. 149−89.

Morris, John W. (ed.), *Geography of Oklahoma*. Oklahoma City: Oklahoma Historical Society, 1983.

Morris, John W.; Charles R. Goins; and Edwin C. McReynolds, *Historical Atlas of Oklahoma*. Norman: Univerity of Oklahoma Press, 1981.

Ruth, Kent, *Oklahoma Travel Handbook*. Norman: University of Oklahoma Press, 1980.

Chapter 2

Currey, Billy R., "Climate of Oklahoma," *Climates of the States*. (Silver Spring, Md.: U.S. Department of Commerce, Environmental Sciences Services Administration). Washington, D.C.: Superintendent of Documents, revised, 1970.

Morris, John W. (ed.), *Geography of Oklahoma*. Oklahoma City: Oklahoma Historical Society, 1983.

Morris, John W.; Charles R. Goins; and Edwin C. McReynolds, *Historical Atlas of Oklahoma*. Norman: University of Oklahoma Press, 1981.

Oklahoma Department of Wildlife Conservation (1801 N. Lincoln, Oklahoma City, OK 73152) pamphlets: *The Bald Eagle in Oklahoma, Sport Fish in Oklahoma, Oklahoma Game Birds*, and *Oklahoma Mammals*.

Chapter 3

Green, Donald E. (ed.), *Rural Oklahoma*. Oklahoma City: Oklahoma Historical Society, 1982.

Morris, John W. (ed.), *Geography of Oklahoma*. Oklahoma City: Oklahoma Historical Society, 1983.

Morris, John W. and Arthur H. Doerr, "Irrigation in Oklahoma," *Journal of Geography*, Vol. LVIII, No. 9 (December, 1959), pp. 421−29.

Skaggs, Jimmy M., *The Ranch and Range in Oklahoma*. Oklahoma City: Oklahoma Historical Society, 1978.

U.S. Bureau of Census, Department of Commerce, *1982 Census of Agriculture*. Vol. 1, Part 36 (Oklahoma: State and County Data). Washington, D.C.: Government Printing Office, 1984.

Chapter 4

Bernard, Richard M., *The Poles in Oklahoma*. Norman: University of Oklahoma Press, 1980.

Blessing, Patrick J., *The British and Irish in Oklahoma*. Norman; University of Oklahoma Press, 1980.

Brown, Kenny L., *The Italians in Oklahoma*. Norman: University of Oklahoma Press, 1980.

Franks, Kenny A., *The Oklahoma Petroleum Industry*. Norman: University of Oklahoma Press, 1980.

Franks, Kenny A.; Paul F. Lambert; and Carl N. Tyson, *Early Oklahoma Oil: A Photographic History, 1859−1936*. College Station: Texas A and M University Press, 1981.

Gibson, Arrell, *Wilderness Bonanza: The Tri-State District of Missouri, Kansas, and Oklahoma*. Norman: University of Oklahoma Press, 1972.

Johnson, Kenneth S., "Minerals, Mineral Industries, and Reclamation in Oklahoma," in John W. Morris (ed.), *Geography of Oklahoma*. Oklahoma City: Oklahoma Historical Society, 1983, pp. 93−111.

Morris, John W. (ed.), *Drill Bits, Picks, and Shovels: A History of Mineral Resources in Oklahoma*. Oklahoma City: Oklahoma Historical Society, 1982.

Rister, Carl C., *Oil! Titan of the Southwest*. Norman: University of Oklahoma Press, 1949.

Chapter 5

Curran, Claude W., "Forests and Forest Industries in Oklahoma," in John W. Morris (ed.), *Geography of Oklahoma*. Oklahoma City: Oklahoma Historical Society, 1983, pp. 83−92.

Dikeman, Neil J., Jr., "Development of Manufacturing in Oklahoma," in John W. Morris (ed.), *Geography of Oklahoma*. Oklahoma City: Oklahoma Historical Society, 1983, pp. 125−37.

Morris, John W. (ed.), *Cities of Oklahoma*. Oklahoma City: Oklahoma Historical Society, 1979.

Neal, H.C., "Historic Autos Made in Oklahoma," *Oklahoma Today*, Autumn, 1973, pp. 28−31.

"Oklahoma's Salesman-Governor," *Business Week*, October 11, 1969.

Chapter 6

Bell, Robert E., *Oklahoma Archaeology*. An annotated bibliography, 2nd edition. Norman: University of Oklahoma Press, 1978.

Bell, Robert E., *Prehistory of Oklahoma*. Orlando, Florida: Academic Press, Inc. (Harcourt Brace Jovanovich Publishers), 1984.

Gibson, Arrell M., *The American Indian: Prehistory to the Present*. Lexington, Mass.: D. C. Heath and Company, 1980.

Holmes, Mary Ann and Marsha Hill, *Prehistoric People of Oklahoma*. Stovall Museum and Archaeological Survey No. 2

"A Young Person's Guide to Oklahoma's Prehistoric People," *Oklahoma Today*, Vol. 22, No. 2 (Spring, 1972), pp. 18−23.

Chapter 7

Allen, Henry E., "The Parrilla Expedition to the Red River in 1759," *Southwestern Historical Quarterly*, Vol. XLIII, No. 1 (July, 1939), pp. 53−71.

Hammond, George P. and Agapito Rey, *Narratives of the Coronade Expedition, 1540−1542*. Albuquerque: University of New Mexico Press, 1940.

"Nativity, Vocations, and Political Views of the Constitution Makers," *The Daily Oklahoman*, December 9, 1906.

Nesbitt, Paul, "Governor Haskell Tells of Two Conventions," *Chronicles of Oklahoma*, Vol. 14, No. 2 (June, 1936), pp. 189−217.

Scales, James R. and Danney Goble, *Oklahoma Politics: A History*. Norman: University of Oklahoma Press, 1982.

Wright, James R., Jr., "The Assiduous Wedge: Woman Suffrage and the Oklahoma Constitutional Convention," *Chronicles of Oklahoma*, Vol. 51, No. 4 (Winter, 1974−1975), pp. 421−43.

Chapter 18

Bilger, Edda, "The Oklahoma Vorwärts: The Voice of German-Americans During World War I," *Chronicles of Oklahoma*, Vol. 54, No. 2 (Summer, 1976), pp. 245−60.

Casey, Orben J., "Governor Lee Cruce and Law Enforcement, 1911−1915," *Chronicles of Oklahoma*, Vol. 54, No. 4 (Winter, 1976−1977), pp. 435−60.

Dale, Edward E. and James D. Morrison, *Pioneer Judge: The Life of Robert Lee Williams*. Cedar Rapids, Iowa: Torch Press, 1958.

Daugherty, Fred A. and Pendleton Woods, "Oklahoma's Military Tradition," *Chronicles of Oklahoma*, Vol. 57, No. 4 (Winter, 1979−1980), pp. 427−45.

Fischer, LeRoy H., *Oklahoma's Governors, 1907−1929: Turbulent Politics*. Oklahoma City: Oklahoma Historical Society, 1981.

Fowler, Oscar P., *The Haskell Regime: The Intimate Life of Charles Nathaniel Haskell*. Oklahoma City: Boles Printing Company, 1933.

Gage, Duane, "Al Jennings, the People's Choice," *Chronicles of Oklahoma*, Vol. 46, No. 3 (Autumn, 1968), pp. 242−48.

Hilton, O. A., "The Oklahoma Council of Defense and the First World War," *Chronicles of Oklahoma*, Vol. 20, No. 1 (March, 1942), pp. 18−42.

Hurst, Irvin, *The 46th Star: A History of Oklahoma's Constitutional Convention and Early Statehood*. Oklahoma City: Semco Color Press, 1957.

Rohrs, Richard C., *The Germans in Oklahoma*. Norman: University of Oklahoma Press, 1980.

Scales, James R. and Danney Goble, *Oklahoma Politics: A History*. Norman: University of Oklahoma Press, 1982.

Warrick, Sherry, "Radical Labor in Oklahoma: The Working Class Union," *Chronicles of Oklahoma*, Vol. 52, No. 2 (Summer, 1974), pp. 180−95.

Chapter 19

Andrews, Bunyan H., "Oklahoma's Red River Boundary," *Chronicles of Oklahoma*, Vol. 44, No. 3 (Autumn, 1966), pp. 246−53.

Bigger, Margaret G., "Send Me Another Set of Chains," *Oklahoma Today*, Vol. 36, No. 6 (November−December, 1986), pp. 36−39.

Ellsworth, Scott, *Death in a Promised Land: The Tulsa Race Riot of 1921*. Baton Rouge: Louisiana State University Press, 1982.

Fischer, LeRoy H. (ed.), *Oklahoma's Governors, 1907−1929: Turbulent Politics*. Oklahoma City: Oklahoma Historical Society, 1981.

Fischer, LeRoy H. (ed.), *Oklahoma's Governors, 1929−1955: Depression to Prosperity*. Oklahoma City: Oklahoma Historical Society, 1983.

Franklin, Jimmie, *The Blacks in Oklahoma*. Norman: University of Oklahoma Press, 1980.

Morgan, Anne Hodges and Rennard Strickland, *Oklahoma Memories*. Norman: University of Oklahoma Press, 1981.

Neuringer, Sheldon, "Governor Walton's War on the Ku Klux Klan: An Episode in Oklahoma History, 1923 to 1924," *Chronicles of Oklahoma*, Vol. 45, No. 2 (Summer, 1967), pp. 153−79.

Scales, James R. and Danney Goble, *Oklahoma Politics: A History* Norman: University of Oklahoma Press, 1982.

Stanley, Ruth Moore, "Alice M. Robertson, Oklahoma's First Congresswoman," *Chronicles of Oklahoma*, Vol. 45, No. 3 (Autumn, 1967), pp. 259−89.

Tobias, Henry J., *The Jews in Oklahoma*. Norman: University of Oklahoma Press, 1980.

Chapter 20

Blackburn, Bob. L., "Law Enforcement in Transition: From Decentralized County Sheriffs to the Highway Patrol," *Chronicles of Oklahoma*, Vol. 56, No. 2 (Summer, 1978) pp. 194−207.

Bryant, Keith L., Jr., *Alfalfa Bill Murray*. Norman: University of Press, 1968.

Clark, Blue, "'To Preserve Local History': The WPA Historical Records Survey in Oklahoma, 1936−1942," *Chronicles of Oklahoma*, Vol. 61, No. 2 (Summer, 1983), pp. 168−79.

Davenport, Walter, "Land Where Our Children Die," *Colliers*, September 18, 1937, pp. 11−13, 73−77.

Fischer, Leroy H., *Oklahoma's Governors, 1929−1955: Depression to Prosperity*. Oklahoma City: Oklahoma Historical Society, 1983.

Fossey, W. Richard, "'Talkin' Dust Bowl Blues': A Study of Oklahoma's Cultural Identity During the Great Depression," *Chronicles of Oklahoma*, Vol. 55, No. 1 (Spring, 1977), pp. 12−33.

Graves, Gregory R., "Exodus From Indian Territory: The Evolution of Cotton Culture in Eastern Oklahoma," *Chronicles of Oklahoma*, Vol. 60, No. 2 (Summer, 1982), pp. 186−209.

Green, Donald E., *Panhandle Pioneer: Henry C. Hitch, His Ranch and His Family*. Norman: University of Oklahoma Press, 1979.

Green, Donald E., *Rural Oklahoma*. Oklahoma City: Oklahoma Historical Society, 1982.

Greenway, John, "Woodrow Wilson Guthrie," *Oklahoma Today*, Autumn, 1971, pp. 18−30, 74−78.

Henderson, Carolyn, "Letters from the Dust Bowl," *Atlantic Monthly*, Vol. 157 (May, 1936), pp. 540−45.

Henderson, Carolyn, "Spring in the Dust Bowl," *Atlantic Monthly*, Vol. 158 (June, 1937), pp. 715−17.

Hendrickson, Kenneth D., Jr. (ed.), *Hard Times in Oklahoma*. Oklahoma City: Oklahoma Historical Society, 1983.

Hibbs, Ben, "The Dust Bowl Can Be Saved," *The Saturday Evening Post*, December 18, 1937.

Holland, Reid, "The Civilian Conservation Corps in the City: Tulsa and Oklahoma City in the 1930s," *Chronicles of Oklahoma*, Vol. 53, No. 3 (Fall, 1975), pp. 367–75.

Holland, Reid, "Life in Oklahoma's Civilian Conservation Corps," *Chronicles of Oklahoma*, Vol. 48, No. 2 (Summer, 1970), pp. 224–34.

Ketchum, Richard M., *Will Rogers: His Life and Times*. New York: Simon and Schuster, 1973.

Mathews, John J., *Life and Death of an Oil Man: The Career of E. W. Marland*. Norman: University of Oklahoma Press, 1951.

Moffett, Hugh, "Dust Bowl Farmer," *Life*, July 28, 1947, pp. 91–101.

Nevin, David, "Globe Girdler from Oklahoma," in *The Pathfinders*. Alexandria, Virginia: Time-Life Books, 1980, pp. 138–61.

Otey, George N., "New Deal for Oklahoma's Children: Federal Day Care Centers, 1933–1946," *Chronicles of Oklahoma*, Vol. 62, No. 3 (Fall, 1984), pp. 296–311.

Purdy, Virginia C. (ed.), "'Dust to Eat': A Document From the Dust Bowl," *Chronicles of Oklahoma*, Vol. 58, No. 4 (Winter, 1980–1981), pp. 440–54.

Scales, James R. and Danney Goble, *Oklahoma Politics: A History*. Norman: University of Oklahoma Press, 1982.

Shockley, Martin S., "The Reception of the Grapes of Wrath in Oklahoma," *American Literature*, January, 1944, pp. 351–61.

Smallwood, James, "Will Rogers: A Centennial Review of His Career," *Chronicles of Oklahoma*, Vol. 57, No. 3 (Fall, 1979), pp. 269–88.

Soden, Dale E., "The New Deal Comes to Shawnee," *Chronicles of Oklahoma*, Vol. 63, No. 2 (Summer, 1985), pp. 116–27.

Steinbeck, John, *Grapes of Wrath*. New York: The Viking Press, 1939.

Ware, James, "The Sooner NRA: New Deal Recovery in Oklahoma," *Chronicles of Oklahoma*, Vol. 54, No. 3 (Fall, 1976), pp. 339–51.

Wilmoth, Carol, "Heavenly Harmony: The WPA Symphony Orchestra, 1937–1942," *Chronicles of Oklahoma*, Vol. 64, No. 2 (Summer, 1986), pp. 35–51.

Winchester, James H., "Wiley Post," *Oklahoma Today*, Summer, 1966, pp. 16–21.

Worster, Donald, *Dust Bowl: The Southern Plains in the 1930s*. New York: Oxford University Press, 1979.

Chapter 21

Billington, Monroe, "Public School Integration in Oklahoma, 1954–1963," *The Historian*, Vol. XXVI, No. 4 (August, 1964), pp. 521–37.

Boulton, Scot W., "Desegreation of the Oklahoma City School System," *Chronicles of Oklahoma*. Vol. 58, No. 2 (Summer, 1980), pp. 192–220.

Childs, Marquis W., "The Big Boom from Oklahoma," *Saturday Evening Post*, April 9, 1949, pp. 22–23, 118–20. (Kerr)

Daugherty, Fred A. and Pendleton Woods, "Oklahoma's Military Tradition," *Chronicles of Oklahoma*, Vol. 57, No. 4 (Winter, 1979–1980), pp. 427–45.

Fischer, LeRoy (ed.), *Oklahoma's Governors, 1929–1955*. Oklahoma City: Oklahoma Historical Society, 1983.

Franklin, Jimmie Lewis, *The Blacks in Oklahoma*. Norman: University of Oklahoma Press, 1980.

Gary, Governor Raymond (as told to Phil Dessaur), "I Say Oklahoma's O.K.!" *Saturday Evening Post*, July 9, 1955, pp. 27, 67–68, 70.

Graves, Carl R., "The Right To Be Served: Oklahoma City's Lunch Counter Sit-ins, 1958–1964," *Chronicles of Oklahoma*, Vol. 59, No. 2 (Summer, 1981), pp. 152–66.

MacKaye, Milton, "The Oklahoma Kid," *Saturday Evening Post*, May 16, 1959, pp. 36–37, 70, 73, 75. (J. Howard Edmondson)

Miller, Ken, "A Spot of England in Oklahoma," *Coronet*, May, 1957, p. 159.

Morgan, Anne Hodges, *Robert S. Kerr: The Senate Years*. Norman: University of Oklahoma Press, 1977.

Murray, Ex-Governor Johnston (as told to Al Dewlen), "Oklahoma is in a Mess!" *Saturday Evening Post*, April 30, 1955, pp. 20–21, 92, 96.

Scales, James R. and Danney Goble, *Oklahoma Politics: A History*. Norman: University of Oklahoma Press, 1982.

Stewart, Roy P., "Raymond S. McLain: America's Greatest Citizen Soldier," *Chronicles of Oklahoma*, Vol. 59, No. 1 (Spring, 1981), pp. 4–29.

Warner, Richard S., "Barbed Wire and Nazilagers, *Chronicles of Oklahoma*, Vol. 64, No. 1 (Spring, 1986), pp. 37–67.

Welsh, Carol H., "Back the Attack: The Sale of War Bonds in Oklahoma," *Chronicles of Oklahoma*, Vol. 61, No. 3 (Fall, 1983), pp. 226–45.

Wilson, Terry P., "The Afrika Korps in Oklahoma: Fort Reno's Prisoner of War Compound," *Chronicles of Oklahoma*, Vol. 52, No. 3 (Fall, 1974), pp. 360–69.

Chapter 22

Bakal, Carl, "The Ocean Comes to Oklahoma," *Reader's Digest*, November, 1970.

"The Credit-Card Governor," *Time*, February 4, 1974. (David Hall)

"The ERA Loses Two More Rounds," *Time*, February 1, 1982.

"I Will Veto Any Tax Increase," *U.S. News and World Report*, May 23, 1983. (George Nigh)

Kirkpatrick, Samuel A.; David R. Morgan; and Thomas G. Kielhorn, *The Oklahoma Voter*. Norman: University of Oklahoma Press, 1977.

Morgan, Anne Hodges, *Robert S. Kerr: The Senate Years*. Norman: University of Oklahoma Press, 1977.

Morgan, Anne Hodges and H. Wayne Morgan (eds.), *Oklahoma: New Views of the Forty-Sixth State.* Norman: University of Oklahoma Press, 1982.

"Oklahoma's Salesman-Governor," *Business Week*, October 11, 1969. (Dewey Bartlett)

"The Port of Muskogee and Tulsa's Port at Catoosa," *Oklahoma Today*, Spring, 1976.

Scales, James R. and Danney Goble, *Oklahoma Politics: A History.* Norman: University of Oklahoma Press, 1982.

"What? Oklahoma A 'Coastal' State?" *U.S. News and World Report*, February 22, 1971.

"Where Graft Reached Epidemic Levels," *U.S. News and World Report*, January 11, 1982.

Chapter 23

Debo, Angie, *And Still the Waters Run: The Betrayal of the Five Civilized Tribes.* Princeton, N.J.: Princeton University Press, 1968. (Paperback edition—Norman: University of Oklahoma Press, 1984)

Debo, Angie, *Oklahoma: Foot-loose and Fancy-free.* Norman: University of Oklahoma Press, 1949. (Reprint, 1987)

Fischer, LeRoy H., "The Historic Preservation Movement in Oklahoma," *Chronicles of Oklahoma*, Vol. 57, No. 1 Spring, 1979, pp. 3–25.

Oklahoma Tourism and Recreation Department, *Oklahoma Museums and Historic Sites.* (pamphlet: 500 Will Rogers Building, Oklahoma City, Oklahoma, 73105)

Olds, Frederick A., "Historians and Art: An Oklahoma Case Study," *Chronicles of Oklahoma*, Vol. 52, No. 2 (Summer, 1974) pp. 196–206.

Shirk, George H., "Oklahomans in Space," *Chronicles of Oklahoma*, vol. 52, No. 2 (Summer, 1974), pp. 139–51.

Terry, Walter, "Four Moons: Oklahoma Indian Ballerina Festival," *Saturday Review*, vol. L, No. 46 (November 18, 1967), pp. 60–61, 96.

(Wilson) "The Charles Banks Wilson Murals," *Oklahoma Today*, Winter, 1975–1976, pp. 36–40.

Wright, Muriel; George H. Shirk; and Kenny A. Franks, *Mark of Heritage.* Norman: University of Oklahoma Press, 1976.

SOME MOTIVATING PROJECTS AND ACTIVITIES

1. *Map and picture postcards.* Put a map of Oklahoma on the bulletin board. Pin or thumbtack Oklahoma postcards around the map. Run a string between each picture and its location on the map. For a more limited project, use only pictures on one topic such as "Oklahoma State Parks" or "Oklahoma Lakes and Recreation."

2. *Resources map.* Do a map showing the location of Oklahoma's main crops, minerals, and other resources. Affix wheat, cotton, peanuts, coal, limestone, etc. in the proper places.

3. *Explorer's map.* Draw a map showing the routes of Spanish, French, and early American explorers across present-day Oklahoma. A different color can be used for each explorer. Alternative: Use colored yarn or string to show the explorer routes on a modern highway map.

4. *Cut jigsaw puzzles.* Use Oklahoma scenes found on old calendars, discarded magazines, or posters. Political campaign posters or sample ballots might be used. An enlarged map of Oklahoma's 77 counties would make a good puzzle; the outside edge could be painted different colors to show the states that border Oklahoma.

5. *Murals.* Do a mural to illustrate some event, person, movement, or era in Oklahoma history. The state's history might be illustrated by a series of murals done on posterboard or a long piece of butcher paper or cloth.

6. *Poster drawings or mosaics.* Make enlargements of the state bird, animal, flower, tree, fish, reptile, flag, seal, rock, etc. The opaque projector might be helpful in doing the drawings or in making a sketch for a mosaic.

7. *Cartoon posters.* Decorate the classroom with current cartoons that are related to state or local topics and can be enlarged on posterboard or paper.

8. *Scrapbook.* Clip newspaper articles, pictures, editorials, and cartoons on Oklahoma's history, geography, recreation, and government. Paste the clippings on loose leaf sheets that can be organized later. Summarize the main points of each clipping in a few sentences and write down its source and date. Alternative: Summarize articles in your own words, each on a separate sheet of paper.

9. *Research paper.* History is a record of people's lives as it is written in diaries, letters, public documents, newspapers, gravestones, photographs, and many other places. Choose a topic related to Oklahoma history and do a research paper, using as many primary sources as possible. A good little inexpensive booklet on style is: William Leahy, *Fundamentals of the Research Paper*, Kenneth Publishing Company, Box 344, Palos Heights, IL 60463.

10. *Current events reports.* Do a current event report on some significant happening in the news. Use as many newspapers and other media sources as are available. Include a title at the beginning and sources at the end of the report.

11. *Project board.* Make a miniature museum on some topic in Oklahoma history. Use pictures, small scale models, family trees, written interviews, gravestone tracings, a research paper, etc. Some possible topics include an important person or family, a Native American tribe or culture, an exploration, early railroad, the buffalo, cattle industry and cowboys, a land run, territorial government, changes in farming, mining, growth of manufacturing or tourism, music and/or art in Oklahoma, McClellan-Kerr waterway, Golden Twenties, Dust Bowl, a war, oil industry, an ethnic group, civil rights struggle, etc. These topics and many others can be limited in scope or broadened according to the resources available.

12. *Original poem or letter.* Pretend you are present at an important Oklahoma historical event. Begin your project by researching all the information you can find on the topic. Then write a letter or poem about your experience at the event. What are some possible topics? Take a plane ride with Wiley Post. Sign on for a cattle drive. Observe a Civil War battle as a reporter. Work on an early railroad. Join a Boomer colony. Take part in a land run. Accept appointment as territorial governor and hold office in Guthrie. Live on a pioneer farm. Go to a pioneer town on Saturday. Be a delegate to the constitutional convention. Celebrate statehood. Mine coal. Strike oil. Build a flood control dam. Travel on the first barge up the McClellan-Kerr waterway. Play a role in the musical "Oklahoma." Live in this area during prehistoric times. Visit the Chouteaus at Saline in 1832 and ride along with Washington Irving on a tour of the Indian Territory.

13. *Contribution (Show and Tell) Day.* Bring to class a family heirloom, old photo, letter, diary, picture postcard, magazine, or document. Show the class a barbed wire collection, antique, an old Oklahoma autombile tag, Indian pottery or basket, soldier's uniform, or stamps—something about life in Oklahoma at an earlier time. A taped or written interview with a pioneer would be a good contribution. Show slides or pictures of historic sites. Wear a costume for some historic era.

14. *Native American handicrafts.* Visit a museum that has Native American handicraft exhibits and write a report. Learn how to weave a basket, to fire pottery in a kiln, to construct an Indian house, to make a bow and arrow with flint arrowhead, etc. Bring your project to class.

15. *Ethnic studies.* Research one of Oklahoma's ethnic groups and do a report or research paper. Present

a class report using pictures; tape recordings of ethnic music, dances, and language; costumes, etc. Books in the *Newcomers to a New Land Series* (Norman: University of Oklahoma Press, 1980) should be useful.

16. *Cowboys.* Collect poems, songs, and pictures related to the life of the cowboy and ranchers in pioneer days.

17. *Oklahoma history in place names.* Make lists of Oklahoma towns, counties, rivers, and lakes that have Spanish, French, and Indian names.

18. *Oklahoma history in advertising.* Make a list of Oklahoma historical names and events used in printed or pictorial advertising. Check the yellow pages for the names of businesses that use historic names. Do a collage or poster with these names, pictures, letterheads, etc.

19. *Oklahoma counties—origin of names.* (a) Do a written report on the origin of county names. A few names like Alfalfa and Rogers may surprise you. (b) Make a chart on the origin of county names. Label the columns thusly: Words of Indian Origin; Rivers; National or Out-of-State Leaders (presidents, generals, *et. al.*); Constitutional Convention Delegates; Oklahoma Pioneers and Railroad Officials; and Others. A good source for this project is Dr. Charles Grady, *County Courthouses of Oklahoma.* Oklahoma City: Oklahoma Historical Society, 1985.

20. *Living history project.* Organize a "living history" project. Visit and report on one of Oklahoma's many living history events. Examples include Rose Hill, a one-room school at Perry which recreates rural education as it was in the early 1900s. The annual Fort Washita rendezvous reenacts activities (trap setting, hide tanning, blacksmithing, etc.) of trappers and traders in the 1830s; the participants have authentic clothing, weapons, and tools. The annual Southern Plains Frontier Encampment at Lawton is another living history reenactment. The Oklahoma Historical Society has sponsored a reenactment of the Civil War battle at Honey Springs. The Rural Museum at Tahlequah recreates Cherokee life in the late 1800s. Downtown Guthrie has a territorial Christmas celebration. For a calendar of events, write to Oklahoma Tourism and Recreation Department, 500 Will Rogers Building, Oklahoma City, OK 73105.

21. *Committee study of legislative bills.* For a class project, get copies of important bills being considered by the state legislature. The class can be divided into committees. Each committee will study a bill and report to the class on it.

22. *Write a letter to your legislator.* Anyone who feels strongly about a bill in the legislature may write his/her representative or senator about it. Write the letter in your own words. Be brief and courteous. Cover one topic and give reasons for your opinion. Be informative by pointing out facts that support your point of view. Address the letter to Honorable (his/her name), State Capitol, Oklahoma City, OK 73105. Begin the letter with Dear

Senator (last name) for a Senate member or Dear Representative (last name) for a House member. A good reference book for current officeholders is the latest edition of *Directory of Oklahoma*, Oklahoma Department of Libraries, Allen Wright Memorial Building, 200 Northeast 18th Street, Oklahoma City, OK 73105.

23. *A war project.* Do a research paper, class report, bulletin board, or other project about a war in which Oklahomans took part. Use books, interviews (if possible), pictures, maps, songs of the time, time line, drawings of heroes or weapons, etc.

24. *Name the faces survey.* Find pictures of ten Oklahomans who should be well-known (governor; U.S. senators; a Congressman; mayor; Oklahoma television, movie, or country music stars; several people from the state's recent history, *et. al.*). Paste the pictures on a cardboard and number them from 1 to 10. Count the number of students who can identify each picture. Several years ago, a newspaper reporter did a similar survey at a shopping center. Some of the wrong answers proved to be interesting.

25. *Who am I? role playing game.* This game can be used for a break in the usual classroom procedure and for review. Names of people studied are drawn from a hat. Each student writes down three clues, arranged progressively from the most difficult to the easiest. Each class member, in turn, comes to the front of the room, gives the first clue, and asks, "How many know who I am?" After the last clue, another student is called on to identify the historical person. Each participant writes his game name on the board before sitting down.

26. *Team review contest.* Appoint two teams of about equal ability with maybe four students on each side. Ask one side a question which they discuss quickly and quietly before giving a team answer. If right, that team gets one point and the second team is given a different question. If wrong, the second team gets the same question that was missed by the first group. Each side is given the same number of chances to answer questions.

27. *Jeopardy game contest.* Write out questions for each of several categories about Oklahoma. Value each question according to difficulty—maybe 80, 60, 40, 20 points. Two teams compete for points. Each side, in turn, chooses a category and a point value. When a question is read, the team which puts up a hand first (or presses a buzzer or light button first) gets to answer. A penalty may be assessed for each wrong answer. The other team is given a chance to answer a missed question.

28. *Open book review contest.* Divide the class into two groups. One student from each side goes, in turn, to the chalkboard to represent his/her side. The contestants, each with a textbook in hand, are given a page number and question. The first student to write the answer, correctly spelled, gets a point for that side. A record of points is kept on the board above the answers.

INDEX